PAINTING ◦ COLOR ◦ HISTORY

COLLECTION PLANNED AND DIRECTED BY
ALBERT SKIRA

FRENCH PAINTING

From Fouquet to Poussin

ALBERT CHÂTELET

JACQUES THUILLIER

Translated from the French by Stuart Gilbert

★

Distributed in the United States by
THE WORLD PUBLISHING COMPANY
2231 West 110th Street, Cleveland 2, Ohio

★

PRINTED IN SWITZERLAND

THE DUCAL WORKSHOPS

★

A PERFECT EQUIPOISE
THE SECRET AND THE STRENGTH OF FOUQUET

★

PROVENÇAL PAINTING FROM CHARONTON TO FROMENT

★

THE RESISTANCE TO ITALY

★

THE ITALIANS AT FONTAINEBLEAU

★

THE PORTRAIT FROM THE CLOUETS TO THE DUMONSTIERS

★

FRENCH AND FLEMISH ARTISTS AT FONTAINEBLEAU

★

THE GREAT GENERATION OF THE SEVENTEENTH CENTURY

Introduction

French painting has two distinctive traits. To the first of these it largely owes its fully justified renown. This is the remarkable continuity which has enabled it, from the revival of art in the Middle Ages to the present day, through periods of full activity and brief relapses, but with a perseverance unequaled by Spain, Germany, Flanders or even Italy, to give the world a constant succession of great masters and of works that rank as landmarks in the history of European painting. The second trait is less commendable. It has attracted less comment and sometimes, despite the proven facts, been called in question or glossed over. This is that no artistic heritage was ever more neglected, belittled, mutilated by vandal ignoramuses than that of France. If we draw attention to these facts at the outset of the present work, it is because, in our opinion, both must be borne in mind in our approach to the history of French art.

Given the multiplicity of painters and art trends, it was impossible to do full justice in three volumes to the huge corpus of French painting. Omissions were necessary. Had we included all the outstanding works, the result would have been a mere anthology on familiar lines. It seemed better to omit some major works so as to make place, in certain cases, for those more intimate canvases which reveal a master's secrets or the inspired moments of an artist of the second rank. Often they reflect more clearly the spirit of an age than do the world-famous masterpieces.

It also seemed wisest to keep to the main stream of French art; some minor tributaries, some little masters born out of their due time have produced charming canvases, the joy of the eclectic connoisseur, but space does not permit us to linger on their work. We have not felt constrained to take into account the frontiers of present-day France. Nor did it seem to us necessary to include in this panoramic view of French art the paintings of such men as Simon Marmion, of the painters at Avignon when it was the papal seat, or of the Primitives of Nice hailing from art centers outside France; any more than of the work of such an artist as "Monsù" Desiderio. On the other hand, the art of Rosso and Primaticcio came to full fruition at Fontainebleau and in virtue of its success and popularity was speedily "naturalized" French. Such men as Valentin, Poussin and Dughet, though they spent much of or all their active life in Rome and in a sense belonged to that great international center, also belong, indispensably, to the domain of French painting.

The same concern for unity has led us, after much reflection, to begin this work with the first easel pictures. True, our opening pages might have been consecrated to the Saint-Germain frescoes at Auxerre and the Gellone Sacramentary or, anyhow, the Epernay Gospel Book. But French book illumination, its splendid flowering and slow decline, fall in a class apart, and by the same token an account of fresco painting would need to cover the arts of the stained-glass window, tapestry and mural decoration in general. Each would require, to do it justice, a volume to itself. Thus we shall allude to these forms of art only in passing, when, as a result of the destruction of the easel pictures, they alone throw light on the activities of an art center or an artist.

No other country has shown as little interest as France in the lives of its painters; we have had no Vasari, no Van Mander. Only at the end of the seventeenth century, in the writings of André Félibien, do we find any factual descriptions of the French masters and their works, and even these are sadly inadequate.

Nor has any other country been so destructive. Some of the most finely executed and longest admired works, such as "the pictures of King René" in Provence, the Galerie d'Ulysse at Fontainebleau and Simon Vouet's large ensembles in Paris were burnt or wantonly destroyed. Of the works of the French Primitives, far more numerous than used to be supposed, and of the Renaissance pictures, only a few waifs and strays (of varying merit) have survived. The most trivial little master of Tuscany or the Tyrol has today more panels to his credit than Jean Fouquet, Jean Perréal or Jean Cousin. Of the canvases of some famous seventeenth- and eighteenth-century artists a bare ten or twenty have come down to us. The rediscovery of Georges de La Tour has proved that even some of the very greatest painters lapsed into total oblivion after a brief hour of glory. Often, too, the art historian can sense a trend, an influence, unevidenced by any extant painting. For no dossier is ever complete, no hierarchy definitive.

Nor can we scan each century from the same angle; for the early periods we have only the works themselves to go on. Exceptionally, Fouquet has for us a personality —almost a biography. But even Enguerrand Charonton is little more than a name to us, that of the painter of the Coronation of the Virgin. *On the other hand, in dealing with the art of men like La Tour and Poussin, it is of prime importance to build up the life story of the artist, that sequence of chance events and deliberate choices which composes a "career" and shapes an artist's genius. This, our first volume, opens with the early anonymous paintings and ends with the first great generation of the seventeenth century. Our aim here is a simple one. It is not to propound in any sense a "method" or to advocate any cut-and-dried approach to French painting and force it into the strait-jacket of one of those abstract generalizations whose attraction lies in their very arbitrariness. And far from pitting it against the art of other lands, we aim, rather, at linking it up with its European context.*

These books will have achieved their purpose if the reader, as his eye moves on from picture to picture, comes to sense an underlying unity in the infinitely varied panorama of French painting, which through the ages has followed its appointed path, despite the idiosyncrasies of individual artists, seeming changes of front and daring innovations: a path forever opening vistas on a new visual apprehension of Man and of the world he lives in. In sum, we have kept in mind that never-ending quest described by Lucien Fèbvre as the hallmark of a great art: "an art that forgetting nothing, missing nothing, making no idle gestures or pointless efforts, weaves incessantly from generation to generation (even when they seem in conflict) a serried tissue of facilities and difficulties—a maze through which the Mind blazes its trail triumphantly, speeding from point to point with the bright alacrity of fire racing up a heather-clad slope."

8

The Ducal Workshops

Anonymous Master.
Portrait of John the Good, about 1360. Wood. (24×16⅛″) Louvre, Paris.

IT was in the Carolingian period that the practice of decorating the walls of churches with frescoes developed throughout France. Thus the great art arose which came to its full flowering when the massive forms of Romanesque architecture provided the painter with long barrel vaults and walls whose uniform expanse was broken only at rare intervals by narrow windows. With the rise of Gothic architecture there came a drastic change; large bays were opened up, continuous surfaces gave place to ribbed vaulting and a complex of pointed arches. This not only reduced the painters' field of action but led to a break in the continuity of the tradition of mural decoration. But alongside the fresco, there developed another form of pictorial art, which found expression in the illuminated manuscripts, and the evolution of this art displayed a remarkable continuity. Both forms of artistic activity were conditioned by their functions; like the Books of Hours, the wall imposed its own laws on the artist.

That is why, despite these impressive precedents, panel painting was essentially a new departure. True, it kept in touch with both illumination and the fresco. But it was not in their direct lineage (as was the case in the Italian domain); this was impossible once Gothic art had made so drastic a break in the evolution of French art. In the present state of our knowledge it is hard to fix the date when panel painting made its first appearance. Of its early manifestations in France, the *Portrait of John the Good* is the sole survivor, but this highly accomplished work bears every indication of being one of a long series of similar works, no longer extant.

It was above all in the reign of Charles VI (1380-1422) that pictorial art came into its own. Despite the ravages of the Hundred Years' War, this was a time when life grew more and more luxurious in the princely courts and a sophisticated art, last flowering of Gothic inspiration, made good in Europe, from Lombardy to France, from Bohemia to Spain. This "International Style" combined elegant arabesques and delicately modulated curves with a new tendency towards naturalism. It was an art well suited to a social order in which a sumptuous way of life was in daily contact with the horrors of war and abject poverty, and which called on its artists to veil the grim reality from the eyes of a privileged élite. In Paris it grew up under the auspices of the royal court, whose tone was set by the prodigal and frivolous Isabella of Bavaria, the king's wife. But even more than in Paris this art was cultivated and brought to a rare perfection in the ducal courts. The king's three uncles, the Duke of Anjou, the Duke of Berry and the Duke of Burgundy, were assiduous patrons of the finest artists of the day and the productions of the ateliers attached to their courts testify to the remarkable progress made by the arts in this period of unbridled luxury and incessant warfare.

Anonymous Master.

The Annunciation, about 1390-1400. Wood. (13⅜×9¾″) Cleveland Museum of Art, Mr and Mrs William H. Marlatt Fund.

The Ducal Workshops

An austere profile, telling out boldly on a gold ground, the *Portrait of John the Good* (Louvre) has long been regarded as the first link in the chain of French easel paintings —or, rather, as the first that has come down to us. The fact that the royal sitter seems to be in his early forties suggests that it may be dated to the 1360s. This has led to a surmise that it was painted when the king was held prisoner in London (1356-1360) and also to its attribution to the painter Girard d'Orléans, who shared his master's captivity. But though generally accepted, this view is purely conjectural and rests on fragile premises. How, for one thing, can we be sure that this aquiline face is really that of a man of forty? The beard is thick, the hair curly and copious, and the forehead unwrinkled; surely it might equally well be the portrait of a man of thirty. But, for our present purposes, this hardly matters; by the nature of the case, ten years one way or the other count for little when it comes to dating the beginning of panel painting in France.

What strikes one first about this portrait is the sureness of the execution. The firmly stated outline compels our attention, but not to the exclusion of the skillful modeling of forms. Of interest, too, is the systematic duplication of the exterior line, at a short distance, by a preliminary zone of shadow anticipating the rendering of the volumes of the face. Thus the salient features seem to be played on by a vivid light that justifies, so to speak, the clear-cut precision of the outer line. We are not surprised to find this distinctively graphic mode of expression employed again, no less rigorously, in the profiles of Charles V and Jeanne de Bourbon, drawn with pen and ink on the silk of the famous altar cloth known as the Parement de Narbonne, now in the Louvre. In this procedure we have yet another proof of the decisive part played by that essentially graphic form of expression, the decoration of manuscripts, in the earliest phase of French painting.

Isolated though it may seem to us today, the *Portrait of John the Good* should not be regarded as a unique work, born out of its due time. The drawings made for the iconographic documentation compiled for the seventeenth-century collector, Gaignières, comprised copies of similar effigies, now lost. They even include reproductions of more elaborate works, where the figures were depicted in interiors. Thus we are shown royal donors in prayer flanked by raised curtains, while another scene shows the Duke of Normandy and Count Eudes IV of Burgundy kneeling at the pope's feet. The inventories are no less explicit. So we can understand why the portrait of "Good King John" is so perfect in its kind. Only for us is it a point of departure;

it must have been, when it was made, only an element, if an outstanding one, in an already long tradition. The artist's choice of a profile portrait must not be taken as a concession to facility or to an archaic convention; it was certainly deliberate. And in this picture, sole of its kind that has come down to us, we cannot but be struck by the artist's masterly combination of scrupulous realism with a will to style.

That a group of professional artists had existed for some time is proved by the many names of painters cited in records of the period. As far back as 1292, according to the Tax Register, there were no less than thirty-three practising in Paris. Evrard d'Orléans was the King's Painter from 1304 to 1357 and after him the post was filled successively by Girard d'Orléans, then Jean d'Orléans. This recurrence of the name "d'Orléans" is intriguing; possibly these men came of the same family, but it may merely mean that all three hailed from the same town, Orléans. Not a single painting by any of these men has survived. And illuminations, it would seem, throw little light on the type of pictures they produced, since this branch of art was still too closely bound up with the technique of the book for the artist to enjoy much scope for personal expression. It is not until the close of the century that we find any further indication of the state of painting proper.

Meanwhile, however, great forward strides in art, preceding the rise of the "School of Paris," had been made in a town now French, but then on foreign soil, Avignon. The popes had made it their capital and under Benedict XII it had developed into a thriving center of artistic activity when that art-loving pope summoned to it a number of Italian painters, most eminent of whom was Simone Martini. Though the great Sienese artist made a relatively short stay in Provence, from 1340 to 1344, those four years sufficed to orient decisively the form of the decorations in the Palace of the Popes, and after him Matteo Giovannetti at the head of a large team of craftsmen, carried on his program. But of their manifold activities only a few panel paintings have survived, though happily some large frescoes are still in situ on the walls of the Palace. Their style, however, shows few signs of French influence. The religious frescoes in the chapels of St John and St Martial, like those in the Audience Hall, are typically Sienese. The only possible exceptions are those in the Robe Room. These superb evocations of hunting and fishing scenes, in which the figures stand out on a tracery of foliage each leaf of which is rendered individually, are so exceptional that they can hardly be assigned exclusively to the Sienese domain. Rather, they bring to mind the tapestries of the next century, but, despite some vague references in old records, there are no good reasons for thinking that the characteristic *verdures* of Arras and Tournai had as yet come into existence. On the contrary, these latter may well have been inspired by the Avignon frescoes. Moreover the attitudes of the figures have not the fluent rhythms and suppleness of Sienese figures, but somewhat rigid inflexions suggesting that French artists had a hand in them. However, this is still a moot point. Mlle Roques has recently maintained that these frescoes were painted by Robin de Romans, but her interpretation of the relevant texts is not entirely convincing.

However this may be, there is no doubt that the Avignon paintings played a decisive role in the first flowering of the art of the Parisian ateliers and that the International Style that characterizes it owed much to them. But influences of fourteenth-century Parisian miniatures and of Lombard art also contributed to this last expression of Gothic art. The smooth flow of lines defining figures, the treatment of drapery folds as decorative volutes, and a fragile grace, fine flower of an aristocratic refinement, are combined, sometimes to curious effect, with frankly realistic touches. This International Style made good from Bohemia to France, from Lombardy to Flanders, with a surprising uniformity. We find indications of it in French illuminations from the late fourteenth century on. As regards the pictures, there is so little trustworthy information as to their provenance that we cannot definitely assign any given one of them to Paris. That charming work, the Wilton Diptych (National Gallery, London), showing Richard II of England kneeling before the Virgin and Child attended by a company of exquisitely graceful, almost diaphanous angels, is presumably of English origin. On the other hand, the small Bargello Altarpiece (Florence), in which the feverish excitement of the Magi hastening towards the Child strikes a very different note, may well be Germanic. The large Bargello Diptych (Florence) in which the elegant figures of the angels combine so closely with the flamboyant architecture of the frame, has obvious affinities with Mosan art. One of the reasons for the "international" nature of this art was the migration of artists from one country to another. Paris was already a lodestone for English, Germanic and Netherlandish craftsmen and some of the works mentioned above, though retaining characteristics of the homelands of their makers, may well have been made in Paris.

The Cleveland *Annunciation* (formerly in the Sachs Collection) belongs to this cosmopolitan milieu. Here, however, all is Gothic elegance and there is no recourse to emotive gestures. The atmosphere of this small, delightful panel is one of pensive calm and dignified repose, and the finesse of the execution does not preclude a very real grandeur. That we have here a manifestation of the International Style is evident in the suppleness of the figures and fluency of the design, as also in the realism and vivacity of the attitude of God the Father. But the concern for order and proportion, the majestic simplicity and forthrightness of the figuration could well be characteristic expressions of the climate of Parisian art.

Meanwhile, apart from the (often problematic) activities of the artists resident in Paris, other art centers were developing. Though the royal court may have been the supreme attraction, other courts were now providing artists with rewarding opportunities. The brothers of King Charles V shared his ambition of figuring as a patron of the arts, and this was specially true of their nephew, the luxury-loving Charles VI. Most eminent undoubtedly was the Duke of Burgundy, Philip the Bold, who in 1384 became Count of Flanders after his marriage with Marguerite, heiress to the county. He gratified his ambition and his taste for art by founding, at the gates of Dijon, the Chartreuse de Champmol, burial place of the Burgundian dynasty; it was brought to completion by John the Fearless. Champmol was one of the busiest workyards of the period; not only architects and masons, but a host of sculptors, painters and glass-workers were employed there. The first stone was laid, with all due pomp and ceremony, in 1383. The building operations were supervised by Raymond du Temple and Drouet de Dammartin. Jean de Marville, first sculptor-in-chief, was replaced in 1389 by Claus Sluter, assisted by Claus de Werwe. The decorative paintings and numerous altarpieces were executed by the Duke's painters, Jean de Beaumetz, Jean Malouel and Henri Bellechose successively. But an "outsider" was also called in. Melchior Broederlam, "town painter" of Ypres, was commissioned to paint the wings of the reredos carved by his compatriot Jacques de Baerze; as Broederlam was detained at Ypres by his other duties, the wings were sent to him there. He spent several years working on them and they were dispatched to Dijon only in 1399.

Charles Sterling has recently identified two panels painted under the supervision of Jean de Beaumetz for cells in the Chartreuse de Champmol (Chalandon Collection, Lyons, and Wildenstein Collection, New York). Their style is slightly disconcerting; there is an effect of overloading in the arrangement of the masses that tends to drain the composition of its expressive power and vitality. Like André Beauneveu, Beaumetz (who was born at Cambrai) had begun by working at Valenciennes. Thus his art had a Flemish background—which may explain why in these works the elegance of the International Style tends to be submerged by violent gestures and a harsh realism. Jean Malouel, another Northerner, who succeeded Beaumetz in 1397, came from Guelders. Born at Nimeguen, he worked in Paris, where mention is made of him in 1396. Only a single work of his exists, its attribution to him being based on a contemporary document; it is the *Crucifixion with the Last Communion and Martyrdom of St Denis* (Louvre). Even this attribution has been called in question, though the record speaks for itself. Malouel died in May 1415 and on May 23 Henri Bellechose succeeded him as Painter to the Duke of Burgundy. In May 1416 Bellechose bought the colors

Jean Malouel and Henri Bellechose.
Crucifixion with the Last Communion
and Martyrdom of St Denis, about 1416.
(63⅜×82¾″) Louvre, Paris.

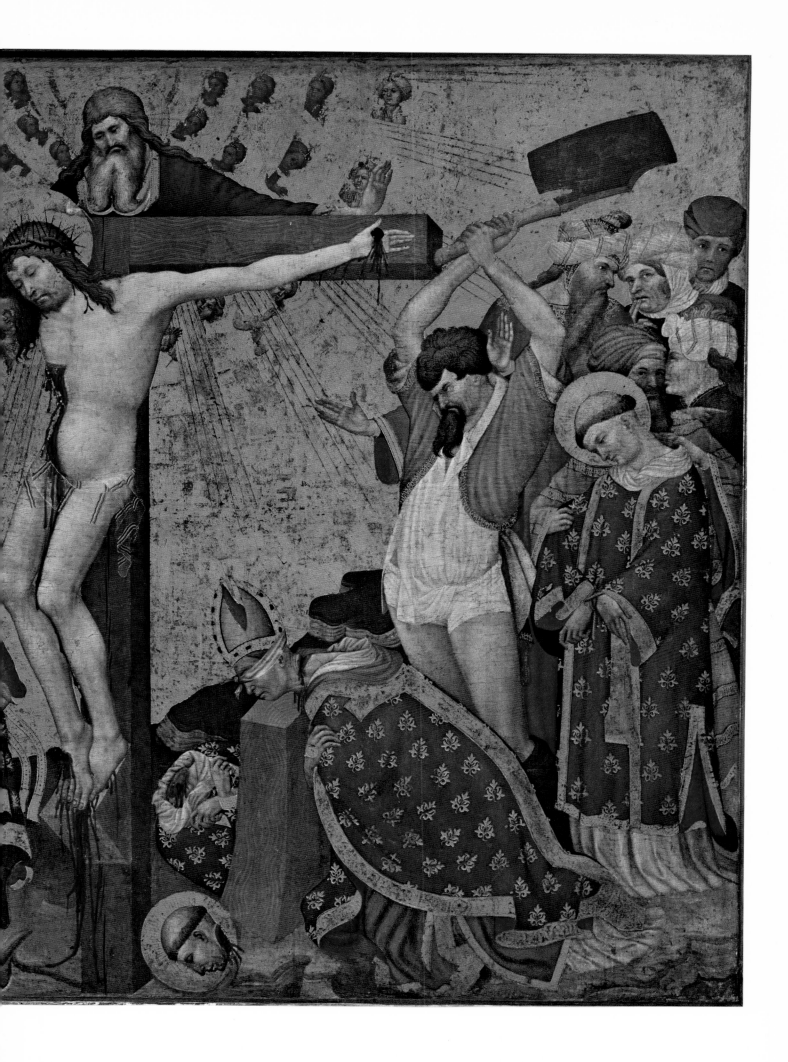

needed "to finish a picture of the life of St Denis." There can be little doubt that this was the work now in the Louvre. This view is supported by the fact that in March 1398 Jean Malouel had bought five panels on which to paint altarpieces; these were certainly intended, along with the reredos by Jacques de Baerze and Broederlam, for the six altars consecrated at Champmol in March 1389. And one of the six, the one above the Chapter Hall, was still dedicated to St Denis in the eighteenth century. Thus there is no good reason to call in question the traditional attribution, especially (as has recently been done) solely on the grounds of the measurements of the panels bought by Malouel; these panels were presumably in the rough when bought, and cut down by him to the required size.

Thus the *Martyrdom of St Denis* is the fruit of a collaboration, but too much stress should not be laid on this. During this period a picture, once it had been begun, comprised all the essential figures, which had to be clearly demarcated in view of the gold ground around them. All that was left undetermined was the final execution of some of them. The general conception, the layout of the picture elements and even the types of personage represented must, then, be assigned to Malouel, not (as many have thought) to Bellechose. Indeed, his style makes itself felt at every point. Like Beaumetz, perhaps even more than he, Malouel accentuates the realism of certain faces, delineates exactly the saint's wrinkles, and closely scrutinizes the warts on an executioner's face, on the theory no doubt that an ugly face often reveals an ugly mind. There is nothing mawkish in this artist's handling of the International Style. He never lapses into such minute refinements as the arrangement of folds in symmetrical volutes. Rather, he applies that style to the organization of the large masses of the composition and imparts to them an elegance that is never merely on the surface.

An exceptionally interesting work in the same style has recently been discovered: the Berlin *Virgin and Child*. The Virgin is shown half-length attended by ten angels, with golden butterflies (a curious attribute, whose symbolism eludes us) hovering above them. The brocade at the bottom of the composition is another unusual feature; its shape suggests the crescent moon referred to in the Litany of the Blessed Virgin. Millard Meiss and Colin Eisler, however, have suggested a more ingenious explanation. They very rightly point out that this strip of cloth acts as a link between the picture space and that of the beholder. But of even greater interest is their discovery of an exactly similar device in a drawing which is a copy of a lost portrait of Duke John the Fearless in prayer. Was this the second wing of a diptych of which the Berlin *Virgin and Child* was the first? This would seem a certainty, were there not another difficulty; the drawing shows the Duke turned to the left whereas, if this portrait figured alongside the panel representing the Virgin, he should be facing right. We would then have to assume that, for some whim of his own, the draftsman reversed the figure in his copy. (As a matter of fact this is not impossible; similar inversions are fairly frequent in fifteenth-century copies.) In any case the affinities between this panel and the *Martyrdom of St Denis* are so numerous that we can safely assign it to a Burgundian workshop. Here, perhaps, the tradition of the International Style makes itself more strongly felt; in the graceful undulations of the Virgin's garment and the somewhat mannered elegance of the slim fingers. But the naturalistic, almost crude directness of the rendering is also more pronounced. Indeed the caricatural treatment of the faces of certain angels has almost its only parallel in a few of the heads in the glory surrounding God the Father in the Louvre picture. And the Child's face with its globular eyes and puffy cheeks seems strangely out of keeping with the gracious features of the Virgin. Brutal, not to say barbaric elements of this kind are also to be found in the *Martyrdom of St Denis*, but there they are offset by a more refined handling, resulting in a better balance between these two conflicting tendencies. May it not be that Bellechose when finishing the picture tried to tone down the asperities and the violent contrasts which disconcert us in the Berlin picture and for which Malouel was, presumably, responsible? This is, of course, a mere hypothesis, but it may help to an understanding of other works emanating from the same milieu.

Anonymous Master.
The Coronation of the Virgin, about 1400-1410. Wood. (Diameter 8″) Staatliche Museen, Berlin.

A case in point is the large tondo in the Louvre, a *Pietà*, in which we find a sort of *détente*, a softening of the more aggressive features and a subtler harmony—developments of the tendency already adumbrated in the *Martyrdom of St Denis*. Very different are the small *Pietà* tondo and the *Entombment* (both in the Louvre), which fall into the category of Malouel's "harsh" productions. All this goes to show that the output of the Burgundian workshops comprised a singular diversity of trends. In the *Coronation of the Virgin* (Berlin) all harshness has been eliminated; the graceful undulations of the bodies and the simplicity of the gestures give this small panel the charm of a courtly poem, and, while imbued with a gravity approaching that of the Cleveland *Annunciation*, the scene is treated in what might pass for the Parisian spirit. Thus in the blend of realism and Gothic idealism, which characterized the International Style, Dijon tended to give priority to the former. A similar balance is struck in Claus Sluter's magnificent statuary and here that priority is even more apparent. Possibly this bias was essentially "nordic," in which case Sluter's art should not be assigned to the French domain properly so called. But the contacts and exchanges of ideas between workshops (confirmed by the records of the time and evident in such works as the *Coronation of the Virgin*) were still so numerous that all the other ducal courts kept in close touch with the activities of Champmol.

It must not be forgotten that those great artists attached to the court of Jean, Duc de Berry, the three Limbourg brothers (Pol, Herman and Jean) were nephews of the Duke of Burgundy's chief painter Jean Malouel. His court was even more magnificent, more refined and more Parisian than that of Burgundy. The Duke, whose face, as depicted by his illuminators, looks so attractive, was in point of fact completely unscrupulous. He exploited his subjects, utilized his Duchy of Guienne for replenishing his treasury, and spent most of the money thus acquired on his ruling passions, works of art and spectacular entertainments. Of his château at Mehun-sur-Yèvre only one tower has survived, but its splendor is immortalized in that paragon of illuminated books, the *Très Riches Heures*, in which we can admire the delicate beauty of its Gothic gables, vying with that of the Louvre of Charles V. And the Sainte-Chapelle which he caused to be built at Bourges for the funeral rites of the ducal House, bore comparison, so far as we can judge, with its celebrated namesake in Paris. The leading painters of the day worked for the Duke. To begin with, there was Jean d'Arbois, Painter to the King, about whom, despite his international renown, little is known. He was summoned to Milan to work on the cathedral, but what exactly were his functions in that gigantic enterprise remains a mystery. André Beauneveu, sculptor and architect, was the Duke's right-hand man. He hailed from Flanders, where he had served Duke Louis de Mâle. At Bourges he supervised building operations, carved the statues of the Sainte-Chapelle, and also, on occasion, worked on illuminated books. He was responsible (according to the ancient inventories) for the grisailles in the Duc de Berry's Psalter (MS fr. 13 091, Bibliothèque Nationale, Paris). These represent prophets and apostles, stately figures seated on thrones of stone adorned with Gothic pinnacles. Typically sculptor's work, they throw more light on that branch of art than on contemporary painting and illumination. Jacquemart de Hesdin is less easy to classify. The *Grandes Heures du Duc de Berry* (MS lat. 919, Bibliothèque Nationale) are presumably the ones referred to in the inventory of 1413 as containing "grandes histoires de la main de Jacquemart de Hodin et autres ouvriers de Monseigneur." But in the form in which they have come down to us these *Heures* contain not "grandes histoires" but only small scenes. Thus the ascription of these miniatures to Jacquemart, though probable, is far from certain. So far as we can judge of his personality, he seems to have been an illuminator whose art fell within the main stream of the International Style.

Regarding the Limbourgs, we are better informed. It is mainly due to Friedrich Gorissen's intensive research-work that so much is now known about their lives. They were the sons of a sculptor residing at Nimeguen, Arnold de Limbourg, whose wife Mechteld was a sister of Jean Malouel the painter. They were still quite young when their father died (in 1399) and it appears that their uncle took them under his care. It was he who apprenticed the two youngest, Herman and Jean, to Albert de Bolure, a Parisian goldsmith, and it was apparently their uncle who arranged for Pol and Jean to enter the service of the Duke of Burgundy. We read of their being engaged in 1402-1403 on the illuminations of "an exceeding fine and noteworthy Bible." Though there is no mention in the records prior to 1410 of their being in the Duke of Berry's service, this does not necessarily mean that they had not been working for him before that date. The Duke presented Pol with a house at Bourges (5, Rue Porte Jaune), and he married a girl from that locality, Gilberte Baston. The brothers did not outlive their patron; all three died, probably in the course of an epidemic, in 1416. Much has been written about the friendliness of the Limbourgs' relations with the Duke, evidenced for example by that "piece of wood painted to look like a book, in which there were no leaves nor any writing," which Pol and his brothers gave the Duke in 1410 as a New Year's present.

However, the making of such gifts, generously recompensed by the patron, we may be sure, seems to have been a tradition. In 1414 Pol gave the Duke a much more valuable present, a salt-cellar in agate with a gold lid inset with a sapphire and four pearls. Such gifts, however, were not so much tokens of any real intimacy as judicious offerings to a prince who liked receiving no less than giving.

Details of this sort have their interest as showing the diversity of the accomplishments of the Limbourg brothers. Herman and Jean, anyhow, were trained goldsmiths and this may account for the taste for minute precision and precious substances so evident in their miniatures. Probably they made panel pictures as well as illuminations, but there are no positive statements in the records to this effect. The circumstances of their life brought them in contact with very varied art milieux. There may well have been more interest in art than is generally supposed in their native Guelders. In Flanders, Paris and Dijon (where their uncle surely took them in their boyhood) they became acquainted with contemporary art trends; and, last but not least, they studied to advantage the recent achievements of Italian art. For the numerous borrowings from this in their works are explicable only on the assumption that at least one of them visited Italy. That they were great travelers is a point stressed by Friedrich Gorissen in the work to which we have already referred, and it is interesting to note how often they returned to their native Guelders, to keep watch on their local interests.

The Limbourg brothers' œuvre has come down to us solely in the form of illuminations, in those superbly illustrated books belonging to the Duc de Berry's well-stocked library whose contents have been determined by the erudite researches of Delisle. It is above all the last Book of Hours commissioned by the Duke, which was still unfinished at his death and took several years to complete (meanwhile the artists engaged on it had died), that repays careful study. Pride of the Musée Condé at Chantilly, the *Très Riches Heures du Duc de Berry* formed part, oddly enough, of a sequence of magnificent Prayer Books. It would seem that the Duke, never satisfied and always hoping for a work more "modern" in conception, asked each of the artists he successively employed to treat the same theme, his "Hours." Some of these books were never finished, as was the case with the *Très Belles Heures de Notre Dame*, which the Duke made over to Robinet d'Estampes, Keeper of the Ducal Jewels. The Limbourgs worked successively on two books: the *Belles Heures* (also known as *Les Heures d'Ailly*) now in The Cloisters, New York, and the *Très Riches Heures* at Chantilly. In this latter we see them at their splendid best; it is indeed the fine flower of the art of book illumination, and this work originally intended solely for the Duke's private devotions has won world-wide celebrity thanks to innumerable reproductions.

It is chiefly to the Calendar pictures at the beginning of the text that the manuscript owes its popularity, though the subsequent pages are well up to the level of the introduction. Each month has a page allotted to it showing the appropriate sign of the zodiac and the seasonal form of human activity. It follows the typology invented for the portals of cathedrals, at Paris and Amiens. But the page of a book gave more scope than stone carving to the artist's creative imagination and here, instead of symbolical figures in medallions, whole scenes are depicted. These twelve pictures form a sort of fresco of the daily life of the Middle Ages, then drawing to a close. They show us the occupations of the poor, such as haymaking and acorn-gathering, and the pastimes of the nobility, and both often figure in a single scene. Yet despite a wealth of realistic details and lifelike renderings of familiar gestures, the world conjured up by the Limbourgs is a dreamworld or, rather, an ideal world. Appearances notwithstanding, the methods of the art of Dijon are transposed; realism is relegated to the background and its place is taken by Gothic stylization. The nobles, often even the peasants, strike more elegant poses than the Virgins of religious art, encumbered with the weight of the Child; fingers are slenderer and suppler than those of the female saints of the previous century. Here, in fact, the exquisitely graceful beings created by Jean Pucelle, most elegant of the Parisian illuminators, return to life. Pucelle, however, stressed the linear aspects of his figures by isolating them on a ground of plain parchment or in purely schematic settings. The Limbourgs integrate theirs into meaningful contexts and locate them in narrative scenes and everyday surroundings, so as to bring them more vividly to life.

Thus under their brush a new world of beauty came into being, full of gay, scintillating color harmonies. The colors indeed have a gem-like luster, reminding us that the Limbourgs' early training was in a goldsmith's workshop. Everything, down to the tiniest detail, has a crystalline, otherworldly purity. Even the manner, empirical as it is, of suggesting space contributes to this idealization. Planes are merely superimposed without any attempt at linking them together. The proportions of figures and objects vary more in terms of the composition than with regard to their positions in space; for instance, in the "April" picture the clumps of trees, though equidistant from the foreground, are sometimes lofty, sometimes scaled down to tiny shrubs. The horizon line is placed as high as possible though the figures in the foreground are represented in front view, and the landscape acts as a sort of backdrop just behind them. Inexpertness? Perhaps, but, above all, a set purpose on the artist's part to confuse the issues; to cut the bridges between the real and the imaginary, so as the better to lure us into the wonderlands he is evoking.

In the *Meeting of the Three Magi at the Crossroads* we have an eloquent demonstration of this power of casting a spell on the beholder and plunging him simultaneously into two worlds. The towers of Notre-Dame de Paris and the Sainte-Chapelle play the same part as the views of the Duc de Berry's châteaux in the Calendar pages. They give the curious rock-formations spanning the horizon, fragments of an alien world, a singular immediacy, and, similarly, the running dogs are so realistically rendered that the three cavalcades seem wholly convincing, exotic yet paradoxically familiar. A sort of ballet, directed by a skilled choreographer, develops with the triple entrance of these picturesque cortèges. One of the mounted figures is exactly copied from a gold medal acquired by the Duke in 1402. The original, one of a set of four medals representing the four Roman emperors—Augustus, Tiberius, Constantine and Heraclius—who played leading roles in the early history of Christendom, is lost, but a cast in bronze preserves its salient features. The provenance of the original model is something of a problem. There is no proof whatever that, as used to be thought, it came from Italy. The fact of its being a "collector's item" admits of the possibility of its having been made by the Limbourgs themselves or by the master-goldsmith to whom they were apprenticed. Its graceful line and rhythm, so closely akin to the Limbourgs' characteristic "mannerism," and its general aspect are so exactly in the spirit of the illuminated page—and indeed the whole work—that it may well have been by the same hand. In which case the Limbourgs' "imitation" here was—of themselves!

Unfortunately none of their paintings proper seems to have survived. One is, however, tempted to assign to them the wholly delightful *Nativity with St Sixtus, St Jerome and a Cardinal* at Glasgow. This is usually dated later, to the second half of the century, and ascribed to the Provençal or Savoyard milieu. Yet the jagged mountains, the elegance of the young cardinal's profile, the flexions of the saints' heads and even the quaint intrusion of a restive donkey in a scene charged with poetic glamour belong to an artistic climate very close to that of the creators of the *Très Riches Heures*.

It is again illuminations, likewise of an exceptionally high quality, that reveal the activities of another great art center, the ducal court of Anjou. Eldest of the brothers of Charles V and a lavish patron, Louis I was famed for his collections of works of art, inventories of which have been preserved. He had a predilection for jewelry, precious stones, rare objects. Less is known of the artistic interests of his son, Louis II. His library does not seem to have been remarkable in any way and he had no great taste for paintings. Very different was his

The Limbourg Brothers.
The Meeting of the Three Magi at the Crossroads, about 1416. (8½×5¾″) Miniature from Les Très Riches Heures
du Duc de Berry, folio 51 verso. Musée Condé, Chantilly.

Entourage of the Limbourg Brothers.

Nativity with St Sixtus (?), St Jerome and a Cardinal, about 1410-1416. (20⅝×16⅛″) Glasgow Art Gallery and Museum.

wife, Yolande d'Aragon, who on his death took over the reins of government. It was she who took in hand the Dauphin Charles, nicknamed the "King of Bourges," whose trusted counselor she remained up to his death. She appears to have been no less interested in art and culture than in affairs of state. Round about 1414-1415 a very fine artist makes his appearance in her entourage. His earliest works figure among the Parisian manuscripts of the beginning of the century, but of the man himself nothing, not even his name, is known. He is styled the Master of the Rohan Hours, after the Book of Hours originally made for the House of Anjou, which passed into the hands of the Rohan family. Like the *Très Riches Heures du Duc de Berry*, the *Grandes Heures du Duc de Rohan*, as it has come to be called, far excells in brilliance and originality the common run of illuminated manuscripts produced in this period.

The first thing to strike us is the unusually large size of the pages and the fact that entire sheets are covered with illuminations. Here once again the miniature has become a self-sufficient picture—even more so perhaps than in the Limbourgs' works. The composition is set out in large masses, which take into account the flat surface of the page. This density of forms implies the work of a large-scale painter rather than a miniaturist; perhaps of a fresco painter adapting monumental figures to the restricted space provided by a book. There is no attempt (as with the Limbourgs) to suggest perspective; and the artist keeps to the medieval tradition, that of the cathedral portals, in which the stature of Christ or God the Father is commensurate with His authority. Likewise he reverts to the Romanesque practice (current in both frescoes and illuminations) of giving backgrounds an abstract, uniform coloration.

But alongside these deliberate reversions to medieval usage we find in the Rohan Master's work an impassioned inward drive that was something new. An example is the image of the Virgin swooning before the body of the Dead Christ, the violence of the effort St John is making to hold up her drooping form, and the cry of indignation he is hurling at the face of God the Father, charged with the elemental grandeur of the Old Testament Jehovah. Indeed each of the compositions in the Rohan Hours voices an anguished protest against the horrors of an age of wars, rebellions and wanton savagery, that age whose grim reality is elegantly camouflaged in the productions of the Duc de Berry's entourage. The very faces represented by the Rohan Master bear the marks of suffering and violence. Here we are poles apart from the ethereal idealization of the *Très Riches Heures*. It has given place to a deliberate, obsessive insistence on the ugliness of life, carrying more conviction than the figurations of an artist such as Malouel. None the less this forcefulness keeps within the ambience of the age; forms retain a Gothic fluency, violence finds expression in the linear rhythms and graceful attitudes of the International Style. How eloquently the anguish of a soul confronting the terrors of the Last Judgment is summed up in the figure in a lower corner of this powerful composition dominated by Christ the Judge seated on a rainbow! The flowing curves of the man's garment and the contracted arm have no less grace, though of a different order, than the form of the naked woman risen from the dead, who is treated in the same style as the Limbourgs' "Eve."

But these extraordinary illuminations raise more than a purely stylistic problem; quite clearly there is a new idea behind them, differing *toto caelo* from the traditional conception of the illustrations appropriate to a Book of Hours. Presumably this novelty and this independence were feasible only on the assumption that the artist was given a specific commission; that this work was "guided." Everything points to the fact that an exceptional climate of taste had developed at the court of Anjou, differing greatly from that prevailing at the courts of King Charles VI, the Duke of Burgundy and the Duke of Berry. True, no definite proof of this is possible; too little is known of the personalities of Louis II and Yolande d'Aragon for us to ascribe with any certainty to either this new art trend. However, there exists a miniature whose inspiration can only have derived from the court of Anjou. This is a highly curious depiction of the "last judgment" of a private individual; he is lying dead on the ground,

Master of the Rohan Hours. The Last Judgment, about 1420. (11⅜×8¼″).

Miniature from Les Grandes Heures du Duc de Rohan, folio 154. MS lat. 9471, Bibliothèque Nationale, Paris.

stripped of his insignia (a large gown in the Angevin colors) and thus reduced to an anonymous cadaver confronting God the Father, who is about to receive his soul. This representation of a naked body is clearly meant to suggest all men's equality in death, the vanity of worldly pomp and power. An interesting point is that this theme reappears in a picture commissioned by King René, son of Louis II and Yolande d'Aragon, for his tomb at Angers. A gaunt, emaciated corpse wearing the royal crown and cloak is shown grotesquely seated on the royal throne. Evidently King René had a special fondness for this motif; during his captivity at Dijon (1435-1437) he had insisted on its figuring in his Book of Hours (now in the British Museum, MS Egerton 1070). The close affinities between these works are evident; all three must have had the same source of inspiration.

There can be little doubt that the Rohan Master made panel paintings; the attribution to him of a shutter in the Laon Museum is certainly correct. Sole surviving element of a large triptych, it owes its preservation to the fact that when the triptych was dismantled it was built into a cupboard. Despite its lamentable condition, this panel has a wonderfully emotive quality. On the obverse is a group of apostles, in wildly billowing robes, framed in an architectural setting. Below them is a row of lunettes with heads of prophets. The general effect is one

Master of the Rohan Hours.
The Angel of the Annunciation and a Donor, about 1420-1430. Wood. (37⅜×40¾") Musée Municipal, Laon (Aisne).

Master of the Rohan Hours.
Portrait of Louis II of Anjou, about 1420 (?). (9×6⅝″) Bibliothèque Nationale, Paris.

of hushed expectancy and religious awe. On the reverse is the Angel of the Annunciation. The reverence of the kneeling angel's attitude, and the pointing fingers, indicate that the adjoining panel (now lost) contained the figure of the Virgin Annunciate. The picture has the same dramatic force as the miniatures in the Book of Hours. Behind the angel kneels the donor, an abbot draped in his cope. His face is portrayed with scrupulous fidelity and without the least attempt to palliate its expressive ugliness.

That in portrait painting the Rohan Master could be more lenient has been proved by Jean Porcher's undoubtedly correct attribution to him of the *Portrait of Louis II of Anjou* (Bibliothèque Nationale). The face is painted on a sheet of parchment with the delicate precision of an illumination; indeed one wonders whether it was intended to figure in a book or (as it has come down to us) in a frame. There is no knowing; but this much is clear: that, whatever its destination, it was treated in the spirit and with the amplitude of an independent portrait. As in the *Portrait of John the Good*, the face is shown in profile, but here the strict linearism this involves, far from being a handicap, serves the artist's turn. Though we have few portraits of the period to go on, it would seem that the profile view (subsequently adopted by Pisanello) was favored by practitioners of the International Style. In the *Portrait of a Woman* in the National Gallery of Art, Washington—certainly a French and probably a Parisian work—this method is employed with even greater subtlety and refinement. It is interesting to note that in the fascinating likeness of Louis II of Anjou the Master of the *Grandes Heures de Rohan* reveals once again this fondness for Gothic procedures. He stresses the linear contours of the face and disposes the headdress and surcoat in such a way as closely to enframe the profile and to emphasize its clear-cut line. By the same token, far from attempting, like the painter of *John the Good*, to bring out volumes, he confines himself to light touches, suggestive rather than explicit, and, as in the illuminated manuscripts, applies the paints in minute dabs. Though the rhythm is essentially linear, it does not preclude expression; as M. Porcher has pointed out, the Duke's gaze has "that air of gravity and melancholy, tempered by the glamour of some secret dream, which distinguishes the major figures of the Rohan Master."

What was the country of origin of this highly original artist, creator of a world so rich in poetic overtones? His vigorous "expressionism" certainly suggests that he was not French born, and in view of his temperament some have thought he may have been a Spaniard. The Duchess, Yolande d'Aragon, was Spanish and this, it is suggested, may account for her patronage of an artist who was her compatriot. Yet nothing in the Rohan Master's art has a parallel in any contemporary Spanish works. In view of the forcefulness of such an artist as the Master of the Trebon Altar, one is, rather, tempted to surmise that the Rohan Master was a Bohemian. But it would be a mistake, in my opinion, to exclude Flanders and the countries of the north, which were giving France so many artists at the time. In the few examples of contemporary works of Dutch or Nordic origin that have been preserved, we sometimes find an emotivity somewhat akin to that of the painter to the Dukes of Anjou. But what is most striking in this context is that the great exponents of the International Style in France were always foreigners. Malouel and the Limbourgs came from Guelders, the Rohan Master from a country so far unidentified. Thus the "internationalism" of this art is not merely a matter of style; it is also a consequence of the fact that more and more artists from many different countries were now being called in by lavish and enlightened French patrons.

The style did not die out abruptly. Time and again artists reverted to it in Paris and elsewhere. One of the most remarkable examples is the little known but highly interesting œuvre of the painter Jacques Iverni. The name suggests that he was born in the neighborhood of Paris, but it is in the records of Avignon between 1411 and 1438 that references to him are found. At that time Avignon was no longer the seat of the papacy and the Italian artists had, it seems, departed. Italian tendencies can, however, be seen in Iverni's art; his use, for example, of greenish shadows in flesh tints for purposes of modeling. Moreover some of the architectural elements in his paintings are clearly due to Sienese influence. None the less the style of his two best known works, the triptych of the *Virgin suckling the Child* (Turin) and the *Annunciation* (Wildenstein Collection, New York), closely resembles that of the painters employed in the workshops of the Dukes. True, Iverni's more pronounced sense of the monumental is an Italian trait, but his arabesques follow the same curves and are also combined with traces of realism. It is above all to his feeling for volume, which seems to have increased with the years, that Iverni's compositions owe their power and majesty. He continued working when Paris was in a state of chaos, under foreign rule, and kept alive in his privileged retreat the tradition that the wars had obliterated in the capital.

A Perfect Equipoise
The Secret and the Strength
of Fouquet

Jean Fouquet (c. 1420-c. 1481).
Pietà (detail), about 1470 (?). Wood. Parish Church, Nouans (Indre-et-Loire).

THE year 1428 witnessed the completion of the decorations of the Brancacci Chapel in Florence, first and fullest expression of Masaccio's genius. His frescoes pointed the way to a new aesthetic in which the human figure played unequivocally the leading role. Four years later the Ghent Altarpiece was installed in the church of Saint-Bavon. Here, completing the work of that enigmatic personality, his brother Hubert, Jan van Eyck gave free scope to his vision of a world of strange enchantments in which the beauties of the here-and-now are sublimated, exalted to the rank of precious objects. Thus two new art languages arose and made good at the two extremities of the continent of Europe.

In this momentous period French art was dormant. War, internecine conflicts, social upheavals had put a stop to the activities of wealthy patrons, artists had fled in all directions. It was not until the kingdom began to re-cement its unity under Charles VII that French art entered on a new lease of life. It then found itself oscillating between two new poles of attraction, Flanders and Italy, and took form under their joint influence.

But no sooner did French art show signs of a revival than a genius in whom all its basic qualities were united came on the scene: Jean Fouquet. It is significant that Fouquet, trained undoubtedly in a Flemish milieu, should have been the first French artist to make the journey to Rome, where he was welcomed as a master. Far from evading the conflict between the painting of the north and that of the south, he faced the problem squarely and solved it by striking a judicious balance between their diverse trends. Isolated masters had already attempted this, at Bourges and in Provence, but it was Fouquet who redressed the balance with a success unparalleled for many years to come. From Flanders he acquired that flair for the savor of quite ordinary things which is basic to his art. To Italy he owed that unfailing sense of human dignity which accounts for the intrinsic nobility of his creations.

A Perfect Equipoise
The Secret and the Strength
of Fouquet

WITH the disaster of Agincourt (1415) France entered on a period of insecurity and nation-wide unrest. John the Fearless, Duke of Burgundy, liege and uncle of the King of France, made terms with the English and ceded French territory to the victors. In 1419 John's assassination by members of the Dauphin's suite made matters worse, the result being that his successor, Philip the Good, openly took sides with the partisans of the English. France capitulated and in pursuance of the Treaty of Troyes (1420) Henry V married Catherine of Valois, daughter of Charles VI, and the right of heirship to the French crown was accorded to the son who was soon to be born to them. The French parliament endorsed this treaty, which stripped the Dauphin Charles (later to reign as Charles VII) of his rights. But events were moving fast; within six months (in 1422) Henry V died and Charles VI followed him to the grave. The terms of the treaty now took effect and the French crown passed to Henry VI, who was then an infant less than two years old. Thus the Court of Paris now came under the domination of the English king represented by his regent, the Duke of Bedford. The Dauphin Charles, backed by a few members of his court, proclaimed himself King of France, but it cost him many years of struggle to get his status recognized by all. This was an outcome of the heroic venture of Joan of Arc, but also of many less well-known campaigns. The signing of the Peace of Arras (1435) was only the first stage in the dénouement of this protracted conflict.

The disturbed state of the country told against any progress in the field of art and, moreover, the great patrons of the previous period, the Dukes, had died: in 1416 the Duke of Berry, in 1417 his nephew Louis II of Anjou, in 1419 John the Fearless, Duke of Burgundy. The only one of their successors to show an active interest in art was Philip the Good, and he employed for the most part Flemish artists, doubtless because his favorite residences were in Flanders. Though Burgundian or Parisian artists were occasionally attached to his household or to that of his son Charles the Bold, they had to live in Flanders. Thus it is not due to chance or merely to the ravages of time that not a single major work in the French domain can be assigned to the period 1420-1445. Not that all artistic activity had ceased; illuminators' workshops continued to flourish in Paris. Most important was the one whose moving spirit was the anonymous artist known as the Bedford Master, after one of his outstanding works, a breviary made for the English Regent, John Plantagenet, Duke of Bedford. But none of the great manuscripts which rank as landmarks in the field of the miniature or painting was executed in his workshop. The Bedford Master excelled in anecdotal figurations, but did little more than exploit in a minor way the discoveries of his great predecessors. It is at a distance from the disturbed areas—in Avignon where Iverni was still working and in Anjou where the Rohan Master carried on for some years—that we find continuing traces of creative activity.

A revival was, however, getting under way, the first signs becoming perceptible at about the time of the Peace of Arras (1435), particularly in the entourage of Charles VII, who had chosen for his residences the château of his uncle, the Duke of Berry, at Mehun-sur-Yèvre and the ducal palace at Bourges. But though he had inherited his uncle's residences, it was beyond his power to play the part of art patron on the same scale, anyhow until the Peace of Arras. The only large commission he gave, before his first victory, was one for the completion of the Duke's tomb by the sculptor Jean de Cambrai.

But now a great art patron came to the fore: this was Jacques Cœur, the fabulously rich financier whom the king appointed master of the mint and (in 1438) steward of the royal

Master of the Aix Annunciation.
The Annunciation, between 1442 and 1445. (61⅛×69⅜″) Church of Sainte-Marie-Madeleine, Aix-en-Provence.

expenditure. In 1443 he built his magnificent private residence at Bourges; well preserved and skillfully restored, this is one of the finest examples of medieval civil architecture. In 1447 he had work started on a chapel in the cathedral, which was to be lavishly decorated with works of art. But in 1451 he fell into disgrace; after a long trial he was imprisoned, but contrived to escape, first to Provence, then to Italy. His career in France was ended.

Very few of the works made to the order of this lavish patron of the arts during his brief years of prosperity have come down to us. However, on the vaulted ceiling of the small, finely laid-out chapel in his house at Bourges, we still see a company of gracious angels, linked by inscribed scrolls, hymning the glory of the Virgin and Child. A work of major importance but too often disregarded, it proves the extent to which Flemish influences had permeated this part of France. The wonderfully elegant rendering of the angels' hands and the curiously rigid fall of the folds of their garments bring at once to mind the art of Rogier van der Weyden. The plenitude of the forms and the skill with which they are fitted into segments of ogival vaults show a highly personal approach to monumental art. But even more surprising is the modeling of the faces with strong contrasts of light and shade, at once gripping our attention and accentuating the pensive gravity of the downcast eyes. Who, one wonders, was the artist who conjured up this vision of a choir of angels hovering in mid-air? Henri Bouchot has proposed Jacob de Littemont and the fact that this artist is known to have worked for the king's financial adviser lends color to his view. De Littemont was Painter to the King from 1451 to 1469. The name, too, suggestive of a northern origin, is another point in favor of Bouchot's theory. But all this is purely speculative; indeed a case might be made out with almost equal plausibility for Conrad de Vulcop, in the king's employ from 1448 on, or the stained-glass painter Henri Mellein.

Of even greater interest, perhaps, than these frescoes is the "Jacques Cœur window" in his private chapel (in Bourges Cathedral). There is no certainty that it was made before 1451 when the great financier's career ended in disaster, for we learn that his son, titular bishop of Bourges, was still engaged in completing the chapel five years later. But anyhow its general conception must have been arrived at some time before, not later anyhow than the years 1447-1450. For the period, the layout was strikingly original, and evidently due to an exceptionally gifted artist. In the wide bays of the wall a simulated architecture has an effect of prolonging and enlarging the restricted space assigned to the Chapel. Situated in the vast perspective vista thus created are four majestic figures, rendered with compelling power: St James, St Catherine, the angel Gabriel and the Virgin. The emergence of a new style is unequivocal. The plenitude of the forms, the artist's feeling for space and his flawless composition invest the ensemble with monumental grandeur and nobility. Here we have qualities of an essentially sculpturesque order; indeed, it seems possible that the formative influences behind this style derived from the workshop of the Duke of Berry's sculptor Jean de Cambrai, in whose art are anticipations of the forceful style which was to prevail at the end of the century. Far from indulging in the realistic or dramatic accents characteristic of such a man as Claus Sluter, he created ample, broadly molded figures, disdained to linger over drapery folds, so as the better to stress the dynamic qualities of forms, and toned down the realistic elements of faces. But the sculpturesque figures of the stained-glass windows are also akin to the frescoed angels in the chapel. Count Durrieu, indeed, surmised that the two works were by the same hand. In that case we have to assume that, when he worked in the cathedral, the artist had evolved, discarded the formulas of his Flemish training, and developed an art that was original through and through.

Unlike northern France, Provence had escaped the turmoil of the war and was now the scene of an artistic revival, oriented towards a broader, fuller handling of form, and this is evidenced in another major work. Though the popes had quitted Avignon, this part of France was prosperous, teeming with energy, and a wealthy middle class had come to the fore.

Pierre Corpici, a draper in Aix-en-Provence, gave instructions in his will (December 9, 1442) for the making of an altarpiece in the Cathedral of Saint-Sauveur representing the Annunciation. In a second will made by Corpici in 1445 (he died in 1449) it is stated that his wishes had been carried out and the altarpiece installed. Unfortunately there is no mention of the artist's name in this or any other document. Jean Boyer has recently advanced a theory that this painter was Guillaume Dombet, basing it on the notable affinities between the Aix *Annunciation* and the windows, for which Dombet was given the commission (in 1442), in the chapel of Saint-Mitre. This attribution, however, is not wholly convincing. For one thing, we question whether Dombet, who was in the prime of life as far back as 1414, could have produced a work at once so boldly experimental and so strongly marked by the art of the great contemporary Flemish masters. Moreover, judging by the records, he seems to have been eminently adaptable, and his work shows few signs of a well-defined artistic personality. Thus we learn that payments were made to him both for the stained-glass windows (these in a "vanguard" style) in the chapel of Saint-Mitre and for Archbishop Nicolaï's tombstone, whose design and execution are traditional and mediocre. If the *Annunciation* really came from his studio it must have been the work of one of his younger assistants, perhaps one of his sons or, more probably, his son-in-law. For when in 1430 Arnolet de Catz, a glass painter from the diocese of Utrecht, married Dombet's daughter Peyronnette, his father-in-law entered into a renewable three years' partnership with him, on the understanding that they were to share equally their emoluments. This younger man from the north—possibly the "Arnoulet" described as a master-painter in the records of the Tournai guild in 1423 and of whom there is no further mention—answers much better than his father-in-law to our conception of that admirable artist, the Master of the Aix *Annunciation*.

Only the central panel is still at Aix, but no longer in the cathedral, having been transferred to the church of Sainte-Marie-Madeleine. The right wing is in the Musée Royal, Brussels. Of the left wing two fragments survive. One, containing the still life on the upper part of the reverse, belongs to the Rijksmuseum, Amsterdam, but has been loaned to the Louvre; the other, representing the prophet Isaiah, after figuring in the Cook and Van Beuningen collections, is now in the Boymans Museum, Rotterdam. The realistic handling and the artist's addiction to heavy drapery and brocades show marked affinities with Flemish art, notably with that of Jan van Eyck and the Master of Flémalle (indeed the Aix *Annunciation* has recently been attributed to the latter). Influences of both are plain to see. The fully rounded forms and vigorous relief derive mainly from the Master of Flémalle, as does the extreme realism of the faces of God the Father and Jeremiah. But it is Van Eyck to whom this artist owes the splendor of the garments and brocades; also the delicate perfection of his surfaces and the elaborate perspective of the background. However, these borrowings do not detract from the originality of the work. The clear-cut composition and the solemn mien of the large figures are in much the same spirit as the stained-glass window at Bourges. While the warm, though muted, color lacks Van Eyck's translucency, it answers better, perhaps, to the artist's concern with volumes. The composition, skillfully combining well-balanced masses with a symbolic content, is no less effective. The picture space is divided into two unequal parts. On the left the angel Gabriel is kneeling in a small, low-roofed recess, while on the right the scene opens out on a far-flung vista, the two long naves behind the Virgin, signifying that the Mother of God is also the Mother of the Church. All the light comes from the left; at the transept crossing where the Virgin is praying it streams down from a small circular window behind which appears God the Father, his hand raised in blessing. Thus it is a divine light that bathes and amplifies the space around her. Here the symbolism, centering on the Church, is unmistakable. The artist did not pick on a religious edifice as a setting for the Annunciation merely because it gave the scene an atmosphere of mystery. We have glimpses of figures at the far end of the nave, persons who have come to worship. They, too, may well have a symbolic purport, but they also serve to enliven the composition, adding a touch of color to the austerity of the background.

Master of the Aix Annunciation.

The Annunciation (detail), between 1442 and 1445. Church of Sainte-Marie-Madeleine, Aix-en-Provence.

On the shutters, in two niches simulating architecture, the prophets Isaiah and Jeremiah are depicted, standing on pedestals. The strongly characterized faces have often been interpreted as portraits, and, as was to be expected, some have seen in the amiable face of Jeremiah a likeness of King René. But the draper had no reason to have his sovereign represented in this guise. If these are really portraits, more weight should be attached to the theory of Jean Boyer, who proposes to identify the two prophets with the draper himself and his only son, Eleazar, who must have been between twenty and twenty-five years of age when the altarpiece was made. But the method of portraying these prophets at once as statues (in an architectural setting and standing on pedestals) and as living beings—an effect enhanced by their costumes, their attitudes and the skillfully contrived disorder of the books piled on shelves above them, to indicate their occupations—is a typically northern, more precisely Flemish, procedure, and one often resorted to by Rogier van der Weyden. The still lifes, too, have a Flemish origin and are a development of the symbolic groups of objects often associated with representations of the Virgin. Thus we are inclined to think that here, too, they have a symbolic purport. But their "message" (assuming they have one) remains to be elucidated.

Though we have constantly to refer to Flanders apropos of the Aix *Annunciation*, this is not the only influence perceptible in it. Elsewhere than in the south of France, saturated with Italian art and in constant touch with Italy, so free an interpretation of Flemish methods could hardly have been feasible. The clear definition of masses, the fully plastic rendering of volumes may well be due to Italian inspiration; also the systematic use of shadows for almost purely decorative purposes. Thus in the art of the Aix master both influences are operative, to superb effect.

Almost simultaneously, then, at the very time when the kingdom was regaining its unity, the first manifestations of a new art were taking place in both northern and southern France, at Bourges and at Aix. It was also the time when Jean Fouquet, the painter who symbolizes *par excellence* and dominates the pictorial art of fifteenth-century France, came on the scene. Fouquet was born at Tours in the troubled period between 1420 and 1425. The illegitimate son of a priest and an unmarried mother, he had to procure a papal dispensation if he was to acquire full status as a member of the Catholic community. It was perhaps for this reason that he went to Rome, where he seems to have lived for some time, previous to 1447. But nothing is known of his youth. The fact that he is referred to in the dispensation as "clericus" has been taken to mean that he had studied at a university. However, this may have been due to a slip of the pen; or else, more likely, was a mere courtesy title. It used to be thought that he was trained as a painter at Paris, in the studio of the Master of the Duke of Bedford. But this opinion was largely based on the attribution to him (as "early works") of a group of illuminations now known to have been made by a painter styled the Master of Juvénal des Ursins, whose art was unprogressive, very different from that of Fouquet, who had already produced the *Hours of Etienne Chevalier*. In any case why assume that Fouquet went to Paris? When he came to manhood the court of Charles VII was still on the move, sometimes in the Berry region, sometimes in Touraine. Several artists were attached to it and Fouquet may well have studied under one of them.

His journey to Italy probably took place between the years 1445 and 1447. Young though he was, he seems to have been hailed as a master, and was commissioned to make the portrait of Pope Eugenius IV attended by two acolytes. It is much to be regretted that this picture is no longer extant; it would have been interesting to observe the reactions of the young artist, newly arrived from France, to the ultra-intellectual Roman milieu. In 1448 we find him back at Tours, in the employ of Charles VII, without, however, holding the official post of Painter to the King. On Charles's death he was assigned the task of coloring his death mask. In 1461 he was deputed to organize the ceremonies accompanying the state reception of the new king, Louis XI, at Tours. Evidently his prestige at Court was steadily rising.

Anonymous Master.
The Annunciation, about 1447-1450. Stained-glass Window. Chapel of Jacques Cœur, Bourges Cathedral.

In 1469, on the foundation of the Order of the Knights of St Michael, he painted a number of pictures for the Order, and in 1474, along with Colin d'Amiens, he designed the tomb in which the king desired to be interred, in the church of Notre-Dame at Cléry. But it is not until 1475 that we hear of his holding the post of Painter to the King. At Tours he made pictures for Notre-Dame-la-Riche (Archbishop Jean Bernard in his will of 1463 had asked him to paint an *Assumption*). In 1476 he designed a dais for the state entrance of Alfonzo V, King of Portugal, into Tours. He married in 1448, and both children of this marriage, François and Michel, became painters. A document dated 1481 refers to "the widow and heirs of Jean Fouquet, Painter to the King." To these few, sadly unrevealing scraps of information is limited our knowledge of the life of this great painter. They differ little from those we have concerning other painters of his time, except for the unusual circumstance of his stay in Italy.

It is not, however, records of the period that have enabled us to identify his œuvre. Neither the pictures in Notre-Dame-la-Riche, nor the *Assumption* commissioned by the archbishop, nor even the pictures made for the Order of St Michael have survived. If we can now assign a number of (anonymous) works to Fouquet, this is solely due to a note that François Robertet, secretary to Pierre II, Duke of Bourbon, had the fortunate idea of inscribing on the end-paper of the *Jewish Antiquities* now in the Bibliothèque Nationale. In this it is stated that nine of the illuminations in the manuscript "are by the hand of Jean Fouquet of Tours." In the light of these nine sheets it has been easy to identify other works as his. These are: (1) the *Hours of Etienne Chevalier* (c. 1450), the greater part of which is in the Musée Condé, Chantilly (the manuscript was unfortunately dismembered in the nineteenth century); (2) a volume of Boccaccio (Munich) which, written in 1458, was probably illustrated forthwith; (3) the *Grandes Chroniques de France* (Bibliothèque Nationale), seemingly executed at almost the same time; and (4) an *Ancient History until Caesar*, only a few pages of which have survived. To these may be added an illumination which would go far to confirm the validity of the attributions, if confirmation were needed: the frontispiece to the "Rules and Regulations of the Order of St Michael," proved to be by Fouquet's hand.

Though all these works are illuminations, one of them, the *Hours of Etienne Chevalier*, has enabled the identification of the diptych made for the same patron, and by the same token of the portraits of Charles VII and Juvénal des Ursins. Finally, in 1931, Paul Vitry discovered another full-size painting in the parish church of Nouans, a *Pietà*, clearly affiliated to this group. Few as these pictures are, their quality makes ample amends for their fewness.

The earliest is doubtless the *Portrait of Charles VII* (Louvre). The absence of any background, the frontal presentation of the king's torso and the symmetrically placed curtains on each side strike an archaic note. Drawings made in the seventeenth century of fourteenth-century portraits no longer extant prove that some of these conventions already obtained in royal portraits, and this is confirmed by the use of a very similar composition in Jean Clouet's *Portrait of Francis I*. Clearly this work fell in line with an old tradition of the royal portrait. Such strict conformity with tradition would be *prima facie* unlikely in the case of a painter who had developed a personality of his own after a sojourn at Rome, where, under Popes Eugenius IV and Nicholas V, art had made such noteworthy advances. We entirely concur with Charles Sterling's dating of this royal portrait to about 1445. For the inscription on the frame (*"le très victorieux roy de France"*) which has puzzled so many art historians, who assumed that it commemorated the reconquest of Guienne (1452), may well have been added later and, in effect, proves nothing.

In this work Fouquet is already in full possession of his means, though still dominated by Flemish influences. The king's rather uncouth face is treated with unflinching candor; the over-large nose, the pouches under the eyes, the thick lips and heavy jowl seem curiously at odds with the laudatory inscription on the frame. Yet, despite its archaism and realism, this portrait has an austere grandeur prefiguring subsequent developments. Pope Eugenius IV may well have been startled by such intransigence. Speaking of the portrait of him which Fouquet made in Rome, Filarete remarked that it was "positively alive," *che veramente vive proprio*. Francesco Florio, too, commented on this singular lifelikeness, perhaps because it contrasted so strongly with Italian idealism. An engraving which probably reproduces this no longer extant work reveals a style very near that of the *Portrait of Charles VII*. We have only to compare it with the face of Eugenius on the bronze door of St Peter's (made by Filarete) to realize how alien to Rome is Fouquet's art. In the painting all the volumes are boldly indicated and features sharply delineated—"his brush is like an engraver's burin"— whereas in Filarete's likeness there is barely a hint of modeling, the face is little more than a profile; here, in short, the sculptured portrait is less plastic than the painting.

These two portraits—or rather this portrait and the shadow of another—help to an understanding of both the importance and the novelty of the diptych made by Fouquet for the church of Melun. The two panels have now been separated. The one representing Etienne Chevalier (who commissioned the diptych) commended by his patron saint is in Berlin; the *Virgin and Child* in the Royal Museum, Antwerp. Our plates restore them to their position side by side. There is no reason to question the truth of the ancient inscription on the back of the Antwerp panel to the effect that the *Virgin and Child* was painted in pursuance of a vow made at the time of the death of Agnès Sorel, one of whose executors was Etienne Chevalier. Copies of contemporary portraits confirm the tradition that the Virgin is a likeness of the famous mistress of King Charles VII. So the diptych may be dated to about 1450 (the year of Agnès Sorel's death), i.e. shortly after Fouquet's return from Italy.

The difference between the two panels comes as a surprise when we see them side by side. The *Virgin and Child*, with its background of cherubs in the colors of the celestial hierarchy, seems like a relic of medievaldom. Its formal dignity and the grave demeanor of the Child have the austere remoteness of an icon, and the pink-and-blue cherubim, despite their plumpness, contribute to this otherworldly effect. On the other panel we see Etienne Chevalier and his patron saint standing in a stately, marble-paved hall. The contrast between these scenes, the hieratic quality of one and the realism of the other, carries a symbolic rather than a stylistic value. On one side is the ideal world, the world of God, on the other that of Man. Each has its own light and its own space, and these alone would suffice to differentiate them.

The pensive air of the angels and the Child and the lowered, inward-turning gaze of the Virgin stress the solemn nature of the moment, transcending the human situation and charged with intimations of divinity. This sublimation is implemented by a vigorous, forthright modeling that generalizes features, presenting them in simple forms; the face of Agnès Sorel is transmuted, given a serene, celestial beauty. Did Fouquet, one wonders, while in Italy, become acquainted with the art of Piero della Francesca? There is nothing against this, chronologically. But tempting as this surmise may be, we must not press the rapprochement too far. Fouquet does not idealize his figures, either in his illuminations or in his paintings, except in evocations of the world of the divine. We have but to turn to Etienne Chevalier to realize that this is a different world; space is unequivocally indicated and the human figures in it have realistically stated volumes. Idealization is reduced to the use of an angle of vision and a light enabling a forceful organization of forms.

There is little probability that Fouquet knew Leon Battista Alberti, and even less that he was initiated into the new theories of perspective and *costruzione legittima*. The most we can say is that he must have seen works in which the new rules were applied, and tried to imitate them; this is proved by the perspective recession of the pavement and the wall, stressed by pilasters spaced at regular intervals, behind St Stephen. But the keen observation so clearly evidenced in his rendering of Chevalier's gravely attentive face and far-away brooding

Jean Fouquet (c. 1420-c. 1481).
The Melun Diptych, left wing: Etienne Chevalier commended by St Stephen, about 1450. (37¾×34⅝″)
Staatliche Museen, Berlin.

Jean Fouquet (c. 1420-c. 1481).

The Melun Diptych, right wing: Virgin and Child, about 1450. (35¾×31⅞″) Musée Royal des Beaux-Arts, Antwerp.

gaze, was doubtless due to a study of the Flemish masters. What, indeed, could be more Eyckian than his depiction of the rock that killed St Stephen, which looks almost like some precious stone and assumes such an oddly innocuous air upon the rich red leather binding of the book the saint is holding?

The portrait of Guillaume Juvénal des Ursins, the king's chancellor, must have occupied one of the panels of a similar diptych. The donor is shown in prayer, gazing at the Virgin and Child. One is tempted to believe that a memory of the *Madonna of Chancellor Rolin*, then in a chapel of Autun Cathedral, prompted not only the commission but even Fouquet's treatment of the subject. The very absence of a patron saint and the emphasis given the donor's cloak, reminding us of his high rank and affluence, cannot but call to mind that other Chancellor, Jan van Eyck's. The face invites comparison with the portrait of Canon van der Paele by the same master. But here wrinkles and slight blemishes are not rendered with the same meticulous precision. Fouquet makes a point of stressing the architectonic planes, so as to impart a monumental grandeur to his figure. Moreover, in the case of this work we have a record of the artist's initial conception; there exists in Berlin an excellent preliminary drawing of the Chancellor's face. Each detail of the features is minutely analysed and delineated in silver-point, enhanced with colored chalk, but these details, when transposed on to the panel, cease to catch the eye and merge into the general color scheme, one of the most striking features of the composition. Thus the richly colored background, inspired by the decorative repertoire of the Italian Renaissance, includes a "reserved" slab of green marble against which the face tells out sharply, as on a medallion.

There is another portrait by Fouquet, of all the greater interest for being a likeness of himself. This small round plaque is executed in an enamel technique hitherto, it seems, unknown in France. The same technique had been employed some years before by Filarete in the decoration of the pedestal of a statue commissioned by Piero II de' Medici. Possibly, indeed probably, it was Filarete who taught him this new technique, for the two artists had become friends when Fouquet was in Rome. Until the Second World War there was another enamel in Berlin, similarly treated, representing the Pentecost. Both may have figured in the frame of the Melun Diptych. For an early description of it states that "it contained small enamel medallions representing some story in the Bible, with most admirably depicted figures." Despite its smallness, the self-portrait is in the lineage of Fouquet's major works. Those watchful eyes gazing at us so intently make us sense a living presence, and no less impressive is the sculpturesque quality of the boldly modeled head backed by a grisaille flecked with gold: "a forthright face," as Focillon has said, "simply and solidly constructed with something in it of a peasant turned townsman and acclimatized to city life." But a preternaturally alert peasant, judging by the tight-set lips and the extreme intensity of the gaze.

Great painter though he was, Fouquet's fame does not rest solely on these pictures. One feels indeed that it was in his illuminations he felt most at ease, less hampered by convention or set programs. Though occasionally he had to allow for a setting placed on the page before he started work, he was usually given a free hand and could break, if he so wished, with the traditions of manuscript illumination. The most revealing instance is the Book of Hours he made, about 1450, soon after his return from Italy, for Etienne Chevalier. Though unfortunately the complete book no longer exists, a considerable number of the detached pages are preserved at Chantilly. Here the miniatures of traditional illuminated manuscripts have given place to pages entirely covered with painting. The text is reduced to a few words, sometimes inscribed in a colored band acting as a sort of base or foundation to the scene, sometimes actually incorporated in the composition. In the latter case Fouquet employs a layout of a most unusual order; the lower part of the picture consists of a relatively narrow foreground, without any hint of depth, which tends to crowd back the leading theme towards the upper part. It is almost as if one were looking at a play in which the forefront of the stage is occupied by two or three supernumeraries holding between them a phylactery, while the action takes place behind and above them. Perhaps, as has been suggested, Fouquet got the idea from the mystery plays for which there was so great a vogue in the fifteenth century (the period of the famous *Mystères* of Arnoul de Gréban).

But the most striking feature of these illuminations is the primacy given Man and the new conception of space, scaled to the human measure. One of the first results of the unusually wide foregrounds in the *Hours of Etienne Chevalier* is to confine the scene depicted to an oblong zone in which figures seem to bulk larger than in the traditional page-high rectangle. This, however, is not the only device employed by Fouquet for giving prominence to the figures. In the *Visitation*, for example, he restricts the space in which they are located by inserting a projecting portico forming a background adjusted to the same scale as the figures. For he also does away with the differences of proportion in the compositional elements, which still existed as a rule in the Limbourgs' compositions. Moreover, though the perspective governing the organization of space does not exactly conform to the rules laid down by Alberti, it approximates to them. The *Visitation* is also significant for the light it throws on Fouquet's highly personal solution of the problems of pictorial construction. At first sight one might think that the architectural elements are conventionally rendered, in terms of receding lines converging on a vanishing point. Actually, however, Fouquet is manipulating perspective in a quite unusual way when he opens up behind the Virgin a narrow couloir flanked by a bare wall flooded with sunlight—an effect striking an Italian note. Moreover these same elements also stress the dualism of the painter's inspiration; he reinterprets in the language of the South two medieval symbols of the virginity of the Virgin: the well and the closed garden.

The artist's overriding interest in the human figure and the vivacity of his compositions cannot fail to remind us of Italian predellas; they have the same poetic narrative quality, are bathed in the same limpid light. More particularly, perhaps, they bring to mind Fra Angelico's predellas. Probably Fouquet was still in Rome when Fra Angelico was painting his frescoes in the Chapel of Nicholas V in the Vatican. Though we have no evidence that the two men actually met, it is clear that Fouquet closely studied the Italian master's work.

Jean Fouquet (c. 1420-c. 1481).
Self-Portrait, about 1450. Enamel Painting.
(Diameter 2¾") Louvre, Paris.

Jean Fouquet (c. 1420-c. 1481).

The Visitation, about 1450. (6½×4¾″) Miniature from Les Heures d'Etienne Chevalier. Musée Condé, Chantilly.

From Fra Angelico he certainly borrowed his method of punctuating space with figures, of giving them thickset bodies draped in heavy garments falling in clear-cut folds, and even his bright colors, his vivid blues. But all these borrowings were integrated into a wholly personal style. Characteristic of Fouquet's miniatures is their gravity, the deep reflection that so clearly lies behind them. Where there is action, it is slow and stately; but more often action is arrested, held in suspense.

Into the *Hours of Etienne Chevalier* Fouquet put the best of himself; none of the other manuscripts he worked on has the same density, the same unity of tone. In the *Grandes Chroniques de France*, made around 1458, perhaps under instructions from Charles VII, the execution shows signs of haste and it is probable that he employed assistants. The same is true of the *Boccaccio* commissioned by Laurens Gyrard, notary and secretary to the king. But, in both manuscripts, we find here and there magnificent, more carefully composed pages, as happily inspired as those in the *Hours of Etienne Chevalier*. One is the well-known miniature depicting the *lit de justice* at the Parlement convened by Charles VII at Vendôme in 1458.

It is, however, in two later manuscripts that we see Fouquet once more at his best: the *Ancient History until Caesar* and the *Jewish Antiquities*. Only a few pages of the former have survived (Louvre). The illustration of the latter (Bibliothèque Nationale), begun by the Duke of Berry's illuminator, was completed between 1461 and 1476 by Fouquet, at the request of Jacques d'Armagnac, a descendant of the Duke. In both cases the layout of the book had been decided on before Fouquet started work, and differed greatly from the one he had employed in the *Hours of Etienne Chevalier*. It consisted of large pages comprising extensive

Jean Fouquet (c. 1420-c. 1481). David given Tidings of the Death of Saul, about 1470. (8⅜×7″)
Miniature from Les Antiquités Judaïques, folio 135 verso. MS fr. 247, Bibliothèque Nationale, Paris.

decorations in the margins and a vertically disposed rectangle left free for the pictures. Fouquet arranged these in such a way as to make the best use of the space available. He gave prominence to the foregrounds and grouped his figures in them, often in a sort of frieze. Above them he usually placed a landscape, as in *David given Tidings of the Death of Saul*.

Already in the *Hours of Etienne Chevalier* some scenes had included fairly large land-scapes. But in the later works this theme is given wider scope. Here and there we still find spectacular rock-formations whose peculiar shapes derive from International Gothic. But these are purely incidental. For the most part planes are rendered in a fluent rhythm, recalling that of the rolling countryside of Touraine, but re-created, idealized in the artist's imagination, and an infinitely gentle light plays on the pale green meadows. Indeed these landscapes are treated in an almost classical spirit, such is their essential purity. But Fouquet's idealization takes its start on typically French soil; these billowy green expanses, friendly hills, and smoothly flowing, pellucid streams have none of the asperity of the Tuscan scene or the Van Eycks' imaginary mountains. True, a complete harmony between the foregrounds crowded with active figures and the placidity of nature is not always achieved. But this break of continuity may be deliberate; by stressing the contrast between the two worlds, it brings out the poetic quality of landscape treated as a thematic element in its own right. Even the battle scenes are pervaded by a curious serenity, tempering their violence.

The most recently discovered work by Fouquet has, once again, a religious theme. This is the *Pietà* piously preserved in the little church at Nouans, a village in Touraine. It was commissioned by the Canon who figures among the participants in the sacred drama, escorted by his patron saint, St James. The fact that the execution falls somewhat short of that of Fouquet's other large-scale pictures has led some to doubt its authenticity. But these blemishes are purely superficial; the composition, the iconography, even the drawing have the intensity characteristic of Fouquet's art. A number of figures are closely grouped together on a slanting plane. Their arrangement recalls that of Flemish sculptured retables, but, even more, that of the northern paintings in which this layout was adopted. A comparison of the Nouans *Pietà* with Rogier van der Weyden's *Descent from the Cross* (Prado, Madrid) helps to an under-standing of Fouquet's artistic personality. Here all anecdotal details are ruled out; no sump-tuous garment clashes with the harmony of simple tones, no theatrical gesture disturbs the atmosphere of meditative calm. By concentrating on the moment following the Descent from the Cross—the moment of hushed repose when the body of Christ is laid in front of the Virgin and all are gazing down in silent grief—the painter has lowered the action, so to speak, towards the ground, and he reduces gestures to a minimum. Only the Canon's figure, clad in a white alb, is shown in its full stature, this difference indicating that he belongs to another world. The Virgin's grief is conveyed quite simply by the tenseness of the finely molded face, the clasped hands, and the slight droop of her body. And her sadness is reflected in the expressions of those around her, especially the touching group of the three Marys.

It was about this period that French sculptors turned to a theme that was to have a great vogue in the near future: the Entombment. This theme had points in common with that of Fouquet's *Pietà* and was invested with similar emotions. However, even in its sparest versions, for example the *Entombment* in the hospice of Tonnerre (1451-1453) and that of Solesmes (1496), the sculptors contented themselves with naïvely emotive gestures or lingering with loving care on details of garments. Nowhere do we find the large veils of the mourning women treated with the fine economy of means distinctive of the Nouans *Pietà*. Doubtless this painting invites comparison with sculpture, by reason of its emphasis on volumes; but no sculpture having the same austerity, dignity and discretion was being produced at the time. The whole work is conceived in the spirit of a bas-relief destined to serve as a frieze on the wall of a religious edifice. In Fouquet's earliest pictures, even his illuminations, we find intimations of this intensity of expression, fruit of a deep meditation on the given theme.

The Nouans *Pietà* is generally thought to mark a final stage of its maker's artistic evolution, but there are too few landmarks on the path from the Melun Diptych to Nouans for us to feel any certainty. Still, it may well be that here we have one of our great artist's last creations.

In some eloquent pages Henri Focillon has shown that Fouquet's place is in the lineage of the cathedral sculptors. "Jean Fouquet owes his compelling power and pre-eminence to the long-enduring tradition of the 'grand style' of French monumental art; and to the fact that he was a direct descendant of the image-sculptors who from the late twelfth to the late fourteenth century made statues to adorn our churches, in strict keeping with their architecture." What better proof of this could there be than the Nouans *Pietà* whose rhythms and massive force are those we associate with a tympanum? It would, however, be a mistake to minimize for this reason the part played by Italian culture in the shaping of Fouquet's art. From his stay in Rome he brought back far more than "some casual reminiscences and a few minor accessories." In his illuminations and panel paintings we occasionally find wreathed columns, antique entablatures and Corinthian capitals encircled by putti, which at first sight may seem out of place in their context. But, looking more closely into these seeming anomalies, we find that he resorts to classical architecture only when evoking the terrestrial world, the world in which (for example) Etienne Chevalier is kneeling as he contemplates the Virgin and Child, whose domain is that of Gothic art. His usage of the Italian style as a symbol of the contemporary world of men testifies to a deep insight into the spirit of the age he lived in. What Fouquet derived from his Italian sojourn was a new vision of Man, and the conception of a world made to the human measure. Hence his break with the medieval *Weltanschauung*,

Jean Fouquet (c. 1420-c. 1481).

Pietà, about 1470-1480 (?). Wood. (63⅛×86⅝″) Parish Church, Nouans (Indre-et-Loire).

a break whose purport may not have been fully understood by his own generation. It well may be that the Nouans *Pietà* could not have come into being but for the artist's contact with Renaissance culture, to which it owes its transference of the sacred scene into a purely human world, and its comprehension of the human emotions of the participants in the divine tragedy.

So peculiar to itself was Fouquet's genius that its influence may seem to have been negligible. There is no denying that all we find, as a rule, are but pale reflections of it. One of the works approximating most closely is a triptych in the church of Saint-Antoine at Loches, in Touraine. It was originally in the Carthusian monastery at Liget and is inscribed with the date 1485, showing it was made after Fouquet's death. In any case there are few traces of any profound inspiration in its three scenes: the Bearing of the Cross, the Crucifixion and the Entombment. What we find are, rather, borrowings of formulas and type-figures, along with a plethora of anecdotal elements. The figures lack grandeur, volumes are stiffly and perfunctorily rendered and look as if they were carved in some hard wood. The same is true of another picture recently discovered in the church at Gonesse, just to the north of Paris, and thought to come from the near-by château of Ecouen. Not that these two works are by the same hand; all they have in common is that both are the work of disciples copying the master's style. In somewhat the same manner his influence makes itself felt in certain illuminations, notably those of Jean Colombe and Jean Bourdichon. These two men, however, assimilated Fouquet's methods to better effect and created a style appropriate to the taste of the last generation of the fifteenth century.

But these are merely superficial resemblances; Fouquet's influence on his generation should surely be traceable at a deeper level. Unfortunately few works of the kind we have in mind are extant. Also we are hampered by the fact that so little is known about his contemporaries and that they are rarely mentioned in documents. However, some outstanding works of the period have survived, and the most remarkable is undoubtedly the *Retable du Parlement de Paris*. This once famous picture was one of the first "French Primitives" to figure on the "line" in a museum of art. It was made for the Grande Chambre of the Parlement between 1453 and 1455, the cost being defrayed by fines judiciously imposed on members of the Bar, with a view to the decoration of the premises occupied by the Supreme Court. The Retable took the place of another picture made at the beginning of the century by the King's Painter, Colart de Laon and, more fortunate than its predecessor, was destined to survive to our time. When, round about 1511, Louis XII commissioned the lavish decoration to which this enormous room was to owe its name, *La chambre dorée*, it was left in situ, and incorporated in the new layout. All the great sessions of the seventeenth and eighteenth centuries took place in front of the retable. During the Revolution it was given shelter in the Louvre; next, under the Empire, it was restored to its former place and this it never left until the memorable Exhibition of French Primitives held in Paris in 1904. Thus this picture has historical associations of unusual interest and its relegation to the class of "minor" works is quite unjustified.

Unfortunately the records of the period, though stating the exact sum paid to the maker of the retable, fail to mention his name. At first sight one might assume he was of Flemish origin. But this assumption would be over-hasty. For the traces of Flemish influence, if unmistakable, are few in number. They are confined to direct imitation of three elements of Rogier van der Weyden's diptych in the Kunsthistorisches Museum, Vienna: the figure of Christ, St John's face and the attitude given the Virgin—no more than these. All they prove is that the masterworks of Flemish art were known in France and, presumably, in high favor; indeed so literal an imitation may well have been specifically provided for in the terms of the contract. The execution, however, reveals a feeling for volumes, a full-bodied rendering of forms, which differ greatly from the essentially linear handling of the Flemish master. It was assuredly from Fouquet that this artist got the idea of the majestic alignment of the four saints beside the Cross and the dramatic grandeur of the group around the Virgin, in which

Philippe de Mazerolles (c. 1420?-1479).
Retable du Parlement de Paris, 1453-1455. (82¾×106″) Louvre, Paris.

Flemish type-forms are wholly recomposed in terms of a new aesthetic. A peculiar feature of this picture is the way in which the artist combines the noble dignity of its leading figures with the vulgarity of minor personages and the unvarnished realism of certain details. Examples are the small figures of the executioners in the background and the blood spurting from the neck of St Denis, whose severed head has already the livid hues of death.

In appraisals of this retable stress is often laid on the documentary value of the detailed depiction of the medieval Louvre in the left-hand background. Actually, however, it is best not to rely over-much on its accuracy. On the right, too, there is a representation of the Paris of the past, but this view of the Palais de la Cité—the present-day Law Courts—is an artificial synthesis of elements rearranged with an eye to the overall effect of the composition. This aspect of the retable is, however, of secondary importance. Far more striking is the artist's handling of color, for example his use of cool flesh tints enhanced with touches of pure color, intense blues in the shading of the eyes of certain figures, and pure reds for blood. The cool

Philippe de Mazerolles (c. 1420?-1479).

Retable du Parlement de Paris (detail), 1453-1455. Louvre, Paris.

flesh tints were something completely new. It is usual to credit Hugo van der Goes with the idea of them, but he was still a child when this work was made. In view of the fact that painters were often makers of stained-glass windows, in which clear glass was sometimes used for the flesh tints, we are, perhaps, justified in seeing here an influence of stained-glass technique. Only an indirect influence, however, for the author of the retable, versatile though he was, does not seem to have practised glass painting.

We are inclined to identify him with that singular fifteenth-century personality Philippe de Mazerolles. In 1454 de Mazerolles was living in Paris, where he seems to have been working as a goldsmith. In 1466 he was at Bruges, where he brought to completion a magnificently illuminated Book of Hours, presented by the city to the Comte de Charolais (subsequently Charles the Bold). Next year he was appointed *valet de chambre* to the Duke of Burgundy and remained at his residence in Flanders until 1479 when both he and his wife died, carried off presumably by an epidemic. Until recently his work remained anonymous and he was described as the Master of Anthony of Burgundy and the Master of the 1476 Boccaccio. His œuvre comprises several superb manuscripts, now grouped alongside the Book of Hours (on black sheets) presented to the Comte de Charolais, and also some striking engravings made for one of the first books printed by Colart Mansion. His artistic career was remarkable not merely for the variety of the works produced, but also because these are assignable to the French and to the Flemish domains, successively. For, just as the *Retable du Parlement de Paris* was often thought to be a Flemish work, so the works he made at Bruges can hardly pass for those of a truly Flemish artist. Possibly this was an exceptional case. But it should warn us against a tendency to distinguish too sharply between "national styles" in a period when the nations were still in the making.

Given the rarity of works contemporary with Fouquet and showing his influence, considerable interest attaches to a picture recently brought to light and now in the Cleveland Museum of Art. It represents the Trinity—God the Father seated, holding forth the Cross, Christ crucified, and the dove of the Holy Spirit flying above. This is a variant of a composition invented by the Master of Flémalle. But here the group stands out against a glory of angels, colored in terms of the heavenly hierarchy, in exactly the same manner as the angels in Fouquet's *Virgin and Child* (Antwerp). But it is the composition, the compact grouping and the unusual fullness given the faces that most clearly recall the right wing of the Melun Diptych. This intermingling of Flemish reminiscences with procedures distinctive of Fouquet comes close, if in a different key, to the art of Philippe de Mazerolles. But here another element is added; the wistful, supramundane grace of the quiring angels has already something of the poetic beauty of the angelic choirs which the Master of Moulins was to paint in the last decades of the century. A link seemed to be missing between the art of the Antwerp *Virgin and Child* and that of the Master of Moulins, and the Cleveland *Trinity* goes far to supply it.

Also in the lineage of Fouquet are three works which have given rise to much discussion and are still something of an enigma. All three are portraits. Perhaps most striking is the one that represents a young man standing behind a parapet on which his left hand rests, only his head and shoulders being visible (Collection of the Prince of Liechtenstein, Vaduz). The date, 1456, is painted behind his head in a flowing Gothic script whose quaint calligraphy has a wonderfully decorative effect, while the square face with an energetic chin and the wide open, slightly squinting eyes has a singularly compelling power. The artist has obviously sought to achieve the forcefulness of Fouquet's modeling, but given it a certain harshness by dint of realistic touches which the Touraine master was always mindful not to overdo. Another, very similar work is the famous *Man with a Glass of Wine* in the Louvre. Here the realistic element is even more pronounced, not only in still-life details—the glass from which the man is about to drink, the bread and cheese, the knife on which his hand is resting, all no doubt having some symbolic significance—but also in the scrupulous rendering of the man's features and in the darkly smoldering gaze. These two portraits have a "family likeness"; we even find traces on the brownish ground of the *Man with a Glass of Wine* of an arabesque (now almost effaced) recalling the writing on the 1456 portrait. A third work of the same type has recently come to light; the curious portrait of a man in the Châteauroux Museum which had passed unnoticed until 1937, and owes its present-day renown chiefly to the erudite study of it (1955) by Jacques Dupont. The man depicted is a member of the Venetian nobility, recognizable as such by his elaborate coiffure, the *zazzera*, which came into fashion at the end of the century. He has the same strangely staring eyes, the same rather prominent features as the young man of the 1456 portrait and his clasped hands rest on a parapet. Though its kinship with the two other portraits is evident, we need not assume it is by the same hand. The execution is dryer, the modeling more linear. Moreover, M. Dupont has detected on the back a seal with the arms of the Contarini and the only member of the family to have any contacts with France was Zaccaria Contarini who came as Venetian ambassador to the court of Charles VIII in 1492. Thus this work is some thirty-five years later in date than the Liechtenstein portrait, a fact that renders its attribution to the same artist still less plausible. In that case the Châteauroux portrait is merely an imitation of the style of the two earlier portraits.

On the strength of the affinities between these three portraits and Fouquet's art, one is tempted to assume that they originated from Touraine, and indeed this was the generally accepted view. Recently, however, the question of their provenance has been reopened as a result, oddly enough, of a close examination of the work of two master-illuminators. Jean Porcher has pointed out that the Master of Juvénal des Ursins inserted faces closely resembling these in the initial letters of one of his illuminated manuscripts (MS 10.474, Bibliothèque Royale, Brussels). As it so happens, these illuminations were at first thought to be youthful works by Fouquet, and in recent studies we find a tendency to assign them to the Loire region. Still, the illuminator does not give the impression, by and large, of being an inventor of new forms, a fact that renders his assimilation to Fouquet highly dubious. Nor has he the power of expression that we find in the initial letters of the Brussels manuscript, which, in turn, lack the solid construction of the portraits we are dealing with. That they stem from a common source seems certain, but it is probably the Master of Juvénal who is imitating in his illuminations the work of the Master of 1456. Paul Wescher, for his part, agreeing in this with Miss Grete Ring, is reminded of another distinguished illuminator of the period, the Master of the Lovesick Heart. But it is difficult to believe, in the absence of any historically authenticated evidence, that works so monumental as the portraits here in question can have been produced by a manuscript illuminator, however expert in that field, and however brilliant and original his contribution to the art of the period.

The so-called Master of the Lovesick Heart owes his appellation—let us hope, provisional—to a manuscript with a wealth of exceptionally fine illustrations. It is a de-luxe copy, probably made for its owner (and author), of a romantic allegory written by King René of Anjou. The text was completed in 1457 and the copy in the Nationalbibliothek, Vienna, was probably made at about that date. The composition of the miniatures was completely new for the period, befitting the novelty of the themes the miniaturist was asked to illustrate for his royal patron. A revival of the allegorical love poetry of the troubadours, the *Lovesick Heart (Le Cuer d'Amours Espris)* describes the adventures of the knight "Cuer" who, accompanied by "Désir," sets forth to rescue the gentle lady "Doulce Mercy" from captivity. The subject called for an entirely new mode of illustration and the artist rose nobly to the occasion. In this renewal he followed in the footsteps of Fouquet; for it was certainly from him that the prominence given the human figure by the René Master derived. Even more than in the *Hours of Etienne Chevalier*, there is a tendency to build up the composition around a few figures, and the surrounding space, even when it is a landscape, is correspondingly reduced. Despite its intrinsic interest, it serves primarily as a frame—almost one might say a casket—for the stately presences of "Cuer" and "Désir."

56

Master of the Lovesick Heart. Meeting of Heart and Humble Request, about 1460.

(11×7⅞″) Miniature from Le Cœur d'Amour Epris, folio 31 verso. Cod. 2597, Nationalbibliothek, Vienna.

The figures themselves are robustly rendered, and their essential volumes given a monumentalism that is frankly sculpturesque. Here the fluent, aerial Gothic line has given place to a massive statement of the human form. Often, too, plastic values are emphasized by bold contrasts of light and shade. Indeed the René Master's handling of light is one, and not the least, of the many surprises of this remarkable volume. Greatly daring, he paints the sun itself, not as a token detail, but as an active source of rays dividing space into zones of light and shadow. He paints darkness, too, intensified by the little pool of brightness around a candle flame. Is this due to an acquaintance with the work of his Italian contemporaries, keen observers of the counterpoint of light and shade? Quite possibly, but in that case it seems strange that he did not also make attempts to render perspective. In this field the René Master is less advanced than Fouquet. He does not even trouble about seeing that proportions are coherent and makes doors lower than his figures, plants symbolic trees at the corners of his compositions and sometimes plays fast and loose with the relative statures of the persons he represents. This is undoubtedly deliberate, a corollary of his *ars poetica*. If he reverts to a Gothic procedure, this is at once to implement the dreamlike quality of his settings and to center attention on the figures.

The brightness of the colors, too, comes as a surprise. Dazzlingly blue skies and vividly green fields predominate in the scenes in which recurs, like a leitmotiv, the white cloak of "Vif Désir." Even the marginal decorations seem to have been devised so as to strike a contrast between the fragile grace of an interlace of flowers and foliage disposed in flowing arabesques and the robustness of the figuration. Moreover margins have been much enlarged; ceasing to frame the picture proper—the traditional practice—they counterbalance it, sometimes acting as a sort of fulcrum. But what strikes us most in these remarkable illuminations is that the man who made them was by nature a poet and brought a poet's vision to his interpretation of King René's allegorical romance; for example in his renderings of the handsome face of "Vif Désir" and its look of poignant melancholy. This manuscript was presumably his master-work. In any case none of the few other extant works by his hand is marked by the same lyrical effusion. For it to have come into existence at all a very special climate of taste was needed. It was what we should describe today as an avant-garde work, and it has the audacity as well as the uniqueness that the epithet implies.

Naturally we desire to know the name of this singularly gifted artist. And here we come up against a highly intriguing problem. For a tradition which, given its antiquity and persistence, cannot be lightly dismissed, assures us that King René himself was a distinguished painter. Hence the obvious temptation to ascribe to him the illuminations figuring in what was seemingly his literary *magnum opus*. To this temptation Dr Otto Pächt has succumbed and there is no denying that his arguments in favor of this attribution have considerable weight. The king's personal *Book of Hours* (MS Egerton 1070, British Museum) contains five illuminations dating beyond all doubt to the period of his captivity in Dijon (1435-1437). He was kept in such strict custody that the possibility of his calling in one of his favorite artists to make them seems to be ruled out—this anyhow is the opinion of Dr Pächt. In that case we have in the *Book of Hours* a set of illuminations undoubtedly by the king's own hand, and a comparison with those in the Vienna manuscript of the *Lovesick Heart* tends (again according to Dr Pächt) to confirm the attribution of the latter to the royal artist. So far, so good. But the weakness of this argument lies precisely in the fact that when the two illuminated manuscripts are compared, it becomes obvious that the London manuscript has relatively few similarities with the one in Vienna. It is still under the influence of the Flemish technique which the René Master so notably transcended in the *Cuer d'Amours Espris*.

Must we, then, reject the legend of the royal painter as a myth? Probably we must, for even allowing for the different conditions of his age, it seems unlikely that after King René had written his novel (or anyhow sketched out its leading episodes), he found time and had the patience himself to paint day after day the pages of his manuscript. That he guided his painter's hand, prescribed the lines on which each episode was to be treated, suggested in some cases the composition of a scene, and even perhaps added a few touches of color on his own, we can readily believe. The fact that in those days far more importance attached to the general conception of a work of art than to the actual execution may well explain why King René was so often described as being himself a painter. Be this as it may, there is no question that this enlightened king played a considerable, indeed a leading role in the evolution of French fifteenth-century art. The mere existence of a tradition of his being a painter suggests, at the very least, that he was keenly appreciative of works of art, and this is confirmed by the number of purchases he made and the commissions he gave to artists. Moreover, he was one of the most traveled princes of his age. During his two-years captivity at Dijon (1435-1437) he probably had opportunities of becoming acquainted with the work of painters employed by his cousin, the Duke of Burgundy. It is quite likely that he met Jan van Eyck himself when he was in Brussels in February 1433 or at the beginning of 1437 when he was at Lille. According to Summonte (whose statement carries all the more weight since he was writing in the fifteenth century), he painted "in the Flemish manner." But King René was soon to go to Naples and in the four years he spent there (1438-1442) must have come in contact with Italian artists. Subsequently, he stayed some four months in Florence, where his friends the Pazzi, lavish patrons of the arts, doubtless familiarized him with the works then being produced in the Tuscan capital. Then again he made a short stay in Lombardy in 1453.

As a prince and art lover, King René may have acted as an intermediary between his homeland, France, and Italy and Flanders where a great flowering of art was then in progress. But he also did much, it seems, to promote the development of French art, for he was constantly traveling back and forth between Anjou and Provence. In Anjou, until the death of Charles VII, his boyhood friend, he was a persona grata at the royal court. He became friendly with that other famous art patron Jacques Coeur and gave him shelter in Provence when the great financier's career ended in disaster. From the records we learn that he often took with him on his travels his favorite artists, one of them being Barthélémy de Clerc (in his employ from 1449 to about 1476), who has often, perhaps rightly, been identified with the Master of the Lovesick Heart. It was only in 1471 that King René took to residing permanently in Provence. Until then he had only made two prolonged stays there, from 1447 to 1449 and from 1457 to 1462. Was his painter, then, an Angevin or a Provençal? More probably the former, even if he accompanied the king and worked for him on his travels.

It is still difficult to determine the exact part played by King René in fifteenth-century art; too little is known as yet about his collections and his painters. And what was evidently a key work—the large painting named *The Dead King* that he commissioned for his tomb in Angers Cathedral—has disappeared. Curiously enough not a scrap of evidence exists pointing to any effective contacts between the king and Fouquet. Yet without doubt these were the two men who did most to orient the evolution of French art in the fifteenth century.

Provençal Painting
from Charonton to Froment

Enguerrand Charonton (c. 1410-c. 1466).

The Coronation of the Virgin (detail), 1453-1454. Hospice of Villeneuve-lès-Avignon.

AVIGNON became an active art center in the fourteenth century when, from 1309 on, it was the papal seat and the popes called in Italian artists to supervise the work of the teams of painters, French, Flemish and Italian, employed on the decorations of their sumptuous palace. Conditions at Avignon were very different in the second half of the fifteenth century, when there was no papal court to commission frescoes, illuminated books, and pictures. The papal legate, sole occupant of the deserted palace, was not in a position to employ the many painters who flocked to the city. Henceforth they catered for an essentially middle-class clientele, consisting of Provençal merchants who, thanks to the flourishing state of trade, had amassed considerable wealth, and there was no shortage of lucrative commissions, judging by the prices quoted in records of the period. This accounts for the continued influx of artists from distant regions, and it was they who were now to shape the course of Provençal art: such men as Enguerrand Charonton (or Quarton) from the diocese of Laon, Pierre Villate from that of Limoges, Josse Lieferinxe who probably hailed from the Netherlands, and Bernardo Simondi, a Piedmontese.

True, the creations of the second half of the century had been preceded by the superb achievement of the Master of the Aix *Annunciation*. But it was a different, more authentically Provençal art that now gained ground. Distinctive of it is a style of a singular austerity, which in its inspired moments attains a compelling grandeur. This art is undeniably Provençal; its austerity stems from the same light as that which, long after, was to guide Cézanne's hand. Intensely vivid, it reduces volumes to their simplest expression, obliterating secondary reliefs; it confronts shadows with clean-cut shafts of light and gives the world of forms that sharpness of definition which is a characteristic trait of the French painting of the fifteenth century.

Enguerrand Charonton (c. 1410-c. 1466).

The Coronation of the Virgin (detail), 1453-1454. Hospice of Villeneuve-lès-Avignon.

Provençal Painting
from Charonton to Froment

THE Master of the Aix *Annunciation* seems to stand outside the main stream of Provençal art; in any case it shows few signs of his direct influence. An exception is the Boulbon Altarpiece (Louvre). Though in poor condition, this work has retained much of its dramatic power. The Christ of the vision of St Gregory, standing in his coffin and surrounded by the instruments of the Passion, reveals himself to a Canon, presented by St Agricola. This iconography (Flemish in origin and conception) is ingeniously combined with that of the Holy Trinity; the wings of the Dove link the face of Christ to that of God the Father, framed in a window in the background. In the course of time, as a result of wear-and-tear and over-paintings, the modeling has lost its pristine vigor. Yet even so we can admire the artist's handling of forms reduced to simply stated planes intersecting at sharp angles. Particularly striking are the faces of the donor and the saint, such is the rigorous asperity of their delineation. Apart from this altarpiece (whose severity and spareness already prefigure the new Provençal school), practically the only other work influenced by the Aix *Annunciation* was a fresco sequence in the Church of the Celestines at Avignon, now known to us only by a sketch made in the nineteenth century. The fact is that a new, quite distinctive type of art emerged in Provence in the second half of the fifteenth century. This art was in some respects a product of Italian and Flemish influences, with, perhaps, some Spanish accents superadded. But only to a limited extent; its main elements are essentially Provençal and in its severity, its ruthless light, we find an instinctive response to the climate of southern France.

The new style makes its first appearance in the work of Enguerrand Charonton. Not that he was a Provençal by birth; he came from the diocese of Laon, but subsequently settled first at Aix, then at Avignon. Records make mention of his presence in Provence from 1444 to 1466. Until recently his only known works were the *Virgin of Mercy* (Musée Condé, Chantilly), painted in 1452, and the celebrated *Coronation of the Virgin* (Hospice of Villeneuve-lès-Avignon) painted in 1453-1454. To these can now be added the *Virgin and Child with Two Saints* recently discovered by Michel Laclotte in a storeroom of the Palace of the Popes. But Charonton's personality is not so easy to determine as one would expect. For the *Virgin of Mercy* was a joint work; in terms of the commission Charonton had a collaborator, Pierre Villate. However, Villate's name does not appear in the order for the *Coronation of the Virgin*, work on which began only a year later. Only a step was needed to ignore his existence, a step taken by most art historians. The discovery of the picture in the Palace of the Popes—let us hope it will be promptly published once it has been restored—will certainly lead to a reopening of the problem. That the newly discovered picture is by the same hand as the Villeneuve and Chantilly panels is evident. But it has a style of its own (both in the composition and the color scheme), a style that gives an added prominence to certain characteristics of the two other works: a simplification of forms, an exact rendering of plastic values and, above all, what may look like an Italian influence. Thus it tends to cast doubt on the unity of conception of the two previously known works. Provisionally, however, pending a detailed comparative study of the three works in question, that unity may be taken for granted, with a view to elucidating the truly original elements in a style that may well prove to be the outcome of a happily inspired collaboration.

In the rather dimly lit room where the Chantilly picture (painted in 1452) is now installed, the first thing that strikes the visitor is the contrast between the gold ground and the fully modeled figures telling out in empty space and disposed with rigorous symmetry on each side of the Virgin of Mercy. Silent and statuesque, they stand or kneel in an abstract space defined by the gold screen, isolating them from the world. The presentation of figures in a restricted space, and on a slanting plane reminiscent of certain carved retables, is in a Flemish spirit. But the layout—the rhythm imposed on the picture surface by the large empty spaces between the figures—is typical of the South of France. For even in the group sheltering under the Virgin's cloak each face is so clearly stated and so effectively contrasted with the neighboring faces that its individuality shines out unmistakably. Even the cast shadows, precisely if sparely represented, heighten the effect of the flooding light that generates these austere volumes.

The *Coronation of the Virgin*, begun in the following year, exhibits similar tendencies. But here the rigorism of the Chantilly picture gives place to a suppler, more anecdotal style. This change may have been necessitated by the extremely detailed instructions given in the contract between Charonton and Jean de Montagnac (preserved in the Archives Notariales of the Bouches-du-Rhône Department). Under its terms the painter was to depict the Holy Trinity, to "see to it there was no difference between the Father and the Son, and to represent the Holy Spirit in the guise of a dove." The contract goes on to list not only the chief saints but also the scenes to be represented, ranging from a depiction of Christ on the Cross to visions of Hell and Purgatory. In the latter, the artist is told to show the angels rejoicing to see the denizens of purgatory making their way to Paradise, "a sight whereat the devils are greatly discomfited." This remarkable document even specifies certain picturesque details to be included, such as "a pine-cone in copper" that the painter should have placed in front of his depiction of St Peter's in Rome—but for some reason omitted.

A curious feature of the composition is that it is divided into two quite distinct parts: above, the Coronation proper, and below, Purgatory and Hell. The narrative elements and the proportions of these lower scenes may, at first sight, bring to mind a predella. But the artist has been at pains to link together the two parts of the composition, the upper and the lower, and a study of the ensemble makes it clear that the highly explicit program set him in the contract of 1453 failed to state an essential point: the basic theme determining the overall structure of the picture. For there is more here than (as is often assumed) a casual association, for purely pictorial purposes, of the Coronation of the Virgin with the Last Judgment. What the artist has in mind is to emphasize the contrast between the celestial Paradise and the ills of the human predicament: Hell, Purgatory, and man's life on earth. The Coronation of the Virgin is treated not as the sole theme but as an incident taking place in Paradise, in which the Virgin plays the leading role. The wording of the contract is precise; the terms Paradise, Hell and Purgatory are employed in it and it also contains a reference to the scenery in the lowest register. "Below the aforesaid Paradise shall be the sky . . . and after the sky the earth in which shall be shown a portion of the City of Rome." The underlying theme of the composition is the lot of the human soul and its destiny after death. What we here are shown is not a

Enguerrand Charonton (c. 1410-c. 1466).
The Coronation of the Virgin, 1453-1454. (71¾×86½″) Hospice of Villeneuve-lès-Avignon.

Last Judgment, but the personal judgment of the individual, the trial of his soul when it has left the body. The painter was told to place "the Cross of our Lord" on earth, "on Mount Olivet" as a reminder of Christ's mission as Redeemer of mankind. And if the Virgin occupies the central place in the composition, this is not only because her coronation is the subject of the picture, but as a reminder of her role as intercessor—a central tenet of the Marian cult— and her function in the celestial hierarchy.

Viewed from this angle, the picture becomes easier to understand. Its gravity, austerity and stately presentation are far more in keeping with the theme of the destiny of the Soul than with the simpler, more joyous imagery of the Coronation of the Virgin and its familiar symbolism. The "pettiness" of man is emphasized by the exaltation of the Blessed and, dominating all, the majesty of godhead. The carefully planned symmetry of the composition resembles that of the Chantilly *Virgin of Mercy* but here is given a still greater expressive value. It was a natural consequence of the injunction in the contract that the figures of Christ

Anonymous Master.
The Villeneuve Pietà, about 1455.
(63½×85¾″)
Louvre, Paris.

Nicolas Froment (active 1461-1483).
The Burning Bush, 1476. (161×119¾″) Cathedral of Saint-Sauveur, Aix-en-Provence.

and God the Father were to be exactly alike. Charonton has made this symmetry essential to the composition by so arranging the "circles" of Paradise that they emanate from the figuration of the Trinity. There are, perhaps, reminiscences of the Master of the Aix *Annunciation* in the massive fullness of the leading figures, but Charonton stresses this fullness to the point of making it an essential element of his style. The decorative details and "Flemish opulence" still persisting in the Aix picture are here almost completely eliminated, so as not to break the continuity and plenitude of the forms; all that remains of them is the gold band set with jewels bordering Christ's cope and the discreet brocade with a broadly spaced design on the Virgin's robe.

All is bathed in a limpid light that sharply facets forms and gives a jewel-like luster to the colors. In these we find an intermingling of the glowing flesh tints of the Master of the Aix *Annunciation* with the bright hues of the frescoes painted by the Sienese in the Palace of the Popes in the previous century. Most striking is the strangely modern aspect they give to the depiction of the world of man in the lower register. Typically Provençal mountains with Cézannesque outlines stand boldly out against a cloudless sky. The ramparts and buildings which evoke, if at a far remove, Jerusalem and Rome are flooded with this vivid Mediterranean light which reduces them to simple forms. There is something of the quality of Corot's Italian landscapes, but it has, here, a certain harshness, partly intentional no doubt, but also due to a less advanced technique inadequate for rendering fine shades of color. The majestic composition, the bright but never garish colors and the extreme precision of the volumes contribute to the high seriousness and expressive power of this remarkable work. The mood of earnest meditation, tinged with melancholy, that pervades it may well express its creator's sense of sin and man's need for redemption from his fallen state.

This capacity for deep thought, combined with so complete a mastery of his means, suggests that Enguerrand Charonton must surely have produced other masterpieces. Should we, then, accept the view of Charles Sterling who no longer hesitates to assign to him that supreme creation of Provençal painting, the Villeneuve *Pietà*? Formerly it figured alongside the *Coronation of the Virgin* in the Hospice of Villeneuve-lès-Avignon. For some sixty years it has been one of the most tantalizing problems of French fifteenth-century art. The eagerness to assign a name to the man of genius who created this deeply moving scene is easily understandable. But always the ground gives way under the feet of the researcher, from the very start. Even the donor has not so far been identified; the most that can be said is that he was almost certainly a Canon. Nor is there any ancient record to show that the *Pietà* was made for the Chartreuse of Villeneuve. Only the date—round about 1455—has been established with some degree of certainty, thanks to the erudite research-work of Charles Sterling. In point of fact, however, this dating rests entirely on an assumption that a *Pietà* in the Musée de Cluny, Paris, is to be identified with the one made for the castle of King René at Tarascon shortly before 1457, a conjecture borne out solely by the proven fact that this *Pietà* was once owned by the Hospice of that city.

It is hard to believe, no doubt, that the *Coronation* and the Villeneuve *Pietà* are by the same hand. The monumental grandeur and poignancy of the *Pietà* are, one feels, unique. Nevertheless it should be noted that here the gold plays much the same part as in the Chantilly *Virgin of Mercy*; it is not purely decorative but, by abstracting the scene from the world of the here-and-now, imparts to it a quality of timelessness. The planes of the symbolic mountain behind the Magdalen are as bare and rugged as those of Charonton, and the flexions of the hands resemble those of the Virgin in the *Coronation*. By and large the view that both works are by the same hand has something to commend it. But if Charonton was indeed the maker of the *Pietà*, he brought to it an intensity of feeling that was new. The perfect balance on which he set such store is broken by the necessity of including the Canon kneeling in prayer. A link between the otherwise isolated figures is established by the convergence of their gestures, creating a symmetry that goes deeper than the obvious contrapposto formed by the attitudes of St John and the Magdalen who reiterate, as it were in a minor key, that supreme, central embodiment of sorrow, the figure of the Mother of Christ. Alone, apart, the Canon is lost in musings on the holy drama that is being enacted beside him, and his white garment strikes a note calling us back to everyday reality. Pervading all is a silent, contained grief, whose inwardness is broken only by the gleam of a tear on the Magdalen's cheek. This atmosphere is sustained by the austere colors, dull carmine reds and dark blues standing out on a brownish soil and lit from above by a shimmering expanse of gold like the last fires of sunset. (The darkness of the colors is not solely due, as once was thought, to accumulated layers of dirt and varnish.) Gazing at this famous picture we cannot fail to be moved by the mood of profound meditation inspiring it, reflected in the expression and demeanor of the reverently kneeling Canon; the mood enjoined by the passage from the Good Friday service inscribed on the gold ground: *O vos omnes qui transitis per viam attendite et videte quod est dolor meus.*

In the Villeneuve *Pietà* we have the supreme expression of Provençal art. The general conception and the execution reveal the deep thought and reverence brought to its making. In no other work of the age are masses so finely balanced, forms so skillfully stylized, reduced to their essential volumes. It has been suggested that this is not a Provençal or even a French work, and that its maker may have been the Portuguese artist Nuño Gonçalves. But the only ground for this surmise is the singular asperity of the faces. The art of the Portuguese painter is very different; he employs serried rhythms and juxtaposes faces, his "asperity" is almost purely linear, and his figures have not the plastic vigor of those of the *Pietà*. No, this work is assuredly Provençal; it has that severity which was to characterize the art of southeastern France and hints of which could already be seen in the Aix *Annunciation*. But such an art as Charonton's or that of the *Pietà* is not assignable to any mere conjuncture of "influences"; it could never have come into being without the emergence of a creative genius, a man whose vision outstripped the limitations of his age. Was this man Charonton himself or his assistant Pierre Villate? Here the records give no help, but the presumption is in favor of the former since his name alone figures in the contract for the *Coronation of the Virgin*. Still, the omission of Villate's name may have been an oversight and in any case its bearing on the problem set by the *Pietà* is inconclusive.

Compared with these noble works, all the other extant paintings seem insignificant. Yet more works of the period have been preserved in Provence than in most parts of France. Moreover the careful surveys made by Canon Requin and L. H. Labande have made it clear that an intense artistic activity prevailed there at the time when these masterpieces were produced. Artists were leaving Aix, where they had settled in great numbers in the first half of the century, and moving to Avignon. This was the case with Charonton himself; he had worked in the Provençal capital from 1444 to 1447 before establishing himself in the City of the Popes. The presence now of a papal legate in the palace until then unoccupied, and probably the hope of a revival of generous patronage, may have led to this influx of painters. But their art was of a very different order from that of the first school of Avignon, for they were now catering for the whole of Provence, not only for the papal court and its entourage. Commissions were given them by the wealthy bourgeoisie then in the ascendant, and also by (now less prosperous) members of the clergy. Though many artists' names figure in the copious records of the period, they are rarely associated with specific works. Among the most eminent contemporaries of Charonton and Villate were, it seems, Changenet and Chapu. For a while there was some question of attributing the Aix *Annunciation* to Chapu. To Changenet, Charles Sterling has tentatively assigned a very fine *St Peter* (Wildenstein Collection, New York) whose Provençal traits are unmistakable. The Tarascon *Pietà* (Musée de Cluny, Paris)—this is doubtless the picture painted in 1457 for King René's palace at Tarascon—includes some compositional elements taken from the Villeneuve *Pietà*, but the dryer execution and particularly the handling of color derive from Flemish art. The large *St Siffrein* in the Carpentras

Nicolas Froment (active 1461-1483).
The Burning Bush (detail), 1476. Cathedral of Saint-Sauveur, Aix-en-Provence.

Master of St Sebastian.

The Marriage of the Virgin, about 1490-1500. Wood. (31½×23⅝″) Musées Royaux des Beaux-Arts, Brussels.

Museum also imitates the style of the great Provençal artists, stiffening not only folds but gestures and facial expressions. But most significant undoubtedly is the vigorous revival of Flemish influence which, already perceptible in the Tarascon *Pietà*, comes to the fore in the work of such men as Nicolas Froment.

In Froment's art we can once again see King René's guidance. For though he does not seem to have exercised any influence on the development of the great Provençal style round about 1450, King René played an active part in shaping the course of art from 1471 on. His quarrel with Louis XI led him to relinquish his Duchy of Anjou, and cede it to the king. Thereafter he lived in Provence and practically never left it until his death in 1480. In 1476 he gave a commission to Nicolas Froment, a newcomer to his court, for the large triptych entitled *The Burning Bush*. Born at Uzès, Froment was a Southerner. His first work, however, *The Raising of Lazarus* (Uffizi, Florence), signed and dated 1461, shows few traces of the Provençal spirit. On the contrary, the feverish gestures, the grotesque expressions of faces and even the overcrowded composition seem, rather, to derive from northern prototypes.

The possibility of Froment's having visited Flanders or Holland cannot be excluded, but it is much more likely that it was from nearby Burgundy that he derived his style. Until the death of Charles the Bold in 1477, Burgundy was ruled by its dukes, the Counts of Flanders, and an independent art took form there (it has not yet been adequately studied) which, while much affected by Flemish influences, was primarily a continuation of the art of the Champmol workshops. Since, presumably, not enough orders were forthcoming in Burgundy, many artists migrated to Flanders or Provence; Guillaume Dombet and Changenet were Burgundians and so was Pierre Coustain, painter and *valet de chambre* to Charles the Bold, whose *Raising of Lazarus* (Louvre) was once attributed to Froment. Pierre Spicre, who worked at Dijon from 1470 to 1478, kept to this tradition. In his frescoes in Cardinal Rolin's chapel in Notre-Dame de Beaune, and the tapestry with scenes from the life of the Virgin in the same church (apparently made after his cartoons), we find the same stylistic tension, the same crowded composition, the same almost caricatural faces. To the same school belong several noble portraits: those of Hugues de Rabutin and his wife Jeanne de Montaigu (John D. Rockefeller Jr. Collection, New York) by the Master of Saint-Jean-de-Luz, and also those of Claude de Toulongeon and Guillemette de Vergy (Art Museum, Worcester, Mass.).

It was, then, in Burgundy or in the studio of some Burgundian artist living in Provence that Froment learnt his craft. None the less the Uffizi triptych bears traces of Provençal inspiration. On the reverse of one of the wings the donor (a Canon) and two friends are represented praying to the Virgin. The style here, though still rather awkward, is freer; there is, also, an effort to achieve a clearer composition and simpler volumes, showing that the artist was now by way of learning the lesson of Provence. In the *Burning Bush*, however, he comes into his own. The composition is better balanced, volumes are less assertive, harshness has almost wholly given place to a gentler mood. If it is a fact that Froment worked in Italy —the Uffizi triptych appears to have been made for the Convento del Bosco at Mugello, but it may have been executed in Provence—this change may have been due in part to his contacts with Florentine art. The landscape background has a strictly ordered yet poetic charm, bringing to mind the landscapes of Piero or Pollaiuolo, so gracefully disposed are the brown cypresses standing out against a limpid sky. Indeed the far-flung plain with its winding roads and streams seems more Florentine than Provençal. But this change of style may owe something to the instructions of King René who made no secret of his taste for a more harmonious art, more restful in its expression. Probably he was also responsible for the iconography of the composition. According to the Bible it was God the Father who manifested Himself to Moses in the Burning Bush. But the theme of the bush that "burned with fire and was not consumed" was held by some to be a prefiguration of the Virgin Birth. None the less this substitution of the Virgin and Child was a bold conception, worthy of that somewhat fantastical monarch King René. Another novelty was the inclusion of a diaphragmatic arch, simulating sculpture, framing the scene and throwing it into the background, a device borrowed from Flemish art but new to Provence. Here it serves to emphasize the distinction between the sacred world and the terrestrial world of the donors figuring on the shutters. Thus Froment's art became both bolder and more pleasing to the eye. While aiming at a more dignified composition, in key with that of the older generation, he gives it a new fluency by a smoother, more delicate handling of plastic values. In his colors, too, he seeks out more elegant harmonies and even tries to create a sort of aerial perspective. Sometimes indeed we have almost the impression of a painstaking imitation of the art of Fouquet.

The Provençal school of the fifteenth century did not end with Froment. It lasted into the first decade of the sixteenth century and a quantity of panels testify to the continued activity of its artists. But no more great painters emerged, and all we find are ever feebler imitations of the masterpieces of the past. Despite the rather naive charm of a landscape evoking the limpid light of Provence, the *Altarpiece of the Pérussis Family* (Metropolitan Museum, New York) is a hard, poorly executed work, a pale reflection of the early phase of Froment's art. The most attractive works dating to the end of the century are those of the artist known as the Master of St Sebastian. This group of seven panels, now dispersed (John G. Johnson Collection, Philadelphia; Walters Art Gallery, Baltimore; Palazzo Venezia, Rome;

Hermitage, Leningrad) illustrates incidents of St Sebastian's life. All have much the same dimensions, and they evidently formed part of an altarpiece. Charles Sterling gives sound reasons for believing them to be fragments of the work for which a contract was given on July 11, 1497, by the prior of the Confrérie du Luminaire de Saint-Sébastien (affiliated to the church of Notre-Dame des Acoules at Marseilles) to two painters, Josse Lieferinxe and Bernardo Simondi. They were commissioned to paint an altar with a central panel showing St Sebastian between St Anthony and St Roch and eight scenes from St Sebastian's life, which may have included the seven panels in question. It has been suggested that the differences of style between them confirm this and, by the same token, the attribution of some of these works to Lieferinxe. But it seems possible that the collaboration of the two artists was of a closer order, for in some of the panels Italian or Lombard elements figure alongside others that have all the air of deriving from the North. A similar ambivalence is found in another group of panels which seemingly formed part of an altarpiece having for its theme the life of the Virgin (Musée Calvet, Avignon; Louvre, Paris; Musées Royaux, Brussels). In the Brussels panel, the *Marriage of the Virgin*, the harshly, not to say grotesquely delineated faces in the background have a distinctly Nordic tang, whereas the buildings and the women's faces remind us of Italian art. It might indeed be wisest perhaps to speak, in the plural, of the Masters of St Sebastian. That the works of these artists are in the main stream of Provençal art is evidenced by the brilliant light dissevering forms in clear-cut facets and by the stiffness of the attitudes. Here the rather peculiar treatment of the narrative elements is due to the studied monumentality of Provençal art; figures seem petrified, all movement suddenly arrested.

A similar approach is found in the attractive panels depicting the *Marriage of the Virgin* which Charles Sterling links up with a fragment of the *Altarpiece of St Anne* painted by Nicolas Dipre in 1499 for the Confrérie de la Conception de la Vierge at the church of Saint-Siffrein, Carpentras. Squat, heavy-headed figures are stiffly posed in a setting that a direct light carves into geometric forms. This artist is less accomplished than the Masters of St Sebastian; his handling of the proportions between figures and architecture is unsure and his attempts to get buildings in correct perspective show a certain awkwardness. His art has, nevertheless, an immediate, popular appeal. Though here we are worlds away from the great Provençal art of such men as Charonton, something of it lingers on in this, its naive aftermath.

The Resistance to Italy

Master of Moulins (active 1475-1505).

Virgin and Child accompanied by Angels, about 1490 (?). Wood. (15⅛×11⅝″) Musées Royaux des Beaux-Arts, Brussels.

Besongnez donc, mes alumnes modernes,
Mes beaux enfants nourris de ma mamelle,
Toy Leonard qui as graces supernes,
Gentil Bellin, dont les loz sont éternes:
Et Perusin, qui si bien couleurs mesle:
Et toi Jean Hay, ta noble main chomme elle?
Vien voir nature avec Jean de Paris
Pour lui donner ombrage et esperits.

IT is interesting to find Jean Lemaire de Belges, court poet to Margaret of Austria, thus associating in his *Plainte du Désiré* (1504) the great Italian painters with the French. It goes to prove that the courts of France and Flanders were already acquainted with Italian art. For though Leonardo was not yet in France, Charles VIII had brought back "masters of the craft" from his campaigns in the lands south of the Alps, and Cardinal d'Amboise was soon to call in some of them to decorate his magnificent château of Gaillon.

However, in this transitional period between the fifteenth and sixteenth centuries, from the close of the reign of Louis XI to the reigns of Charles VIII (1483-1498) and Louis XII (1498-1514), French artists, far from adopting the Italian manner, resolutely fought against it. Confident in their own methods, they had no truck with foreign trends. And this very resistance to southern influences seems to have predisposed them to welcome those of the north. The Master of Moulins, Jean Perréal, the Master of St Giles, Jean Hay and their contemporaries had more in common with the painters of Bruges and Ghent than with those of Florence and Milan. While deigning to accept from Italy some decorative motifs, they rejected the conceptions basic to Italian art. Paradoxically enough, at the very time when the region south of the Alps was becoming familiar and easy of access, they were further from it than Fouquet was in the days when Rome seemed so remote.

This attitude is well conveyed by Jean Lemaire's poem. He obviously regards French and Italian artists as being on an equal footing, almost, indeed, as if there were nothing to choose between them. But it is only the French artists, Jean Perréal and Jean Hay, whom he bids "come look at nature"; all he concedes to the Italians are "supernal graces" and "harmoniously mingled colors." Reading between the lines, may we not see in this a profession of faith in northern realism as opposed to Italian art, whose qualities, to the poet's thinking, are evidently of an exclusively idealist order?

Master of Moulins (active 1475-1505).

The Moulins Triptych, central panel: Virgin and Child in Glory, about 1498. (62¾×111½″) Moulins Cathedral.

The Resistance to Italy

A<small>T</small> the close of the fifteenth century, when the country was still suffering from the effects of the Hundred Years' War, Paris had not yet fully regained its status as capital of France. The royal court was usually resident in Touraine, chosen perforce as his domicile by Charles VII, favored for political reasons by Louis XI, cherished for its own sake by Charles VIII and Louis XII. Meanwhile, more nomadic than ever, the court made frequent stays in Lyons, at once a flourishing commercial city and a half-way stage to Italy, the land which was soon to become the lodestar of the French king's aspirations. It was at this central point of France that the artists now forgathered. True, Fouquet's successors—the illuminator Jean Colombe, Jean Bourdichon, painter to the king, and that enigmatic personage Jean Hay —still resided in Touraine. But there were quite as many practitioners of the arts at Lyons, where a well-organized guild of painters had developed, and it was there that Jean de Paris (Jean Perréal) laid the foundations of his fame. Jean Bourdichon, too, came to work there.

Circumstances favored the rise of Lyons. Louis XI took an active interest in the city and did much to stimulate its commerce. On his death in 1483 the regency of the Beaujeu family was another favorable factor; the Duke and Duchess of Bourbon could not fail to concern themselves with the fortunes of the great city so near their duchy. The rise of a wealthy and powerful middle class, together with the frequent sojourns of the court, ensured an abundance of commissions for the local artists. But except for a few outstanding men, such as Perréal, little more is known than the names of most of the members of the Lyons painters' guild. One of them, however, has recently attracted the attention of art historians: this is Jean Prévost. If we are to judge by the extant records, there was nothing exceptional about his career. In 1471 he succeeded his father-in-law as "artist and glass-painter to the Cathedral of Lyons." The tasks allotted to him were those of all the "official" painters of the time: preparations for the state entry of Louis XI into Lyons in 1476, scenery and costumes for morality plays, royal coats-of-arms for boats, the painting of a canopy, collaboration on the decorations for the entry of Charles VIII—nothing, in short, of an exceptional order. In 1498 he made over his duties in connection with the Cathedral to Pierre de Paix (Pierre d'Aubenas). But he seems to have gone on painting. In 1502 we hear of a "Maître Jehan le peintre" attached to the Beaujeu family at the court of Moulins as a servant of superior rank; and it seems probable that this man was none other than Jean Prévost (whose name, however, still figured in the tax registers of Lyons). He died in 1504. The records have no more and no less to say about him than about the common run of contemporary painters.

Master of Moulins (active 1475-1505).
The Moulins Triptych, detail of the central panel, about 1498. Moulins Cathedral.

Nevertheless it seems quite possible that this artist, whose name is mentioned neither in Jean Lemaire's poem nor in the writings of any of the chroniclers, was the best painter of his day, the man who is still entitled, provisionally, the Master of Moulins. It was thought at first that, given the superlative qualities of this artist's work, he could safely be identified with the Jean Perréal of whom contemporary records speak in glowing terms. But there are so many facts militating against this conjecture that it is now regarded as untenable. To begin with, the very nature of the œuvre indicates a man of a very different caliber from that of a successful, much admired court painter like Jean Perréal; a man who shunned publicity and would certainly have disdained the servitudes attaching to an official status. There is not a trace of ostentation or display in the art of the Master of Moulins. It is essentially contemplative, discreet, imbued throughout with a high seriousness which, however, does not preclude a delicate grace, and with the melancholy gravity of a mind forever haunted by a rankling unrest.

One of his earliest works, a *Nativity* (Musée Rolin, Autun), commissioned by Cardinal Jean Rolin, gives at first sight an impression of being essentially Flemish in spirit. The name of Hugo van der Goes is often cited in explanation of its mood of intense meditation. Yet this work does not stem directly from the Flemish master; it is, rather, the result of similar causes. In the boldly modeled rendering of figures in space we can see the influence of Fouquet (paralleled in the case of Van der Goes by the latter's close contacts with Florentine painting). The general arrangement, however, of the *Nativity* has much in common with the layouts of Dirk Bouts, who did so much to shape the style of Van der Goes. Both the color scheme and its superb handling remind us, once again, of Jan van Eyck; what more natural than that Cardinal Rolin should ask his painter to model his work on the famous picture made for his father, the Chancellor, and figuring on the walls of his chapel in the cathedral? Nor, as is sometimes said, does the pallor of the Virgin's face, matched here by the cool tint of her robe, go to show the influence of Van der Goes; these pale flesh tints were a convention of the period and we find them, if rarely, in the work of Fouquet, as also in the *Retable du Parlement de Paris* and in Dirk Bouts' entourage. Moreover, it may have derived from the glass-workers' practice of using plain glass for flesh tints.

Master of Moulins (active 1475-1505).
The Moulins Triptych, detail of the central panel, about 1498. Moulins Cathedral.

Master of Moulins (active 1475-1505). Charlemagne and the Meeting of St Joachim and St Anne at the Golden Gate, about 1488. (28¼×23¼″) By Courtesy of the Trustees, National Gallery, London.

The contacts of the Moulins Master with the court of the Beaujeu family went back much earlier than 1502, the year when the presence of "Maître Jehan" at Moulins is first recorded. They had begun about 1488. This is the date inscribed on two wings of an altar-piece—the central panel of which is missing—in the Louvre. They represent the Duke and Duchess of Bourbon in prayer, presented by St Peter and St John the Evangelist. However, since this was the year of the accession of Pierre II to the duchy, the date need not be taken literally as that of the execution of the work; it may relate to the event commemorated by the triptych. On the reverse of these panels there figured probably two scenes, now much damaged, *Charlemagne and the Meeting of St Joachim and St Anne at the Golden Gate* (National Gallery, London) and the *Annunciation* (Art Institute of Chicago), and a (missing) fragment representing St Louis counterbalanced the figure of Charlemagne on the London panel. This association of two scenes relating to the virgin births of Christ and Mary suggests that the central panel of the triptych represented the Virgin and Child, depicted (in accordance with the then current symbolic figuration of the Immaculate Conception) above the crescent moon. This is all the more likely since the Duke and Duchess of Bourbon seem to have attached particular importance to that dogma, soon to be authoritatively endorsed by the Sorbonne. Moreover, many years before, in 1474, the Duke's father Jean II had erected an altar dedicated to the Immaculate Conception in Moulins Cathedral. Between the treatment of the panels in London and Chicago and that of the Autun *Nativity* there are marked differences, their style being predominantly narrative. The setting of the *Annunciation* is a charming interior and the momentous encounter of Anne and Joachim takes place in front of the massive entrance of a castle. Despite some slight indications of perspective, the space in which the figures move seems curiously restricted. Rejecting Fouquet's far-flung vistas, the Moulins Master elects for a more artificial space, that of the carved retables which just then were having a great vogue in Flanders. Though he applies his high technical proficiency to making the backgrounds less stereotyped and even to rendering the atmosphere enveloping them, he keeps to a compact grouping of the figures and gives their gestures a sculpturesque immobility. The inclusion of Charlemagne, like St Louis patron of the royal dynasty, derives from the same traditions. Here there is hardly any trace of Italianism; it is limited to such minor details as the putti holding garlands and the medallions in the antique manner adorning the Golden Gate.

The second triptych made by the Master of Moulins for the House of Bourbon has the same theme, the Immaculate Conception. It has been preserved intact (except for the frames of its wings) in the Cathedral of Moulins. Here narrative elements are omitted, doubtless because the frankly monumental nature of the layout called for their suppression. The "Golden Gate" theme has accordingly disappeared; all that remains is that of the Annunciation, reduced to a few large figures in grisaille on the outside wings. In the central panel the Virgin is shown seated, with the crescent moon beneath her feet and surrounded by a glory of angels, while on the wings are the Duke and Duchess presented by their patron saints. It is to this work that the master owes his (provisional) appellation. But another, more poetic name had been suggested by it, and we can but regret that it was not adopted: the Master of the Angels. For this name would have laid stress on what was one of this great painter's essential traits, his rapturous delight in childhood. In that religious-minded century, it was only in depictions of angels and the Child Jesus that he had occasions for expressing that emotion; had he lived two centuries later he would surely have vied with Louis Le Nain. For the theme of the Immaculate Conception no "crown" of angels was needed; the Master included it on his own initiative. A medieval tradition of the distinctive hues of the hierarchy of cherubim guided his choice of the colors for the angels' robes. The elongation of their bodies, the supple flexions of their limbs, indicated by rippling folds of their garments, remind us of another key work of late medieval France, the vault of Jacques Coeur's chapel in his house at Bourges. It was Henri Bouchot who first pointed out, at the end of the nineteenth century, the close affinity between these works, too often overlooked. This is of much interest as proving that the Moulins Master had contacts both with Touraine and with contemporary art of Flemish inspiration. It is in the angels' faces that we see the fullest expression of his personality. He so disposes the lighting as to bring out to best effect the innocent charm of these young faces, so much like those of the children we still see in the French countryside. One has almost the impression that they have just been serving at mass beside the altar, then been suddenly translated by some miraculous intervention on to the celestial plane. The small, childishly chubby hands, too, raised or clasped in impulsive gestures of adoration, bewilderment and awe, are wonderfully expressive.

But while the angels recall those of Bourges, the Virgin and Child remind us of Fouquet. This Child Jesus is twin brother of the Antwerp Child and the Virgin has the same graceful pose, the same contemplative air as the idealized Agnès Sorel in the Melun Diptych. But these reminiscences, however precise, do not obtrude themselves; they are too closely bound up with another way of seeing more in keeping with medieval tradition and Flemish art trends, whose influence can be seen even in the portrayals of the donors. Pierre II de Bourbon and his wife Anne de Beaujeu are shown kneeling before their patron saints in a confined space demarcated by the heavy curtains which already in the fourteenth century were being used in portraits of royalty. This preference for a depthless space is one of the Moulins Master's idiosyncrasies. He gives ample scope to the volumes of his figures, but when he locates them in the open he usually resorts to an abstract or indefinite space, such as that of the sky in the center of the Moulins triptych. When, as in the donor panels, space is more positively indicated, it often seems curiously cramped. Frequently his composition reminds us of a bas-relief, more precisely a bas-relief in inverse, sunk into the surface.

We find a similar emotional approach in an enchanting panel of the *Virgin and Child* (Musées Royaux, Brussels). This was probably one wing of a diptych; the other, showing perhaps a patron saint, is lost. Here, again, the painter has grouped some angels with plump, almost babyish faces around the Virgin. What could be more charming than the gesture of the angel in the top right-hand corner, who is holding up both hands, with the palms turned towards us, in delighted wonderment? Even the Virgin has the face of a little girl; a frail, slender figure bowed by the weight of her veil, she seems lost in a brown study; and yet one somehow feels that she is curbing, only for this solemn moment, a juvenile vivaciousness.

The Master of Moulins was also a delicately perceptive portrait painter; his œuvre is studded with faces in which we trace his ever-growing skill in this domain. The earliest known portrait is a fragment of a diptych representing Cardinal Charles II of Bourbon, which Mlle Huillet d'Istria dates on good grounds to about 1476, the year when Charles was elevated to the purple. More than any other work, this portrait shows to what extent the painter's early style was affected by Flemish art. The close-set modeling and crisp outlines remind us of Dirk Bouts and also, if to a less degree, of Rogier van der Weyden. But already there are signs of that insight into the psychology of the model—here, the far-away, brooding gaze—which was to characterize the later portraits. Similar, if somewhat bolder, is a panel of another diptych (Louvre, formerly Somzée Collection) on which we see a winsome St Mary Magdalen beside a female donor with an unattractive, not to say forbidding face. The painter seems to have taken pleasure in contrasting the girlish grace of a young saint with the ugliness of her companion. Here, too, Flemish influence is perceptible and this portrayal of the Magdalen definitely reminds us of that in the Jean de Braque triptych in the Louvre. However, the modeling is more emphatic, the space around the figures, though still compact, is clearly indicated, and air circulates more freely.

But it is above all in the portraits of the Duke and Duchess of Bourbon (1488, Louvre) and in those of the Moulins triptych (c. 1498) that a new tendency becomes apparent. The line becomes less precise, modeling more fluid, even the realism is attenuated. Most striking of all, a trend that was merely hinted at in the treatment of the eyes of Cardinal de Bourbon is

Master of Moulins (active 1475-1505).

François de Chateaubriand commended by St Maurice, about 1500. (22×18¼″) Glasgow Art Gallery and Museum.

Master of St Giles (active 1490-1510). St Giles protecting the Hind wounded by Charles Martel, about 1500. (24¼×16″)
By Courtesy of the Trustees, National Gallery, London.

carried a stage further, and the artist studies the expression of his model's face with keener insight, seeking to interpret the significance behind the gaze. But it is in the famous picture in the Glasgow Art Gallery that this trend reaches its culminating point. St Maurice is shown presenting a donor, an elderly Canon whose face shows the ravages of age. This Canon may be identified with François de Chateaubriand, abbot of Evron and Canon of St Maurice's Cathedral at Angers. A wealthy patron of the arts, he spent large sums on improvements of the Cathedral and was also famed for his luxurious way of life. He was involved in a somewhat mysterious law suit; the monks under his charge accused him of appropriating jewels from the Cathedral Treasure and (if our identification is correct) their suspicions may have had some foundation, judging by the pearls and precious stones with which, in the portrait, he is bedecked. But the face tells as much as the costume about this man; we feel that he is at once shrewd and something of a dreamer, greedy for the good things of this world but gifted with a high intelligence. In the œuvre of the Master of Moulins we see the beginnings of a new approach to the art of portraiture. For he strikes an admirable balance between the meticulous realism of the Flemish artists who scanned faces like physicians looking for symptoms of an ailment and the Italian style which concerned itself primarily with stressing their essential forms. But what most of all the French painter sought to discern was the inner man and with this in mind he gave particular attention to the gaze.

A remarkable thing about his figures, whether saints, angels or living persons, is their uniformity of mood—a mood of melancholy tinged with anxiety and dark forebodings. Here we are worlds away from Fouquet's serenity; this spiritual unrest is reminiscent, rather, of Hugo van der Goes. Is his malaise, one wonders, personal or a reflection of the age he lived in? (In the case of Van der Goes it was certainly due to the religious conflicts of the troubled years preceding the Reformation.)

Can this great artist, the Master of Moulins, be identified with Jean Prévost, artist and glass painter to Cardinal de Bourbon at Lyons? This identification is, in our opinion, justified but there is no denying that the arguments in its favor are essentially cumulative; singly, they carry less conviction. None of Prévost's work in Lyons Cathedral has survived, but the stained-glass windows made by his successor Pierre de Paix are known to have kept closely

ws, too, in Moulins Cathedral, though not by his hand, are so much in Master's paintings as to support the view that the pictures grouped ptych were the work of a stained-glass painter. That the Master of ons seems reasonably certain, given the affinities between his style and s we can isolate his share in the tomb of François II de Bretagne in eover, there are two mentions of Prévost's presence at Moulins; in the state entry of Charles VIII, and again in 1502. These mentions ive since the dates may well be those of the completion of the two Dukes, the first begun about 1488 and the second (whose execution in view of its size) about 1498.

ed Jean Perréal was an outstanding figure of the age. On intimate s VIII, Louis XII and Francis I, he even accompanied them on some 502 he was in Italy where he was no doubt one of the first French da Vinci, to whom he explained the technique of drawing in three white chalk—which was to have so great a vogue in France in the their conversations were not limited to art. Perréal fancied himself er, was interested in astronomy, practised as an architect and an rdo's notebooks tells us that Perréal promised to give him the is desire for an encyclopedic knowledge comes as a surprise in France, a contemporary of the Master of Moulins. Yet Perréal's life followed that of his brother artists. We hear of him for the first time in Lyons in 1483, when he was employed on painting the chariot in which the hermit St Francis of Paola traveled from Italy when King Louis XI invited him to France. There is no knowing if he was trained in Paris or in Lyons. In the latter city he made the decorations for numerous state entries, including those of Charles II de Bourbon, the Duke of Savoy and Charles VIII. King Charles attached him to his household at the end of the century, and one of his first missions involved a journey to Germany to paint a lady's portrait. But he never lost touch with Lyons and was often there in the following years. During his stay in Italy in 1502 he selected the marbles for the tomb of François II, Duke of Brittany, whose model he drafted on the order of Anne de Bretagne. He returned to Italy in 1509 as a member of the king's suite. There was keen competition for his services, Margaret of Austria commissioned him to design the tomb of her deceased husband, Philibert II, Duke of Savoy, in the church of Brou at Bourg-en-Bresse. On the deaths of Anne de Bretagne and Louis XII he worked on the funeral ceremonies and made casts of the faces of the deceased. Under the next king, Francis I, he seems to have been less active, but he retained his post of *valet de chambre* to the king until his death (some time between 1527 and 1529).

What is most striking about the mentions of Perréal in the records is that—except when they concern his much-admired decorations for state entries—they relate to his activities as a portrait painter. There are of course the cartoons he made for the tomb of François II at Nantes, but it is hard to distinguish his share in what was a collective enterprise and the actual execution was left to a highly independent artist, Michel Colombe. The ornamental program, of Italian inspiration, may well have been due to him, even though Italian artisans worked on it. But the statuary still wavers between emphatic modeling and Gothic hieraticism. No contemporary painting has any affiliations with this sculpture. Probably it is the portraits that can tell us most about this eminent fifteenth-century artist. For example, the *Portrait of Louis XII* (Windsor Castle) is mentioned as included in the Crown collections of England (inventory of 1543) as far back as the reign of Henry VIII, brother of Mary Tudor whose portrait Perréal painted at the order of his master, Louis XII. Thus there can be no doubt that this work is by his hand. But in some respects it is disappointing. Its thoroughgoing realism seems a little prosaic, and though the style may superficially resemble that of the Master of Moulins, the handling is less refined, above all less sensitive. Should we then assume it to be a copy? This is probably unnecessary; Perréal's celebrity is no guarantee of his abilities as an artist; all it proves is that he enjoyed the favor of the great, fallible like all mortals. This may explain the puzzling fact that, despite Perréal's fame, efforts to trace his œuvre have led to nothing; perhaps they were looked for on too high a level. Some other portraits, however, have been ascribed to him, one being the likeness of Pierre Sala in an illuminated manuscript in the British Museum. The fact that Sala was a close friend of Perréal lends color to the attribution.

It is much to be regretted that fifteenth- and sixteenth-century France had no Vasari or Van Mander to write the lives of her painters—a circumstance that greatly complicates the task of the art historian. One of his problems is the painter Jean Hay whose name figures alongside those of the greatest artists of his day in the poem by Lemaire at the head of this chapter. The reverse of an *Ecce Homo* (Musées Royaux, Brussels) bears an inscription to the effect that it was painted by "Maître Jehan Hay" in 1494. But nothing is known about the man himself. This, his only documented picture, has the strong but delicate modeling characteristic of the Moulins Master. With it may probably be associated the attractive *Portrait of the Dauphin Charles-Orlant* (Louvre), dated to the same year. This is, however, the only picture, apart from the *Ecce Homo*, which can be safely attributed to Hay. Perhaps there was a break in his career, as seems to be implied in Lemaire's line: *Et toi, Jehan Hay, ta noble main chomme elle?* (And you, Jean Hay, is your noble hand idle?). But a possibility remains that the name "Jehan Hay" is the French form of a foreign name (cf. "Jean de la Haye"), in which case a close study of the records may one day give a clue to his identity.

Jean Perréal (c. 1455-1530). Portrait of Louis XII, about 1514 (?). (12×9″).
By Gracious Permission of Her Majesty the Queen, Royal Collections, Windsor Castle.

Recently, however, a suggestion has been made throwing perhaps some light on this elusive painter: the proposal of Professor Van Regteren Altena to identify him with the Master of St Giles. Against this view is the fact that the works ascribed to this master consist of narrative panels with small figures and one has difficulty in believing these to be by the same hand as the Brussels *Ecce Homo*. All the same, the theory has much to commend it. The four pictures basic to the reconstruction of this master's œuvre themselves raise some curious problems. Two of them (National Gallery, London) depict episodes in the life of St Giles; the two others (National Gallery, Washington) contain scenes of the life of St Remi. That all four pictures once formed the wings of an altarpiece, whose central panel is missing, is proved by the saints in similar architectural niches on the reverse (in grisaille). The settings of the incidents are real places depicted with much dexterity. Three of them are located in or near Paris: the Abbey of St Denis, the Sainte-Chapelle and the parvis of Notre-Dame. The

Jean Bourdichon (c. 1457-1521).
Triptych, detail of the right wing: St John the Evangelist, about 1494 (?).
Museo di Capodimonte, Naples.

background of the fourth scene, *St Giles protecting the Hind*, has recently been identified by Prof. Altena and Vallery Radot as the town of Loches, in Touraine. The fact that all these sites fell within the royal domain suggests that the commission for the altarpiece emanated from the king or one of his intimates. It follows that the artist concerned was someone attached to the royal court, and this applies to Jean Hay, who painted the Brussels picture for a notary and secretary to the king.

Be this as it may, the art of the Master of St Giles clearly belongs to this, the final flowering of medieval painting. Northern influences are so manifest that some have thought he was of Dutch or Flemish extraction. The handling of perspective is still unsure, empirical, and he has a typically Flemish fondness for using a high horizon line. Such Italian elements as we find are merely incidental. Yet on one occasion this artist exactly copied, as the setting for his *Presentation in the Temple*, a print by Bramante. The composition, anyhow, is definitely of Flemish inspiration. But it must have been to France that he owed that feeling for just balance which prevented him from pressing his realism too far and also led him so harmoniously to calibrate the masses. The spirit of his art has affinities with that of the Master of Moulins; the austere figures he depicts seem marked by that haunting dissatisfaction with the age which characterizes the work of "the Master of the Angels."

The art of Jean Bourdichon, another painter attached to the court *("peintre et valet du roi")* has an engaging grace peculiar to itself. He was born about 1457 and lived at Tours. In his youth he worked for Louis XI who commissioned him in 1478 to decorate the chapel in his château at Plessis-les-Tours. It was Anne de Beaujeu who appointed him Painter to the King (in 1484), a post which he held under Charles VIII, Louis XII and Francis I, until his death in 1521. His activities, according to the records, were very varied: decorations for state entries and festivals (under Francis I he adorned a tent for the famous Field of the Cloth of Gold), illuminations, altarpieces, portraits. His style can be best determined by the illuminations of the *Hours of Anne de Bretagne* (Bibliothèque Nationale, Paris), whose ascription to him is fully documented. Jacques Dupont has also identified a triptych formerly in the Chapel of San Martino at Naples and now in the Museo di Capodimonte of that city, as being by his hand; it may have been made for Ferdinand I of Aragon. Bourdichon's compositions are still medieval in style, though his forms have a new suppleness. Figures acquire a certain amplitude by the use of simplified folds, but one feels he is consciously seeking to flatter the eye. There are faint reminiscences of Fouquet's art but its grandeur is far to seek. Bourdichon's was a courtly art, made to please—and that it pleased is certain. Its defect, for us, lies in its lack of power. With him an ancient tradition was dying out and, unlike some of his contemporaries, he did not take to heart the lesson of Italian art; all he owed to it can be seen in a rather weak attempt to render aerial perspective.

The Italians at Fontainebleau

Niccolò dell'Abbate (c. 1509-1571).
The Continence of Scipio (detail), about 1560. Louvre, Paris.

IT was under the auspices of Francis I (1515-1547) that Italianism found its way to France. During his reign medievaldom, already in decline, gave place to a new culture, a new climate of opinion. This change had a decisive effect on the arts, but its effect on men's minds was no less marked. To it was due the foundation of the Collège de France, intended to promote a wider freedom of thought untrammeled by the rigidly pedantic disciplines of the Sorbonne. That the French king set himself the highest possible standard is proved by the welcome he gave Leonardo, most eminent man of his age both for his breadth of mind and for the variety of his achievements.

Despite his far-ranging activities, it was on one spot that Francis I focused his enthusiasm for the arts. The small medieval château at Fontainebleau, his favorite residence, was converted in a few years' time into a splendid palace; architects, masons, painters and sculptors were kept busy beautifying it throughout the king's lifetime, and his son Henry II (1547-1559) followed his example. "A Treasure-house of Wonders," was the heading Père Dan gave his description, written in 1642, of the château of Fontaine-bleau. So widespread was the renown of this royal abode and of its decorations that it soon became a place of pilgrimage for artists from the north of Europe. Flemings, Germans and, needless to say, French artists wishing to profit by the discoveries of their elders, flocked to Fontainebleau; Poussin in his youth was one of them.

For the decoration of his château Francis called in Italian masters, probably with a view to breaking with the "old-fashioned" art practised by their French contemporaries. Rosso, Primaticcio and Niccolò dell'Abbate were in general control and as regards the style of the decorations their will was law throughout their lives. The result was that in the reigns of four kings, Francis I, Henry II, Francis II and Charles IX—from about 1530 to 1570—the fortunes of French art were in Italian hands. For, though these masters' style was of foreign origin, it made good in France, gave a new direction to the evolution of the previous century's art and even became a vital element of French aesthetic.

This change had far-reaching effects. For one thing, the art of Fontainebleau, ceasing to give priority to religious themes, indulged in frankly pagan subjects. Losing its erstwhile prestige, Realism gave place to an art "of imagination all compact," the magic of melodious arabesques, the glamour of ethereal colors. Mannerism made headway and, paradoxically enough, France was overrun with formulas of the great art of the classical Renaissance which she had never known.

Giovanni Battista Rosso (1494-1540).

The Fountain of Youth (detail), between 1534 and 1537. Fresco. Galerie François I, Château de Fontainebleau.

The Italians at Fontainebleau

THE "Italian program" of King René, who was bent on making good his claim to the throne of Naples, must have occasioned some of the first artistic contacts between France and Italy. The same policy was followed by Charles VIII, his heir, and after him by Louis XII and Francis I, but in a more vigorous manner. In 1494 Charles VIII successfully invaded Italy, entering Naples "in great pomp" in 1495. He followed this up by bringing back with him to France "twenty-two skilled craftsmen" to work on the château of Amboise. He was the first French king to enlist the services of distinguished Italian artists, such as the architect Fra Giocondo, who stayed in France from 1495 to 1505, another architect Domenico da Cortona, and Guido Mazzoni, a sculptor, who stayed in France until 1507. Cardinal d'Amboise followed the king's example, calling in Andrea Solario to make the decorations of the chapel of the magnificent Château de Gaillon he was then having built near Rouen. Aiming still higher, Francis I summoned Leonardo da Vinci to France, and it was on French soil that the great painter spent the last years of his life (1516-1519). But the first manifestations of Italian art in France had surprisingly little effect. The influence of the architects made itself felt very slowly; that of the painters was almost imperceptible. Andrea Solario's sojourn at Gaillon was too brief and Leonardo led a secluded life at Cloux in the château given him by the king, devoting himself to scientific speculations and perhaps working on some of the paintings that were left unfinished at his death.

Under Louis XII there were signs of a reaction against this trend. When the king went to Italy he took with him his favorite painter Perréal, and he summoned to France only the artists who had already been employed by Charles VIII. Not until the reign of Francis I do we find Italian influences predominant—more specifically after his captivity in Madrid (1524-1526). It was then that he started converting his château at Fontainebleau into a truly palatial residence. Work began in 1528 and painters soon joined forces with the architects and masons employed at Fontainebleau, which now became both the capital of the arts in France and a symbol of the triumph of the Italian style. Rosso settled there in 1530, Primaticcio in 1532 and Niccolò dell'Abbate in 1552.

When Giovanni Battista di Jacopo di Gasparre, better known as Rosso Fiorentino, came to France he already had a long career behind him. He was born at Florence in 1494. Vasari tells us that already in his youth he was highly temperamental, and he put in only a brief stay in Andrea del Sarto's studio. It was, rather, to Michelangelo's cartoon for the *Battle of*

Giovanni Battista Rosso (1494-1540).

The Fountain of Youth, between 1534 and 1537. Fresco. Galerie François I, Château de Fontainebleau.

Cascina and Dürer's engravings that he looked for guidance. From 1523 to 1527 he worked in Rome; then, before setting out for France, traveled extensively in Italy. The work he produced in Italy is typically mannerist. Most striking in his pictures is the acidity of the colors, stressed by an accurate but somewhat harsh line. His figures, too, have an emotive, indeed neurotic quality that puts them in a class apart. According to an old tradition, it was thanks to Aretino that he entered the service of the French king. The poet sent Francis I a drawing by Rosso on a theme he had himself suggested, *Mars led to Venus by Cupids and the Graces:* an ingeniously flattering allusion to the marriage of the king to Eleanor, sister of the Emperor Charles V. This was the first of the pagan allegories which Rosso was to paint in such numbers on the walls of the palace of Fontainebleau. Favorably impressed by the drawing, the king summoned him to the French court, where he soon made a great name for himself. He was placed in general charge of the decorations of the palace and until his death in 1540 directed the activities of the stucco workers and fresco painters in the king's employ.

Changes in taste led to the disappearance of much of the work he carried out at Fontaine-bleau. But his *magnum opus*, the mural decorations of the Galerie François I, have survived. The original frescoes were defaced in the nineteenth century by injudicious over-paintings; these have been removed under instructions from the Minister of Culture, M. André Malraux, and we can now see Rosso's work for what it is, one of the finest decorative achievements of its age. The overall conception of the decorations of this long gallery was strikingly original. The painted panels, executed in fresco, are each surrounded by stucco work and, aligned along the walls, produce the effect of rows of easel paintings. Between and around them are figures culled from pagan antiquity—nudes, naiads, goddesses and putti—executed in stucco and standing out from the walls in high relief. We cannot but be struck by the skill with which, around scenes treated as isolated pictorial units, Rosso combined reliefs and simulated reliefs, stucco work and painting, mosaics and painted medallions, realistic details and decorative strap-work in which the stucco imitates strips of leather rolled up and cut into arresting shapes—an infinite diversity of forms and colors. The decorative arrangement varies from one panel to the other; indeed this variety seems to be the very essence of the layout. Aligned between a beamed ceiling and a high wooden plinth of finely executed paneling (the work of the wood-carver Scibec de Carpi), this long frieze constitutes a world in itself. The arrangement of the pictures between the woodwork and the ceiling recalls that of the *studiolo* of Isabella d'Este at Mantua, while the way they are enframed by allegorical nudes interspersed with fruit swags probably derives from the ceiling of the Sistine Chapel. None the less there are many innovations. One is the use of this layout on the wall of a gallery instead of on a vault where effects of depth would be produced automatically. Another is the allegorical significance of the stucco figures which, ceasing to be purely decorative, are related to the theme figuring on the adjacent painted panel. But most novel and original of all is Rosso's curious idea of inserting high reliefs whose purpose seems to be deliberately to confuse the planes and to mislead the eye. For while they implement the plastic effects of the painting, their pale alabaster hue betrays their unreality. It is to this interplay of conflicting illusions that the composition owes its essentially symbolic, dreamlike quality.

Vasari attributes these stuccos to Primaticcio, who had come to Fontainebleau in 1532. But there are few signs of his style in the Galerie François I and the guiding spirit here was certainly Rosso. Primaticcio may have supervised the execution; he had been one of the team of artists headed by Giulio Romano who went to Mantua to make the decorations of the Palazzo del Tè, so presumably he was used to this type of work. But for the planning of the gallery as a whole, and even of its stuccos and paintings, Rosso was certainly responsible. How drastic was the break, here, with the still medieval world of the painters employed by Charles VIII and Louis XII! In this new language we find artists using for the first time a vocabulary based on the nude figure, and drawing their themes from the mythology of classical antiquity. Everywhere, both in the decorative figures and the painted panels, naked bodies play a leading role. But there is nothing as yet of the marked eroticism which was soon to prevail at Fontainebleau. There are more putti and male nudes than naiads or goddesses, and all are in active movement, every muscle on the stretch. Here once again the figural rhythms remind us of Michelangelo.

The subjects of the pictures in this, the first of the Fontainebleau galleries, are sometimes esoteric and presuppose a knowledge of the byways of classical mythology that today is rare. Some were seldom if ever used even in antique monuments; for instance the *Fountain of Youth*, culled from that little-read work, the *Theriaca* of Nicander of Colophon. Even more baffling to the modern beholder are the veiled allusions to contemporary events, and all the erudition and perspicacity of M. de Tervarent and Erwin and Dora Panofsky was needed to unravel the tangled skein. It is now clear that the Ariadne's clue to this labyrinth of ancient lore is none other than the life of King Francis I. But the significance of these mythological discursions relates not so much to incidents of the king's life as to his personality—they give what might be described as a philosophic portrait of the enlightened monarch who holds so high a place in the history of humanism in France. The gallery begins with a scene, *Ignorance expelled from the Kingdom*, which clearly strikes the keynote of the sequence. It shows artists rendering thanks to the king who has invoked their aid and under whose guidance art is now to be permeated with humanist ideals and a better understanding of antiquity. The *Ancient Sacrifice* seems to be an evocation of the circumstances attending the king's birth. Next, the *Unity of the State* extols his statesmanship, and that strange scene the *Elephant Fleurdelysé* alludes to his virtue and sagacity, his power over the elements (with the exception of the air), his eminence as "a new Alexander." Then come allusions to more personal matters, the king's domestic virtues and his devotion to his mother, while his sons' filial affection is evoked in two scenes, *Cleobis and Biton drawing their Mother's Chariot* and the *Twins of Catania*. The *Death of Adonis*, which comes next, appears to be one of the very few scenes related to a specific event; in this case the death of the Dauphin, on August 10, 1536. Since work on the gallery had begun in 1534 (it lasted three years), this proves that the program of the picture sequence was not definitively fixed in the first instance. The *Vengeance of Nauplius* may be another topical allusion, motivated by the treacherous conduct of the Constable de Bourbon. But the scene, it should be noted, stresses the moral issues involved in this political crisis. The *Fountain of Youth*, however, illustrates only the infirmities of old age and the *Education of Achilles*, facing it, only the joys of youth (even if the youth in question is the Dauphin's). The last two pictures of the series are concerned with warfare. The *Battle of the Centaurs and Lapiths* represents the struggle of an advanced civilization (the Centaurs', here assimilated to the French) against a backward race, and *Venus Frustrated* symbolizes the king's enforced abstinence from love when his military duties call him to the field of battle. The portrait of Francis I given us here is that of a powerful, authoritarian ruler, but above all a thoughtful man having much of the ancient wisdom of the sages of the past. At the same time he is thoroughly human; endowed with strong family feeling and sense of honor, he mourns alike his son's death and the treachery of a trusted servitor and friend.

Admittedly there is nothing French in the sources of this art, except its themes. None the less this purely Italian decoration was destined to play a leading part in the orientation of French art. We do not find, however, the Fontainebleau style in its definitive form in the Galerie François I; the inspiration here is in the main Florentine. The emphasis on muscular structure, the curiously twisted bodies, and these dynamic compositions whose execution is as unusual as their subjects—all are peculiar to Rosso and constitute one of the most brilliant achievements of Florentine Mannerism. For the contemporary French painters this art came as the revelation of an undreamt-of world. Everywhere a clear-cut line brings out with elegant precision the curves and convolutions of interlocking arabesques, and an acidulous color transposes rather than interprets effects of light. The dramatic power of this art and its singularly haunting quality are due to the nervous tension pervading it through and through. For there is little lightheartedness in the artist's treatment of these mythologies. Indeed it makes us feel that the life of Francis I, so gloriously allegorized, cannot have been a happy one, and the tone of the ensemble is set by that pictorial elegy, the *Death of Adonis*.

Rosso died in 1540 at the early age of forty-six. There was a tradition, according to Vasari, that he killed himself out of remorse for having caused the execution of Francesco Pellegrino, his collaborator, whom he mistakenly suspected of having robbed him. Whether the story is true or not, this end was quite in character. His highly moralistic interpretation of the king's personality seems like a reflection of his own unswerving rectitude. Rosso's death gave Primaticcio his chance, and for thirty years he was the moving spirit of the Fontainebleau decorations. Francesco Primaticcio, styled Il Bolognese, was born at Bologna in 1504. It was in Mantua, at the Palazzo del Tè, as a member of the group of artists headed by Giulio Romano, that he had his real training. During the six years he worked there he was initiated into the secrets of Raphael's art. Little if at all influenced by the Rococo Mannerism of his immediate master, he was drawn to a more amiable and eye-pleasing type of art such as that of Giovanni da Udine, one of his co-workers at Mantua. But it was the art of Parmigianino that left the deepest imprint on his work. Primaticcio came to Fontainebleau two years after Rosso. To start with, he held a post much inferior to that of the older artist but he quickly rose to equal favor with the king. In 1544 Francis I, who twelve years before had conferred a canonry at the Sainte-Chapelle on his predecessor, appointed Primaticcio beneficiary abbot of the Abbey of Saint-Martin de Troyes.

His œuvre has suffered greater injury than Rosso's. Of the work he turned out during Rosso's lifetime hardly a trace remains, except certain portions of the Galerie François I which were by his hand, and even these—except for the *Danae* medallion needed to complete the sequence—are hard to distinguish from the rest. It is known that, far from working merely as a collaborator, he executed single-handed the decorations of the Chambre du Roi and those of the Porte d'Or. These are still extant, but altered out of recognition by lavish over-paintings and the ravages of time. It is in the decoration of the Chambre de la Duchesse d'Etampes (transformed in the eighteenth century into a landing on a flight of stairs) that we have the most complete example of his style. He worked on it from 1541 to 1544. Here again paintings are combined with high reliefs in stucco, but quite otherwise than those of Rosso. Far from aiming at a constant association, a give-and-take, so to say, between painting and relief, Primaticcio inserts painted scenes in semi-independent stucco settings. Also, the

Francesco Primaticcio (1504-1570).

Ulysses and Penelope, about 1560. (44×48″) Wildenstein and Co., Inc.

youths of Rosso's compositions are replaced by graceful women with sinuous bodies clinging to the frames and cartouches. The languid elegance of their outspread arms and long, tapering limbs sets the rhythm of the mural decorations. Nothing is here of the ingenious program Rosso had devised for his synthesis of stucco work and pictures in the Galerie François I. Women, putti and garlands of fruit are disposed solely with an eye to decorative effect, while allegorical or moral allusions have given place to an art of a purely sensuous appeal. The "Fontainebleau style" has come into its own with its distinctive cult of feminine beauty and voluptuous nudity, elegantly suggestive attitudes. In this new development the great Florentine goldsmith Benvenuto Cellini may well have played an active part. In 1540, on the death of Rosso, he came to Fontainebleau and continued working there for nearly five years. It was at Fontainebleau that Cellini produced his masterpiece, the magnificent salt-cellar of Francis I now in Vienna and the equally famous *Nymph of Fontainebleau* (Louvre), either or both of which may have suggested the daring elongations of the caryatids' bodies in the Chambre de la Duchesse d'Etampes.

Francesco Primaticcio (1504-1570).
The Masquerade of Persepolis, between 1541 and 1544. Drawing. (10×12″) Louvre, Paris.

Niccolò dell'Abbate (c. 1509-1571).
Eurydice and Aristaeus, about 1558-1560. (74⅛×93″) By Courtesy of the Trustees, National Gallery, London.

The sophisticated elegance of the paintings has suffered much from drastic restoration. Fortunately the preliminary sketches still exist and they bring out delightfully the rare perfection of the drawing. An example is the finished drawing for the *Masquerade of Persepolis* (Louvre), whose delicate and detailed execution conjures up so skillfully the picture in its original state. Despite the rigorously mathematical perspective projection, the linear rhythms move freely, following the curves of naked bodies, the slope of a bent back, the ripple of tensed limbs on the point, one would say, of joining in the figures of a dance. A skillfully disposed chiaroscuro stresses the fluent arabesques formed by the contour lines of bodies. We may assume that in the final painting the acidulous color favored by Primaticcio attenuated emphatic contrasts, and gave free play to the delicate linearism of the forms. Here we have the style of Fontainebleau at its best. And this art, based on a scale of values remote from everyday reality, with its "intellectual" eroticism and its charming allegories, pretexts for taking parades of nudity, has a heady fragrance peculiar to itself.

It is most regrettable that the Galerie d'Ulysse, which contained the finest decorations (their execution took nearly thirty years) was destroyed under Louis XV. The vault, designed by Fantuzzi, was decorated with grotesques inspired by Raphael's in the Vatican Loggie.

On the walls were compositions illustrating the story of Ulysses in fifty-eight episodes. Most of these scenes are known to us by drawings, engravings and even some painted copies. But of outstanding interest is the oil painting, doubtless by Primaticcio's own hand, based on a scene whose actual execution in the gallery, however, was left to Niccolò dell'Abbate. It represents Ulysses and Penelope, at long last reunited, talking in the cool of the evening. Rosso would have treated the theme in depth, but Primaticcio weaves a network of arabesques, a filigree of fluttering hands and sharp profiles, while in the distance, framed in a narrow doorway, two small graceful figures are outlined against the sunset.

This poetic-minded artist could not have found a more congenial helper than Niccolò dell'Abbate, who had been trained on much the same lines as himself. Born at Modena about 1509, he went to Bologna, then to Parma, where he familiarized himself both with the fragile grace of Parmigianino's art and with the more vigorous inventions of the school of Giulio Romano. When in 1552 he came to Fontainebleau he had already a solid reputation and several large-scale decorations in Italy to his credit. Still he always took his lead from Primaticcio, accepted his ideas wholeheartedly and faithfully transposed the cartoons given him on to the walls. He arrived just at the time when two great decorative projects were under way: the Galerie d'Ulysse, work on which, begun ten years before, had been delayed for various reasons; and, secondly, the Ball Room started the year before. He flung himself into these tasks enthusiastically, enhancing Primaticcio's clear-cut design with a fluent tracery of brushstrokes and building forms with interlaces of ribboned colors. Of his frescoes at Fontainebleau only those in the Ball Room have survived. There are grounds for hoping that the ill-advised "improvements" to which they have been subjected will shortly be eliminated and we shall see them as they originally were. It will then be possible to get a better idea of the lines on which these two highly gifted artists, Primaticcio and Niccolò, collaborated.

For Niccolò's contribution was not limited to the execution of another man's ideas. He had not the slightest difficulty in adapting his style to that of Fontainebleau and the type of feminine beauty he delighted in found a place quite readily among the gracious figures peopling its walls. None the less Niccolò dell'Abbate's version of this ideal woman is highly personal; the curious movement he gives her hands, prolonging the slightly swelling muscles of the arms, is peculiar to himself. Often her head is drooping with a flower-like grace and over the slim beauty of her body hover veils so gossamer-light as to be imperceptible, except where they gather in loosely flowing folds. Sometimes, like the girl confronting Scipio's brutal guardsmen, she introduces a dreamlike quality into an otherwise realistic scene. She figures, too, in Niccolò's landscapes which, charged with poetic intimations, were something new in the art of the age. They usually consist of panoramic vistas bounded by lofty mountains. There is nothing disquieting or desolate about these vast expanses. Everywhere are tokens of man's presence: temples, obelisks, pyramids, antique edifices, all brushed in as lightly as the gauzy veils of the young girl. Rolling hills and valleys, softly undulating woodlands, are echeloned in deep recession towards a blue horizon. The scenery brings to mind the "antique landscapes" made by Roman artists for Nero's Domus Aurea. But here what had been only a compositional accessory is more broadly treated and promoted to a work of art in its own right. And here, too, fantasy reigns supreme; in the enchanted world of Fontainebleau, a new Broceliande is conjured into being.

These three men, Rosso, Primaticcio and Niccolò dell'Abbate, could not have coped unaided with an enterprise of such magnitude, and a number of minor artists joined forces with them. There were several other Italians, but relatively little is known about them. One was Fantuzzi who, like Primaticcio, hailed from Bologna; he was responsible for some of the ornaments and arabesques in the Galerie d'Ulysse. Another Italian, Luca Penni, seems to have been highly thought of. His name occurs for the first time in the royal accounts for 1537, but he had then, apparently, been living several years in France. Of the same age as

Primaticcio and presumably a Florentine, he had received his training first in the team of artists employed by Raphael at the Vatican, then at Genoa with Perino del Vaga. After Rosso's death nothing more is heard of him at Fontainebleau; perhaps he incurred the jealousy of Primaticcio who would tolerate no rival. He continued working in France, probably in Paris, until his death in 1556. While at Fontainebleau he had made decorations (now destroyed) for the rooms giving on the façade, for the Salle Haute and the Pavillon des Poêles, as well as for the Galerie François I. He had engravings made of his own works, also of those of Rosso and Primaticcio, and these did much to propagate the style of Fontainebleau. None of his paintings has so far been identified; there are no good grounds for attributing to him (as has recently been done) the *Diana the Huntress* in the Louvre. There are perhaps better reasons for seeing his hand in the frescoes adorning the fireplace of the Salle du Connétable at Ecouen. They contain a landscape of a rather unusual type, more in the spirit of the school of Titian than in that of Niccolò dell'Abbate. Perhaps, as Mme Lucile Golson has suggested, the cartoons for the "Diana suite" of tapestries, made for Diane de Poitiers some time before 1552, may also be assigned to him. If these attributions were confirmed, they would show that he played a part of some importance as a continuator of Rosso's art at the time when Primaticcio was in the saddle.

Giulio Camillo, another Italian, is known to have collaborated with his father, Niccolò dell'Abbate. Mme Sylvie Béguin, who has made a thorough study of the facts of his career, believes she can detect his hand in the famous *Landscape with Men threshing Wheat* (Musée du Château, Fontainebleau), hitherto thought to have been his father's work. This opinion seems well founded and we owe to Mme Béguin the discovery of an attractive "little master." Of his father's vivacity he retains only the dry bones; his execution is less spontaneous, dryer, but there is no denying it a certain charm, for all its gaucherie. At the least we may assume that Giulio was one of the men who perpetuated the methods of the first School of Fontainebleau after the deaths of his father and Primaticcio.

To the same generation belonged another Italian artist, Ruggiero de Ruggieri, who came to Fontainebleau in 1557, and is mentioned in the accounts as being employed on various decorations. The fact that Primaticcio bequeathed to him all his pictures and painter's kit suggests that the two artists were close friends. Ruggiero's masterwork was unquestionably the *Life of Hercules* decorating the Pavillon des Poêles. He was active till nearly the end of the century (his death, it seems, took place in 1596 or 1597). There is no direct evidence enabling us positively to identify his productions, but Mme Béguin, by an ingenious chain of reasoning, has been led to attribute to him, tentatively, the pictures grouped together by Charles Sterling as being the work of the anonymous Master of Flora. The conjecture is certainly attractive, since, for one thing, it helps towards the dating of these exceptionally charming works, but so far there is little to confirm it. Indisputably the *Triumph of Flora* now in a private collection at Vicenza, like the *Birth of Love* (Metropolitan Museum, New York) and even the *Abundance* (Accademia, Ravenna), have many Italian characteristics. The suppleness of the nude bodies, the sharply flexed hands and fingers, and the oddly splayed-out toes are quite in the Primaticcio manner, but here his idiosyncrasies are carried a stage further. In the composition itself there are few innovations; the figure of Flora and the putto bringing flowers are taken directly from Bronzino's *Allegory of Love (Venus, Cupid, Folly and Time)* in the National Gallery, London. But the delicate handling of the figures makes them seem more immaterial. There is, however, a curious ambivalence in the New York and Vicenza pictures; the evanescence of the figures is counterbalanced by the precise rendering of the flowers and the care with which they are arranged, as in a well-planned still life. One is tempted to see in them the hand of a Flemish painter. A possible solution is that two painters took part in these works; this might account for their peculiar, somewhat ambiguous charm. For we must not forget that Flemish painters, already called in at the early stages of the Fontainebleau decorations, were even more in demand in the second half of the century.

Of the many French artists who were employed, certainly in equal numbers, along with the Italians, it is hard to single out the work of any. The name of Geoffroy Dumoustier, one of the oldest members of a family of painters, crops up in the accounts of expenditures on royal buildings for the year 1540. There exists a portrait drawing of him in the Hermitage, Leningrad, on which he is described as "painter and illuminator." Only a very few, however, of his works have so far been identified: some engravings, a design for a stained-glass window and, possibly, some illuminations in the Book of Hours of the Constable of Montmorency. In all of these

Master of Flora (active 1540-1560).

The Triumph of Flora. (51½×43¼") Private Collection, Vicenza.

108

Fr. I 46

School of Fontainebleau.
Diana the Huntress, about 1550. (75⅝×52⅜″) Louvre, Paris.

Rosso's influence is preponderant. Another French painter, Claude Badoin, was given a commission to make cartoons for tapestries after the pictures in the Galerie François I, but these copies are too literal to throw any real light on his artistic personality. Though these names mean little to us today, there are a number of anonymous works having every appearance of being by French hands, and they constitute a far from negligible element of the richly diverse art of the School of Fontainebleau. Characteristic of them is their imitation of the compositional schemes of the Italian masters, but the execution betrays an imperfect

School of Fontainebleau.

Lady at her Toilet, mid-sixteenth century. (41⅜×27⅞″) Musée des Beaux-Arts, Dijon.

assimilation of their style. These artists' knowledge of anatomy is less thorough, their drawing less assured, their handling of perspective less expert, and the traditional French realism with its insistence on exact modeling constantly asserts itself in their works.

Most famous, perhaps, is *Diana the Huntress* (Louvre), thought to be a portrait of Diane de Poitiers, mistress of King Henry II. The style is, on the face of it, Italian, but we also find a preoccupation with modeling that leads the artist to shade off outlines, to the detriment of linear precision. Clearly he is not at ease in his handling of a foreign mode of presentation but it is to this very indecision that the figure owes its naive charm and noteworthy originality. The curious placing of the breast and the unsuccessful foreshortening of the back (an idea taken from Rosso) contrast with the robustness of the limbs and still more with the conventional arrangement of the drapery. Even the color, less translucent, shows a tendency to realism and green foliage is used as a foil to the creamy-white flesh tints. A similar approach can be seen in *Sabina Poppea* (Musée d'Art et d'Histoire, Geneva). The rendering of the flimsy veil covering the nude body obviously derives from Niccolò dell'Abbate but here the folds seem even more insubstantial than the lightly floating veils in the *Continence of Scipio*. Yet the body beneath this tenuous tracery has nothing of the evanescence of Primaticcio's figures; it is amply molded, solidly constructed. In this group of anonymous works such tendencies are so frequent that we may well attribute them to the French artists who, while overawed by the Italian masters and trying their best to imitate them, retained a certain independence.

A recurring theme is that of the naked woman, shown half-figure, in her bath, or dressing, or with a purely allegorical significance (as in the Geneva picture). The popularity of the theme may have been due to the vast renown of a work by, or anyhow attributed to, Leonardo: the nude version of the *Monna Lisa*. None of the pictures claiming to be the original can be regarded as authentic; only in a drawing (heavily retouched, however) at Chantilly do we find approximations to his technique. But the motif evidently appealed strongly to the court of Fontainebleau, already familiarized with the nudes of the Italian artists. Quite possibly Leonardo's picture suggested not only the theme but its combination with a portrait; after all, was not the *Monna Lisa* a portrait? François Clouet was perhaps the first to follow this illustrious lead, with his *Diane de Poitiers in her Bath* (National Gallery, Washington). The *Lady at her Toilet* (Musée des Beaux-Arts, Dijon) is a variant of this theme. Its composition was evidently much admired, for two replicas of it exist, one at Worcester (Mass.), the other at Basel. Here again, perhaps, we have the likeness of some beauty of the day. The artist exploits the sensual possibilities of the subject with an elegant distinction deriving from Primaticcio. The treatment of the hands and fingers has the slightly affected grace characteristic of the art of Fontainebleau, and in the same spirit is the ingenious reflection of the face in the mirror, where the baroque luxuriance of the frame brings out the pure line of the features. Yet here again the charm of the work owes much to the ambivalence of its structure. The concern for style and deft economy apparent in the treatment of the woman's figure and especially her hands is countered by the naively minute depiction of the still life composed of odds and ends strewn in contrived disorder on her toilet table. Presumably there are symbols here the key to which is lost today; the only one we can readily interpret is the ring she is holding out, token of a hoped-for marriage. But why look further? We can surely appreciate the delicate grace of this somewhat enigmatic figure without caring for its "message."

The "bath theme" remained in vogue long after all the leading figures of the first School of Fontainebleau had disappeared. One of its best known examples is a double portrait, *The Duchesse de Villars and Gabrielle d'Estrées* (Louvre). Its composition combines that of Clouet's *Lady in her Bath* and that of the Dijon *Lady at her Toilet*. For once the meaning is crystal clear; the Duchess's gesture indicates that her sister is soon to have a child, a theme that is carried on by the servant preparing baby linen. Here, too, the ring may hint at a desire for marriage, and allude to the birth of the Duc de Vendôme, the king's bastard child (in 1594).

Once again the graceful flow of the design is checked by a scrupulous concern for realism and an insistence on volumes. It has been suggested that *Sabina Poppea* and the *Lady at her Toilet* should be assigned to the same (late) date as the double portrait. However, we cannot agree with Charles Sterling when he attributes all these works to the same master, whom he proposes to identify with François Bunel the Younger. Despite a similarity of style they do not seem to be by the same hand. Even the technique differs, and the creamy flesh tints of Gabrielle d'Estrées are distinctly unlike the livelier coloring of the lady at her toilet. Nor are there any reasons for giving so late a date either to the Dijon picture or to *Sabina Poppea*. Both seem to be more or less contemporary with Clouet's picture, and this has to be dated earlier than 1559 if the traditional identification of the lady with Diane de Poitiers is relied on.

Other themes make their appearance in the anonymous works of the School of Fontaine-bleau. The female nude reappears in pictures of a woman flanked by a youth and an old man, the best known specimen of which is the one in the Rennes Museum. Given a moral or satirical slant, this subject seems to have been taken over from the Italian Commedia dell'Arte. But the Italian actors themselves form the subject of other works, notably those in the museums of Béziers and Sarasota. All the compositions of this type containing half-length figures have a family likeness and are clearly influenced by Primaticcio's figures.

But alongside these anonymous works stylistically associated with the School of Fontaine-bleau we find productions of other artists who took a more independent line. One of them was Jean Cousin. Born at Sens about 1490, he began his career in his hometown, where he combined the activities of geometer and painter. He moved to Paris in about 1540 but he never lost touch with his birthplace until his death, in 1560. While in Paris he worked chiefly on commissions given by religious organizations, such as tapestry cartoons for the Confraternity of Sainte-Geneviève (1541), stained-glass windows for the Notre-Dame de Lorette chapel in the Cathedral of Sens (1542) and for the Goldsmiths' Guild (1557). Nothing is known about Cousin's early training. He is spoken of as a practising painter in 1526, that is to say before the Fontainebleau ateliers had got under way. Did he, then, make the journey to Italy or, after receiving a traditional training, did he succeed in catching up with the new developments in art sponsored by Primaticcio, his exact contemporary? There is, so far, no knowing. That this man whom early writers were fond of describing as "the French Michel-angelo" kept abreast of his times is certain. Some months before his death he published a *Traité de perspective*, one of the first books of the kind to appear in France.

Nothing definite was known about Jean Cousin's œuvre until the discovery in an ancient record of a statement that in 1541 he was given a commission by Cardinal de Givry, Bishop of Langres, for three tapestries illustrating the life of St Mammas. Two of them are still preserved in Langres Cathedral, and a third has recently entered the Louvre. The border decora-tions derive from Rosso's strap-work, but in the figures Cousin is clearly aiming at a classical mode of presentation that he may well have taken over from Raphael. Something of the forcefulness of the original composition must have been lost in its transposition into tapestry. But even so we can admire the dignified handling and the skill with which the landscape is disposed in solidly, harmoniously ordered planes. The quality of these tapestries lends color to the tradition attributing to Cousin that remarkable work, charged with esoteric symbolism, *Eva Prima Pandora* (Louvre). The supple line of the elongated body keeps to the rhythm of the art of Fontainebleau, but the classical rigidity of the woman's profile stems from a different source and the background of leafy rocks seems to owe something to the art of the North, more specifically perhaps to Jan van Scorel.

Cousin's work, moreover, reminds us that Fontainebleau was not the only place in France where Renaissance culture struck root. We can see its influence in a highly curious picture which ever since it was brought to notice in the early years of this century has been much

Jean Cousin (c. 1490-1560).
St Mammas appearing before Duke Alexander, 1541. Tapestry. (14′ 5⅜″ × 14′ 9⅜″) Louvre, Paris.

commented on by art historians. This is the *Moses and Aaron before Pharaoh* dated 1537, now in the Metropolitan Museum, New York. Completely independent of the Fontainebleau School, it shows more affinities with Roman painting; in particular, the crowded composition and the treatment of muscles remind us of Giulio Romano. This picture was probably intended by its first owner, Cardinal de Dinteville, Bishop of Auxerre, or by his brother, to serve as a companion piece to Holbein's famous *Ambassadors*. A comparison with a triptych in the church at Varzy (Nièvre) seemed to supply a clue to the artist's name: Félix Chrétien. This theory was based on a statement by a local eighteenth-century authority that Chrétien was the maker of the triptych (and also of a picture in Auxerre Cathedral, now known to be by a different hand). This discovery was particularly welcome since it furnished another name and another work to add to the meager tally of French art for the period—apart of course from Fontainebleau. But our confidence in this attractive theory has been shaken by Jacques Thuillier's masterly researches. For, as he points out, no trace of a painter of this name exists; Félix Chrétien was the name of a canon attached to the Cathedral Chapter and an intimate friend of Cardinal de Dinteville. He was not even one of the beneficed canons who drew their stipend without cure of souls, nor is there any evidence that he had a talent for painting, rare in any case among the clergy. Presumably the "authority" in question made a slip. As a result these pictures have reverted to anonymity, though needless to say that does not detract from their significance. The Varzy triptych was made in 1535 and the New York picture in 1537, that is to say at the very time when Rosso was decorating the Galerie François I.

Master of Auxerre (active 1535-1537).
Descent into the Cellar, 1537. (22⅞×22½") Städelsches Kunstinstitut, Frankfort.

But they have nothing in common with the art of Fontainebleau, their inspiration stems from a different source. Space is rendered in correct perspective, figures are given salient muscles, gestures are of the type in vogue with the Roman Mannerists. All the same, the cool tones and "far-away melancholy gaze" of some of the figures savor, rather, of the art of the North and the origins of these intriguing works must be sought for in an ambience combining the influences of such men as Lucas van Leyden and Jan van Scorel.

With these two pictures may be associated another, even more curious composition, also dating to 1537 and bearing the de Dinteville arms. This is the panel in the Städelsches Institut, Frankfort, showing three men lowering wine barrels into a cellar. Here we have what looks like a technical study by an artist who is a past-master of perspective. But a study with a difference; the peculiar starkness of the decor, and the lowered gaze of the two men watching their companion climbing down into the gaping darkness creates an atmosphere of mystery quite in tune with present-day taste. Obviously the subject might appeal to the de Dintevilles who had large estates in Burgundy where incidents of this sort were everyday occurrences. Yet so unconventional a work could have come into existence only in a special intellectual climate, favorable to aesthetic innovation and advanced ideas, and such was evidently the milieu of these enlightened art patrons, the de Dintevilles.

In short, the productions of Cousin and of the artist once thought to be Félix Chrétien were not isolated phenomena. It is evident that creative activity was far from being confined to Fontainebleau and that many painters whose names and, in many cases, works are unknown to us flourished in this period. Before being rightly attributed to the Master of Auxerre the *Descent into the Cellar* was thought to be the work of one of those sixteenth-century painters of whom so little is known: Jean de Gourmont. Member of a well-known family of Paris printers, he worked first in Paris, then at Lyons, where his name crops up sometimes in the records. He was chiefly famed for his engravings, which likewise bring to mind experiments in perspective. In the eighteenth century Mariette saw his hand in an *Annunciation* (now in the Louvre) originally painted for the chapel of the château of Ecouen. Here another curious edifice is represented, in which the classical orders and their Renaissance interpretations are intermingled, and this building not only dominates the sacred figures but reduces them to mere details. Similar tendencies can be seen in the work of another Lyonese painter, Georges Reverdy. In short, the few French artists contemporary with the Fontainebleau group whose work is fairly well known today seem to have been obsessed with the new-found wonders of perspective and the problems of geometrical drawing which it involved. And the revelation of these new, exciting discoveries was largely due, we may be sure, to the admirable treatise by Jean Pelerin published at Toul in 1501.

The Portrait from the Clouets
to the Dumonstiers

Jean Clouet (c. 1485?-1540).
Francis I, about 1520-1525. (37¾×29⅛″) Louvre, Paris.

VERY few of the portraits that have come down to us from the fifteenth century are independent paintings of an isolated figure. Most are donor portraits included in devotional pictures or figure on the wings of diptychs or triptychs on religious themes. This close association with religious painting, usually with prayer and private devotion, means that the demeanor of the personage portrayed has always a gravity appropriate to the occasion. Only towards the end of the century do independent portraits become slightly more frequent. Even then, however, their emancipation was still so recent that they retained much of the solemnity of the earlier works. Gazing into the middle distance, the models seem to be searching in vain for a Virgin and Child who are not there; the high earnestness remains, though the divine beings are no longer present.

This conception of the portrait was extremely popular at court. The king had portraits made of his courtiers and his family, while his own likeness was so much in demand that his court painter was compelled to produce copy after copy. As the demand increased, artists began to specialize in this new type of painting. Among these specialists we find no Italian painters, only French, Flemish and Dutch. To the Italians belonged the realm of the decorative and fanciful; there, with their teeming imagination and unfailing sense of style, they were unrivaled. In portraiture, however, they were thought less satisfactory; more confidence was felt in painters who worked "from the life" and whose powers of observation and respect for visual reality could be depended on.

Nevertheless, for all their realism and the conventionally stiff attitudes they had to give their models, the painters of this long line of portraitists were not impervious to style. The success of the Italians impelled them to combine, as best they could, a faithful rendering of reality with certain refinements of line and design, and this precarious path was followed by several generations of artists, all of whom conformed to a set formula. While this type of portraiture had already been inaugurated by Perréal, it was Jean Clouet above all who, in the second decade of the sixteenth century, gave it currency. The tradition thus established proved to be long-lived and held the field until the mid-seventeenth century, when it was finally supplanted by a more ornate type of portrait.

Jean Clouet (c. 1485?-1540).

Guillaume Budé, about 1535. (15⅝×13½″) The Metropolitan Museum of Art, New York.

The Portrait from the Clouets
to the Dumonstiers

Portraits figured in the royal collections of France well before the sixteenth century. Records of the fourteenth century show that even in those early days Charles V took pleasure in adorning his residences with likenesses of members of his family and peers of the realm. And even before that his father John the Good seems to have had similar tastes, though perhaps he indulged them less. But the accounts that have come down to us of these vanished collections are too meager to give any clear idea of their extent and value. We do know, however, that the taste for portraits persisted throughout the fifteenth century: the Duke of Burgundy and the Duke of Berry both owned some, while King René of Anjou, himself a painter, is said to have painted his contemporaries and, when a prisoner at Dijon, even made an imaginary portrait of his cousin, the Duke of Burgundy, before meeting him personally. At the end of the century Jean Perréal seems to have owed his fame above all to the "pourtraictures" he made under express instructions from his royal patron. This interest in portraiture was even more pronounced at the court of Fontainebleau. Now it was not only the king himself, princesses of marriageable age and heirs to the throne who had their portraits made, but the whole court was invited to pose for the artist. Renaissance humanism, with its ever-increasing interest in the human personality, no doubt contributed to the development of this new taste. Moreover, the growing interest in the pagan world of classical antiquity, by diverting art from the religious domain to which it had hitherto been limited, helped to establish the portrait as an independent art form, for which the pretext of portraying a donor had now ceased to be necessary.

Under these circumstances, eminently favorable to its growth, there developed what was nothing short of a passion for the portrait. King Francis I commissioned an illuminated manuscript of Caesar's *Gallic War* in which the figures of Roman heroes were replaced by portraits of his own generals (British Museum, London; Musée Condé, Chantilly). Queen Catherine de' Medici formed a whole collection of portraits, and many of her contemporaries followed suit. To meet the ever-increasing demand, Corneille de Lyon kept on permanent display in his studio a veritable gallery of portraits of the great men of the day. But this passion for collecting did not mean that the painter was free to cultivate style at the expense of verisimilitude. Thus we are told that Catherine de' Medici sent an artist in her employ to make portraits of her absent children, in order to make sure that they were in good health. The portrait, then, though it might be a work of art and a collector's piece, was expected to be strictly true to life.

Jean Clouet (c. 1485?-1540).
Admiral Bonnivet, about 1516. Chalk Drawing. (9⅞×7⅝″) Musée Condé, Chantilly.

This principle was, indeed, fundamental to a style of portraiture which none the less achieved a high artistic standard within these narrow bounds, and which in fact stands out as one of the most significant expressions of the French Renaissance. It is summed up in a single name: Clouet. But that name covers two different artists, Jean (or Janet) and his son and successor François, whom his contemporaries also referred to as Janet. The career of Jean Clouet long remained something of a mystery. Thanks to the research work of Dimier and Moreau-Nélaton, however, we now know considerably more about his life, though many of its phases remain obscure. Though not a Frenchman by birth, he was enrolled in the service of the King of France (in 1516). At first he lived and worked at Tours, where he married Jeanne Boucault, daughter of a local goldsmith. In 1529 at the latest he was living in Paris. He must have died about 1540, for shortly after that date his son succeeded him in the post of court painter. It is clear from records of the period that he did not confine himself to portrait painting. In 1522, for example, he was commissioned to paint a St Jerome for the church of Saint-Pierre du Boile at Tours, and in the following year he supplied some embroidery designs. But of such works as these nothing has survived, or has yet come to light. Even as regards his portraits, only two are fully documented as being by his hand. The first is that of the mathematician Oronce Finé, which was engraved under Clouet's name in 1584; the original painting is lost. The other is a portrait of the famous French humanist Guillaume Budé, who made a note on a page of the manuscript of his *Adversaria*: "*Pictor iconicus qui me pinxit, Me Genet Clouet vocatur*" (The portrait painter who painted me is called Master Genet Clouet). This note has proved instrumental in saving a substantial body of Clouet's work from anonymity, for the preliminary chalk drawing for Budé's portrait is preserved at Chantilly and is one of a set of portrait drawings forming an homogeneous group, which can therefore be reliably identified as the work of Jean Clouet. Since then, in fact, the painting itself has been brought to light; it is now in the Metropolitan Museum, New York. Otherwise, however, it has been possible to supplement the drawings with only a very few paintings: the *Portrait of Francis II as a Child* (Musée Royal, Antwerp), the *Portrait of Madame de Canaples* (National Gallery, Edinburgh) and the *Man with a Petrarch* (Windsor Castle).

The fine *Portrait of Francis I* in the Louvre has long been attributed to Clouet, and indeed was described as early as 1642 by Le Père Dan, who saw it at Fontainebleau, as being by his hand. Today, however, it has become the fashion to cast doubt on this attribution despite its antiquity. Actually there is no real difference between this state portrait and those related to the Chantilly drawings—no difference beyond what would normally be called for in a royal portrait. The gorgeous curtains drawn back on each side and the grandiose presentation of the figure are quite in keeping with the official character of the work; they are not to be regarded as indications of a style of portraiture inconsistent with Clouet's. The sedulous care devoted to the sumptuous costume may indeed seem unusual for him, but this too was necessitated by the setting (which follows that of Fouquet's *Portrait of Charles VII*) and, in some measure no doubt, by the fashion of the day. The rendering of the king's face is manifestly based on one of the chalk drawings at Chantilly, whose severe expression and sharpness of definition it reflects. The refinement and preciosity of the treatment of the hands may seem a little overdone, but similar gestures occur in other portraits by Clouet, though they do not catch the eye to the same extent. It has been suggested that the work may well be by a Flemish artist, and the somewhat acidulous colors and the precision with which embroideries are rendered tend to bear this out. Here then is evidence—slender evidence, admittedly—in favor of the traditional attribution to Clouet. For he was not a Frenchman; the documents in which he is mentioned expressly refer to him as a foreigner, and his name and style make it fairly certain that he came from the Low Countries. The portrait of Francis I, being that of a young man, is almost certainly anterior to the period of captivity in Madrid; it may therefore be dated to the years 1520-1525, immediately following Clouet's arrival at the French court, its markedly Flemish qualities being just such as we might expect to find in work of this relatively early period of his career.

Given, then, the well-established tradition behind the attribution to Clouet, and the corroborative evidence set forth above, let us look again at the portrait and see whether stylistic analysis tends to confirm the attribution or not. One is struck first of all by characteristically Mannerist touches, particularly evident in the preciosity of the gesture and the rendering of the garment. This applies also to the treatment of the face, with its sharpness of outline and extreme precision. These make it still more evident that Mannerism lay at the very source of Clouet's style. His conception of portraiture differs in no essential respect from that of the School of Fontainebleau: he may almost be said to represent that School in a domain virtually unexplored by the Fontainebleau painters. But the peculiar nature of this Mannerism is worth analysing. It cannot have stemmed from the Florentine portraitists, such as Bronzino, who were all younger than Clouet and who, in the second decade of the century, had hardly yet begun their careers. What we find in Clouet is, rather, an embryonic Mannerism, or an imitation by a northern master, committed to realism and accurate modeling, of the procedures of a great Renaissance master, who can only be Leonardo. Clouet could easily have met Leonardo in France and was certainly familiar with his work. In fact the large folds of drapery enveloping the king's arms are a transposition—hardened and tightened by a less supple technique—of those of the angel in the *Virgin of the Rocks*. Even the hands, despite the essentially linear treatment, remind us of those of Leonardo's figures.

This Mannerist trend is also noticeable in other known works by Jean Clouet. It grows, however, less emphatic as his style acquires its definitive form. The pose of the figure is simplified, attitudes become firmer, and the hands are joined. But his color schemes remain the same throughout, invariably high-pitched in tone. The backgrounds are of a strident blue or green, much like those of contemporary Florentine painting. Such, for example, is the style of the *Portrait of Guillaume Budé*, so fortunately rediscovered some years ago, which can scarcely be dated any earlier than 1535.

No wonder that in an art like this, where so much depends on line, the preliminary designs are works of so high an order. The tradition of the preliminary study, drawn in black chalk or more often in black, red and white chalks, seems to be anterior to Clouet. Some of the earliest of such studies may well be works by Perréal or his contemporaries, and it was this technique of drawing in three chalks that the Lyonese master is said to have brought to Leonardo's notice. But it was given its full development only by Jean Clouet and it remained in favor for the rest of the century. Such studies soon became collector's pieces; they were obviously less expensive than finished paintings, were less fragile, more easily transported from one place to another—and of course much more rapidly executed. Queen Catherine de' Medici collected them, and so perhaps did Francis I before her. So great was the demand that artists not only had to increase the number of their studies but had to produce copy after copy of them. As a result they have come down to us in large numbers, sometimes forming entire collections, providing both an invaluable pictorial record of the age and a unique source of information. The most extensive sets of these drawings are preserved in the Musée Condé at Chantilly and the Bibliothèque Nationale, Paris; many of those at Chantilly appear to have belonged to Catherine de' Medici.

The material conditions that favored the production and sale of these drawings were seconded by an aesthetic factor. A portrait by Clouet—if to a less degree than those of his successors—is above all a "speaking" likeness. He was chiefly interested, not in attitudes and costumes, but in the human face, and he sought to record the model's features with the utmost verisimilitude. But at the same time he was much concerned with the definition of contours, of the essential element, in other words, of a composition in which line was all-important. Strangely enough, this ambivalence, the dual emphasis on style on the one hand and lifelikeness on the other, was furthered by the three-crayon technique. The reduction of his means of expression to line alone fully satisfied the artist's austere concern for purity of

François Clouet (c. 1515-1572).
Queen Marguerite as a Girl, about 1560. Chalk Drawing. (11⅝×8″) Musée Condé, Chantilly.

style, while the three different chalks, by introducing color, enabled him to achieve lifelikeness and so to avoid the abstraction of a charcoal or pen drawing. Thus it was that the portrait drawing acquired its letters patent of nobility. It became an end in itself, not just a preliminary study, and was sought after for its own sake, often in preference to actual paintings.

Divested of the tonal richness of oils or tempera, the chalk drawing exemplifies the narrow path trodden by the artists of the sixteenth century and reveals better perhaps than any other medium the delicate perfection of their art. All the resources of gesture, movement, emotional expression and anecdote are spurned. The pose of the head is confined within narrow limits, varying only from the frontal to the three-quarter view, and set at just the right angle to display the beauty of the outline. Under these conditions a man's whole character (or a woman's) had to be summed up in the precision of the drawing and a faithful rendering of the model's gaze. For us today, the names of any predecessors he may have had being unrecorded, Jean Clouet is the creator of this type of portraiture; his drawings, anyhow, set the standards by which it must be judged. His flawless outlines enclose a discreet network of hatchings which he models by variations in their intensity. The face itself is delineated and characterized by a few lines, and similar lines serve to suggest the bust. Yet it was not with him that the portrait drawing developed the extreme linearism which was to characterize it. Hatchings and sometimes even stumped outlines envelop forms, blur them a little, and impart fluidity to the atmosphere. Here again, as Sir Anthony Blunt has pointed out, the influence of Leonardo, particularly of his later drawings, is unmistakable. There is, nevertheless, a highly personal touch in Clouet's use of sfumato effects.

The handling of line by his son, François Clouet, is markedly different. Drier, more precise, but arresting in its very severity, it records the sitter's features in exhaustive detail, as finished as a full-dress painting. The charming *Portrait of Queen Marguerite as a Girl* is a significant example. The red, white and black chalks, washed with watercolor, give the work a self-completeness that could scarcely be excelled in any other medium. As it stands, the portrait might have served as a model for a panel painting by some brother-artist. François' modeling, unlike his father's, is not obtained by clear-cut hatchings, but by very tenuous strokes that are often stumped. But these shadings are restricted to the interior of the figure and do not impair the essential purity of the contour. This linear clarity and sharpness of definition largely accounts for the curiously hieratic quality of his drawings.

The name of François Clouet first appears in the royal accounts for December 1540; he is there described as his father's successor, on the same salary, two hundred and forty livres. Presumably he was born some twenty-five or thirty years earlier, perhaps at Tours. In the course of his career he served as court painter under four successive monarchs, Francis I, Henry II, Francis II and Charles IX, and in this capacity was called upon to execute the paintings and banners used at the funeral ceremonies of two of them, Francis I and Henry II. Very little is known about his life. He had two natural daughters, but it was his sister who inherited his estate when he died on September 22, 1572. The records have little more to tell us than that he produced the usual series of portraits and decorations. We do learn, however, that he was summoned to the Royal Mint in 1570 to give his opinion of a new coin bearing the king's effigy. Who indeed could be better fitted than he to judge of the qualities of a portrait struck on a coin?

François Clouet's work is better documented than his father's. Two signed paintings have come down to us: the *Lady in her Bath* (National Gallery, Washington) and the *Portrait of Pierre Quthe* (Louvre, Paris). A third, the *Portrait of Charles IX* (Kunsthistorisches Museum, Vienna), bears an ancient signature which has every air of being authentic. The Louvre portrait is dated 1562 and, since it was painted twenty-two years after his appointment as court painter, may certainly be regarded as an example of his mature style. This,

François Clouet (c. 1515-1572).
Pierre Quthe, 1562. (35¾×27½″) Louvre, Paris.

as was to be expected, diverged widely from his father's. The sitter was a neighbor of his in Paris, living in the Rue Sainte-Avoye. A well-known apothecary, Pierre Quthe had a garden famed for its rare medicinal plants; hence the open herbal beside him, indicating his profession. In representing his learned neighbor, who was no doubt a personal friend, François Clouet thought fit to depart from the traditional half-length portrait. The unusual pose and layout were probably taken over from some Italian artist, perhaps Bronzino or Salviati. The curtain, however, which mitigates the abruptness of the angle in one corner of the picture, stems directly from the tradition of the previous century, while the face is shown at exactly the same angle as in the chalk drawings. Perhaps the closest link with the Italians is to be found in François Clouet's color scheme, where he abandons cold precision in favor of warmer tones bringing to mind the Brescian painters.

But this picture appears to be a departure from the artist's usual practice; for the most part he keeps to the tradition of the half-length portrait. Such is the case, for example, in the *Portrait of Queen Elizabeth of Austria* (the wife of Charles IX), which, being datable to 1571,

François Clouet (c. 1515-1572).

A Lady in her Bath, about 1550. (36¼×32¼″) Samuel H. Kress Collection, National Gallery of Art, Washington, D.C.

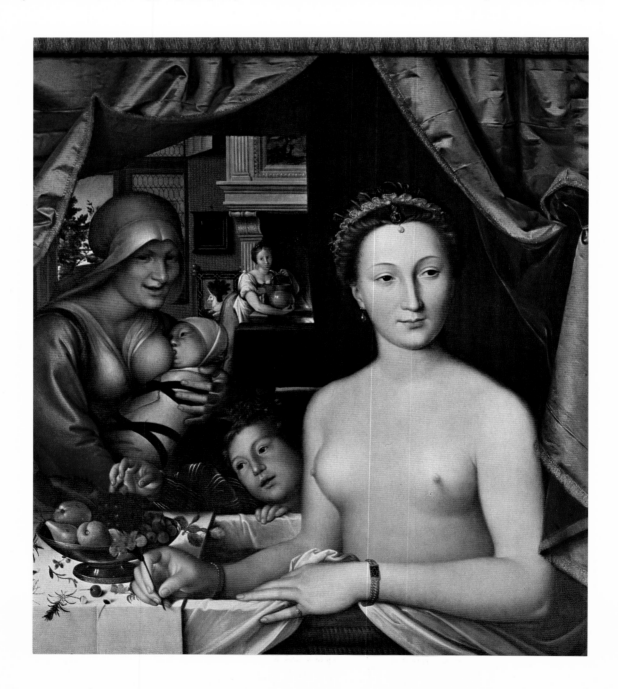

may be regarded as one of his last works. The same is true of the *Portrait of Charles IX as a Child* (Kunsthistorisches Museum, Vienna). Distinctive of both these portraits is the minutely detailed rendering of the costumes which, carried almost to the point of preciosity, act as a foil to the severity of the faces. But François Clouet was also the creator of the full-length portrait. Two examples have survived which, excellent though they are, may only be studio copies: the *Portrait of Henry II* (Uffizi, Florence) and the *Portrait of Charles IX* (Kunsthistorisches Museum, Vienna). In both the figure of the king is framed by drawn curtains—a setting frequently employed in royal portraits. Perspective is roughly indicated by the receding lines of the floor and emphasized—rather pedantically—in the *Portrait of Charles IX* by the chair on which the king rests his arm. But line is so preponderant that the attempts to suggest depth miss fire to some extent; the figures are no more than colorful silhouettes whose only sign of life is in the faces. But there is no question of their delicate grace, and this is enhanced by the "period" costumes.

Again we have a portrait, but one of a rather special kind, in the *Lady in her Bath* (National Gallery, Washington). Some doubt still persists as to the identity of the model. It was suggested in 1929 by Irene Adler that she was probably Marie Touchet, the mistress of Charles IX. Yet there are no very cogent reasons for rejecting the tradition that it was Diane de Poitiers who posed for the picture. The face is the same as that in the *Diana the Huntress* in the Louvre, and the same too as in the many tapestries woven for the royal favorite. But this curious picture sets many more problems than the identity of the lady represented. Her pose, as we have already noted, is taken from the undraped version of the *Monna Lisa*. The actual theme, that of a lady in her bath, may be a boldly realistic transposition of Venus rising from the sea; by thus assimilating his sitter to the most seductive of goddesses, the artist justified his boldness. But there is also an allusion to fecundity—an allusion made quite explicit by such details as the nurse suckling a child and the bowl of ripe fruit in the foreground. The uplifted curtains may be no more than decorative adjuncts; nevertheless, they bring to mind the similar curtains in royal portraits, and may have been an allusion to the royal favor in which the model basked. The presence of children remains a problem. Diane de Poitiers bore two daughters to her husband, Louis de Brézé, but it can scarcely be they who are represented here, for in that case the picture would have to be dated earlier, prior to her liaison with the king. It was suggested by Georges Guiffrey that the picture was intended to allude to the part played by the king's mistress in the education of the royal children (the future Francis II and his sister Elizabeth). But other details defy interpretation. The pink the lady is holding may perhaps refer to the brevity of life—a gesture of defiant coquetry on the part of a woman proud of her enduring charm. The representation of a child reaching for the fruit may hint at the function of the mother, provider of nourishment for her babe. But what of the unicorn represented on the back wall? How is this symbol to be explained? Guiffrey's theory, that it is a reminder of a nostrum recommended by Diane de Poitiers for the royal children, seems a shade far-fetched.

By and large this singular picture remains something of an enigma. One cannot help being struck, for example, by the curious contrast between the nude figure and the accessories around it. Diane is obviously idealized, with her fair complexion, the harmonious proportions of her body, the pure, regular features of her face. If Guiffrey's hypothesis is to be trusted, she must have been forty-six years old at the time the portrait was painted. But she evidently had retained her beauty, for the idealization of her person is no more pronounced here than in the Louvre picture or the Anet tapestries. The other elements of the composition heighten that idealization by contrast, while also stressing her assimilation to a pagan goddess. The nurse has the florid complexion and deeply lined face of a peasant woman. The still life of minutely delineated fruit has all the precision of a Flemish painting, as has the sumptuous interior depicted in the background. This latter brings to mind Titian's *Urbino Venus*, in which, beyond the bed on which the goddess is lying, we also see a richly furnished inner

Corneille de Lyon (active 1540-1574).
Clément Marot, about 1540. (4¾×3⅞″) Louvre, Paris.

chamber where a maid-servant is attending to her duties. But however similar the theme, Clouet handles the background scene very differently, depicting it with a minuteness of detail that is typically Flemish and much in the spirit of the coulisses in Jan van Eyck's paintings. Thus there is a duality of style in the handling of this allegorical figuration whose basic referents, anyhow, are fairly clear: the divinity of woman, with allusions to a royal liaison and to motherhood. To the fact that an idealized figure, marked by influences of the Italians at Fontainebleau, is placed in surroundings executed with the vigorous realism of a Flemish master, is due the ambivalence of the overall effect. The essential qualities of Clouet's style are revealed here still more clearly than in his more conventional portraits.

Corneille de Lyon, a contemporary of Clouet's, was another portrait painter whose work was much sought after in his lifetime. He was not French by birth, for references to him in documents of the period go to show that he was of Dutch origin and born at The Hague. He is first recorded as being in Lyons in 1540, and four years later, in his capacity of painter to the dauphin (later Henry II), he was already exempted from the wine tax, though he was not naturalized French until 1547. In 1551 he is described as painter to the king, and he seems to have remained in favor, for in 1564 he was donated with the property of a foreign weaver lately deceased which had reverted to the Crown. Brantôme tells of a visit paid him in June of that same year by Catherine de' Medici herself. In 1569, as a result of the rising tide of religious persecution, he abjured Protestantism and, with his wife, daughter and servants, joined the Catholic Church. The last recorded mention of him is in the tax registers of Lyons for 1574, probably the year of his death. Such, in brief, are the known facts of the life of the Clouet's great rival. The celebrity he enjoyed, though resident in Lyons, is a further indication of the prestige of this great commercial city as an art center.

But while the essential dates and facts of Corneille de Lyon's life can be determined with some certainty, the identification of his œuvre is no easy matter. Not a single portrait, or picture of any kind, has come down to us with an authenticated pedigree. The only clue we have to the nature of his work is an account by the Venetian ambassador, Giovanni Capelli, describing a visit to his studio in 1551. "We paid a call on an excellent painter who, in addition to other fine paintings he let us see, showed us the whole Court of France, both gentlemen and ladies, depicted with the utmost lifelikeness on a great many small panels." Despite its vagueness, this statement has led to the attribution to him of a whole group of portraits hitherto anonymous and cast into the shade by the achievements of the Clouets in this field. All are painted in a smooth, enamel-like technique and are smaller than the panels of the Parisian painters. Given the fact that they are so uneven in quality, and that the same portrait sometimes exists in several copies, it is obvious that the use of the name "Corneille de Lyon" as a general label for this group of portraits is purely speculative. Nevertheless we may assume that, if not their maker, he was in charge of the studio responsible for these remarkably attractive works, though no conclusive evidence is so far available in support of this conjecture.

Corneille de Lyon (active 1540-1574).
Gabrielle de Rochechouart, about 1547. (6½×5½″) Musée Condé, Chantilly.

Pierre Dumonstier the Uncle (c. 1540-c. 1600). Portrait of a Man, about 1580 (?).
Chalk Drawing washed with Watercolor. (12¼×9¾″) Musée Jacquemart-André, Chaalis (Oise).

The style of these portraits is easily distinguishable from that of the Clouets. Emphasis is laid on the face, even more so than in their work. Hands are rarely visible, the figure generally being cut short at the waist. Very often, too, so as to give it more prominence, the head is slightly enlarged at the expense of the torso. Painted on small panels which they fill almost entirely, reducing margins to a minimum, these faces acquire an astonishing actuality. The best hand of the group, presumably that of Corneille de Lyon himself, models the features in smooth, thin glazes which recall the textural refinements of Jan van Eyck, but the color schemes are restricted to a narrow range of cold tones in which the muted greens and acid blues of the grounds tell out effectively. By contrast the flesh tints gain in delicacy and the eyes acquire a deeper glow. Unfortunately these sensitively executed panels have suffered from excessive cleaning and the surfaces are sometimes much worn and scratched. Hence the unwonted pallor of the faces in which shadows are indicated by blue or greenish hues whose intensity had been attenuated by the original glazes. Many of the portraits, too, are mere replicas perfunctorily executed, meager in texture and less expressive. Thus, to appreciate Corneille de Lyon, an effort has to be made to sort out the best specimens of the works grouped under his name. One of the finest, undoubtedly, is the *Portrait of Clément Marot* (Louvre, Schloss Donation). The poet's finely molded face, set off by a thick black beard, has a strangely dream-like quality. But underneath this realistic, minutely delineated exterior, does the personality of the man himself really shine through? The mildness, the poetic serenity of the gaze, is almost enough to convince us—but not quite. When we remember the facts of Marot's life, his taste for dissolute living, we may wonder whether the painter has not played the poet's part and portrayed his sitter not as he actually was, but rather as he imagined him. For that dreamy gaze is out of keeping; here, as in so many of his portraits, Corneille de Lyon has "thought himself" into his model. The descriptive element is limited to the physical aspect of his figures. His portraits of women, too, have a singular delicacy. The flesh tints are remarkably translucent, lifelike, but the gaze has always something of that wistfulness to which his portraits of Gabrielle de Rochechouart and Louise de Rieux (Louvre) owe their ethereal purity.

True, Corneille de Lyon's art does not in any sense derive from that of the Clouets; it merely reflects the climate of taste of the period. All that they have in common is a fine spareness of means and strict precision. The execution, at once sophisticated and a trifle frigid, suggests a Flemish origin. We are unable to endorse the view recently given currency that Corneille was in the lineage of Perréal, that other Lyonese painter. On the other hand, his affinities with Joos van Cleve have often been pointed out and it seems more likely that he spent his formative years among the Antwerp group. Their reputation stood high in France when he was invited to that country by King Francis I to make his portrait and that of his second wife, Eleanor of Portugal. Corneille de Lyon acclimatized Flemish methods in France by adapting them to that conception of the portrait pure and simple—centered on the face—which was so characteristic of the time.

After a careful survey of the large body of work attributed to Corneille de Lyon, Louis Dimier came to the conclusion that several artists had a share in it. In particular he singled out the work of two anonymous painters, the Master of Rieux-Châteauneuf and the Brissac Master. These groupings are, however, difficult to establish, indeed most of the works assigned to the Brissac Master should in our opinion be restored to the "studio of Corneille de Lyon." As for those grouped under the name of the Master of Rieux-Châteauneuf (e.g. the male portraits in the Musée Ingres at Montauban and the Musée Calvet at Avignon, and, still more notably, the work of a remarkable anonymous artist now in the museum of Toledo, Ohio), we quite agree that they are by a different hand, having affinities, however, with that of Corneille de Lyon. These faces have an intenser life and are executed in a more spontaneous, more impulsive manner and the artist is less preoccupied with studiously polished execution. Here we may have the work of an artist in the master's entourage, perhaps a younger man.

For the interest in portrait painting of this order outlasted the Clouets and indeed continued until the mid-seventeenth century—until, that is to say, a more decorative type of portrait won favor at the court of Louis XIV. François Clouet's successor as painter to the king was Jean Decourt who had already a well-established reputation. Born about 1530 and hailing, it seems, from Limoges, he had begun by working for Marie Stuart and remained in her service in France after her departure to Scotland. He survived his predecessor only by thirteen years. It is, unfortunately, impossible to assign to him any specific painting or drawing. Some have, however, thought to see his hand in a group of crayon drawings remarkable for the firmness and extreme precision, verging on dryness, of the linework. If this attribution be correct, Decourt's work carried François Clouet's a stage further. Clouet had already applied himself to rendering details of costumes with extreme fidelity, but with Decourt they ranked as basic elements of the composition; hence the preciosity of his art and its "fashionable" appeal. A few paintings seem in keeping with these drawings, among them the *Portrait of Henry III* (when he was still Duke of Anjou) and the elegant depiction of a young nobleman in the Hermitage, Leningrad.

Another of Clouet's successors, Benjamin Foulon, his nephew and also his heir, has not fared better. Though he did not immediately succeed his uncle, he became painter to the king under Henry III and retained the post under Henry IV. He lived until 1623 and presumably produced a large quantity of work, but nothing remains of it today except a batch of drawings preserved in the Bibliothèque Nationale. They do not show signs of any great talent. His line has a certain vagueness, as though he were deliberately softening it down with an eye to an effect of modeling; but, in practice, owing to his inexpertness, it seems merely blurred. The portraits of the period are known to us today chiefly by groups of drawings, as in the case of Foulon. Despite the scholarly research work of Dimier and Moreau-Nélaton, much still remains to be done in this field. In a brilliant article Sheila M. Percival has suggested the lines on which to proceed in view of a better comprehension of these hundreds of sheets of portrait drawings. What is needed is to prosecute inquiries still further so as to segregate more surely the work of each of these mostly anonymous artists. Dimier, for example, rightly differentiates from François Clouet's œuvre that of the master whom he names "Anonyme Lécurieux." Like Decourt and doubtless his contemporary, this man rendered details of costumes with finicking precision, but his drawing is far less accomplished.

Among these anonymous draftsmen one calls for special mention, that enigmatic artist styled the Master of the Monogram I.D.C. He owes this appellation to the initials inscribed on one of his drawings (in the Bibliothèque Nationale). Henri Bouchot, who first drew attention to his work, proposed to interpret this inscription as Jean Decourt's signature; unfortunately the persons portrayed do not bear out this identification; it is clear that these drawings were made between the years 1573 and 1600. Here we find a return to the practice of Jean Clouet, who centered attention on the face alone. Bodies are indicated by a design so tenuous as to be almost imperceptible. The linework has an extreme subtlety, sometimes almost producing an effect of painting; its variations of intensity conjure up the forms from the paper support as on a painted panel. This delicate handling is seconded by a nicety of observation to which his portraits owe their taking charm; indeed, as Sheila Percival has aptly pointed out, those of Gabrielle d'Estrées and Mademoiselle d'Urfé have all the refinement of eighteenth-century portraits.

Apart from these anonymous artists and others whose œuvre has not as yet been positively identified—for example Marc Duval who made the portrait of the three Coligny brothers—two families of artists active towards the close of the century call for mention: the Dumonstiers and the Quesnels. The former were descendants of Geoffroy Dumonstier, one of Rosso's fellow-workers at Fontainebleau. He had three sons, Etienne, Pierre and Côme, all of whom were portrait painters. The two elder sons were *valets de chambre* to Catherine de' Medici, won

François Quesnel (1543-1619).

Mary Ann Waltham, 1572. (22×17½″) By Courtesy of The Earl Spencer, Althorp (Northamptonshire).

high renown and had the honor of being sent on a special mission to the imperial court of Vienna. What has survived of Etienne's work is almost exclusively confined to drawings, but these are enlivened by the use of colored chalks. His art has a pleasing frankness, he obviously aims at infusing the maximum of life into his portrait drawings and there is a new intensity in the forthright gaze of his sitters. Of the work of his brother Pierre (styled "Dumonstier the Uncle" to distinguish him from his nephew Pierre II, Etienne's son) several drawings have come down to us, among them being the portrait of the Duc de Sully, chief minister to Henry IV. Like his brother he had recourse to color, some of his portraits might almost pass for paintings. An example is the *Portrait of a Man* (Musée Jacquemart-André, Chaalis), a chalk drawing washed with watercolor. There is less emphasis on line, and the precise linearism of the first portraitists of the sixteenth century gives place to fluent modeling and above all a concern for the expression of life at its most intense. The piercing gaze of this grim-faced man, whose identity is a mystery, tells us more about the sitter than we learn from Clouet's portraits. Yet the spirit is still the same; once again a face is isolated on an abstract ground and subjected to a rigorous analysis. Daniel Dumonstier, Côme's son, also had a successful career. Painter and *valet de chambre* to Louis XIII, he was a friend of Malherbe and of the famous collector Peiresc who lived in Aix-en-Provence. His cousin Pierre II led a more nomadic existence; he spent many years in Italy, first at Turin (where mention is made of him round about 1625), then in Rome. But before these sojourns in the south he had made a trip to Flanders, in 1603. Few of his works have survived; they are limited, once again, to portrait drawings and keep to the tradition of his father and his uncle.

The Quesnel family of painters, fewer in number, produced work of no less interest. Little is known of the first of them, Pierre Quesnel, except the fact that he was court painter to James II of Scotland. Of recent years attention has been directed to his sons François and Nicolas. Many drawings by François (1543-1619) are preserved in the Bibliothèque Nationale. Their identification has been enabled by the signature on one of them and by the attractive portrait drawing in M. Jacques Dupont's collection, *Demoiselle Marie Bourdineau*, recently published by Sheila Percival. They show reminiscences of the art of that brilliantly original draftsman the I.D.C. Master, but here it seems curiously petrified; the artist has evidently applied himself by dint of patient industry to mastering the superb craftsmanship of the portrait of Gabrielle d'Estrées. The painted portrait of Mary Ann Waltham (signed and dated 1572) has a touching gaucherie. The artist has concentrated his attention on the face, delicately modeled and given a smooth enamel-like finish, whereas the body is merely outlined, then summarily blocked in with no attempt at modeling. The explanation of this anomaly may be that the artist was trained to the use of the crayon and felt ill at ease with brushwork; the body is treated with the same perfunctoriness, not to say indifference, as in the drawings on paper. Or it may be that Quesnel left its execution to an unskilled assistant. The work of his brother, Nicolas Quesnel (died 1632) has not yet come under study; Dimier thought little of it, yet the portrait drawing (dated 1574) of the artist's father is remarkably effective. The delicacy of the passages of shading, in particular, suggests that Nicolas may have been an excellent painter and that his œuvre would be well worth tracing.

In the domain of the sixteenth-century portrait another artist, Lagneau, calls for mention. Nothing is known of his career and even his name would probably be unknown but for a brief mention of him by the Abbé of Marolles. He seems to have worked exclusively with chalks, but he struck a new note in his portraits, which tend towards the genre scene, the models being often taken from "low life." Indeed they are not so much portraits as frankly grotesque figurations. None the less their layout and form are still in the Clouet tradition. Where they diverge from it is in a systematic emphasis on shading due to the use of broadly laid-in black chalk strokes, set off with occasional dabs of red. With him sixteenth-century portraiture entered on a decline; departing from the severe disciplines that had hitherto prevailed, it now aimed chiefly at striking effects.

French and Flemish Artists
at Fontainebleau

Frans Pourbus the Younger (1569-1622). The Last Supper (detail), 1618. Louvre, Paris.

THE death of the Italian masters who had made the large frescoes in Fontainebleau during the reigns of Francis I and Henry II did not bring to a stop the decoration of the château. The Italians were now succeeded by French and Flemish artists. The break between the two groups is the less noticeable because the newcomers, like their predecessors, were in the main stream of International Mannerism. However, the influence of Parmigianino, preponderant in Primaticcio's art, now gave place to a wider range of Italian influences. The Northerners, for their part, contributed their personal interpretations of visual actuality, in which Mannerist figurations were combined with a typically Flemish realism often verging on caricature.

After a temporary setback due to the Wars of Religion, artistic activities at Fontainebleau were resumed when Henry IV came to the throne and continued as vigorously as ever during the first two decades of the seventeenth century. The operations of this second School of Fontainebleau, whose leading figures were Toussaint Dubreuil, Ambroise Dubois and Martin Fréminet, were, moreover, less restricted to the château than in the past. Work on the Louvre was speeded up by Henry IV and Marie de' Medici, with the result that artists flocked more and more to Paris and the capital regained little by little its primacy in the field of creative art.

Alongside this second flowering of Mannerism, other tendencies gained ground, more or less discreetly. In some of Toussaint Dubreuil's works and more especially in those of Pourbus we find intimations of that classical approach to art in which the century was subsequently to see its true "vocation" and supreme achievement. In the studios of men like Lallemant realism and romanticism sometimes conflicted, sometimes joined forces. In the entourage of Marie de' Medici and at Saint-Germain-des-Prés, Florentine and Flemish traditions competed for ascendancy. In the provinces hosts of little masters experimented with the new procedures. For, far from showing signs of exhaustion (as we are too often told), French painting in the early decades of the seventeenth century was striking out in many directions though, owing to the prevailing unrest and the divided purposes of that age of anxiety, most of these essays proved abortive. A master was needed. Rubens might well have supplied a lead when in 1625 he installed his cycle of large panels on the theme of the Life of Marie de' Medici in the Luxembourg Palace (now in the Louvre). But, for all its splendor, Rubens' work did not have the effects that might have been expected. A new generation was knocking at the door; a group of clear-visioned young men were readying themselves to shape the course of French painting.

French and Flemish Artists
at Fontainebleau

PRIMATICCIO's death in 1570 deprived the Fontainebleau artists of their Italian inspiration. True, Niccolò dell'Abbate survived his elder by two years, but he had nothing in him of a master spirit, capable of orienting the activities of a team of artists. The times, moreover, were unpropitious for large-scale enterprises. The Wars of Religion continued and on August 24, 1572, came the fateful St Bartholomew's Eve. Still there was no real break in the artistic production of the age; merely a slowing down. The influence of the Italians gradually declined and French and Flemish artists stepped into their places. The Italians who remained at Fontainebleau, for example Ruggiero de Ruggieri and Giulio Camillo, were relegated to minor functions, such as the upkeep of works made by their predecessors.

This re-orientation did not lead immediately to a change of style. To begin with, it operated almost imperceptibly. In the work of Antoine Caron we see the first indications of the evolution that now was getting under way. Caron was born at Beauvais in 1521. When in 1540 he began work at Fontainebleau he was allotted quite unimportant tasks. Strangely enough, it was an Italian lady who gave him his start in life; in 1559 Catherine de' Medici enrolled him in her household as one of her court painters and for the next twenty years he played a leading part in the art of the day. Apparently he was particularly in demand as an organizer of the festivities which continued to take place at the court and in the larger towns despite the bitter religious conflicts of the period. In 1561 he made preparations for the state entry of Charles IX into Paris—this was, however, postponed to happier times— and in 1572 he supervised the fêtes attending the marriage of Henri de Navarre (later King Henry IV) to Marguerite de Valois. In 1573 he organized the reception of the Polish embassy and in 1581 collaborated in the preparations for the wedding of the Duc de Joyeuse. His art is a reflection of these public rejoicings. His color has a theatrical brilliance and his architectural settings have the meticulous precision and emphatic perspective effects of maquettes for stage sets, while the clean-cut, rhythmic grouping of his tiny figures recalls the ballets then so much *à la mode*. The style lacks spaciousness and owes much to the decorators of the time, such as his contemporary Etienne Delaune and the Dutchman Vredeman de Vries. Caron's art reflects the combined influences of these men and of the Italians, from whom he derives the elegant affectation of the gestures. But he keeps to an anecdotal method of expression which differentiates his paintings from the broadly conceived allegories of his elders. Moreover, the slightly meretricious charm of his small figures does not preclude suggestions of a rankling malaise significant of the age he lived in.

Caron's themes, too, are somewhat in the spirit of the state receptions and pageantry in which outstanding events of the time were transmuted into allegories, based on mythology or famous episodes of ancient history. *The Massacres under the Triumvirs* (1566), though representing little actual bloodshed, recalls, like the works of other painters who had treated similar subjects, the earliest hecatombs of the Wars of Religion. Along with other artists he illustrated the *Histoire d'Artémise* (1562), the text of which, a glorification of the widow of King Mausolus, was written by the apothecary Nicolas Houel with a view to providing Queen Catherine de' Medici with an allegory ranking beside that of her bygone rival Diane de Poitiers. About 1588 he made preliminary designs for the tapestries representing fêtes at the Valois Court, in transcribing which the cartoon-maker took considerable liberties. Do his most freely executed compositions, the *Triumph of Summer* and the *Triumph of Winter*, the only surviving elements of a sequence of the Four Seasons, contain any contemporary allusions? This remains a moot point, though Jean Ehrmann opines that in the *Triumph of Winter* the representation of Janus approaching the temple, about to close its door, may well be an allusion to the Peace of Longjumeau (1568).

The illustrative art which Caron gradually developed from the 1560s onwards seems also to have been the speciality of a Flemish artist younger than he who came to the fore in France at about the same time. Born in Herenthals in 1540, Jerome Francken is mentioned as resident at Fontainebleau from 1566. He seems, however, to have kept in touch with Flanders, since he completed and signed in 1571 the *Adoration of the Magi* (Musée Royal des Beaux-Arts, Brussels) which his teacher Frans Floris had left unfinished at his death. In 1585 he painted a *Nativity* (now in Notre-Dame, Paris) for the church of the Franciscan friars. Apart from large-scale compositions in which he still was dominated by his master's influence, he painted scenes with diminutive figures much in the spirit of Caron: a *Venetian*

Antoine Caron (1521-1599).

The Triumph of Winter, about 1568 (?). (40½×70″) Jean Ehrmann Collection, Paris.

Jerome Francken (1540-1610).

Venus mourning for the Death of Adonis, about 1570 (?). (21¼×16½″) Musée des Beaux-Arts, Algiers.

Carnival dated 1564 (Aachen), the *Elegant Reunion* (Stockholm), and the *Musical Party* (Warsaw)—to which must be added that somewhat intriguing work *Venus mourning for the Death of Adonis* (Algiers). The exact part played by Francken in French art is hard to determine. But it seems that he contributed to perpetuating the first Mannerist style until a quite late date (he died in 1610) and also to the development of the small genre scene containing a number of figures, then in great demand. He also did much to promote in France a typically Flemish taste for realistic details and, reciprocally, transmitted to Flanders the characteristic stylizations of French Mannerism.

To the same generation belonged François Bunel, a French artist, born about 1552, whose style was similar. In 1583 he was appointed painter to Henri de Navarre. Except for the portraits of his royal patron, his œuvre is difficult to classify. A number of engravings of his portraits and a signed drawing, *The Pentecost* (Albertina, Vienna), demonstrate the

Entourage of Toussaint Dubreuil (1561-1602).
Leda and the Swan, about 1600 (?). (57×79″) Wildenstein and Co., London.

persistence in his art of the Fontainebleau tradition, but blunted and emasculated by less forceful execution. What we find in the work of the artists of this generation is an essentially transitional art, often hardly distinguishable from the last productions of the first School of Fontainebleau; of Niccolò dell'Abbate, his son Giulio Camillo and such men as Ruggiero de Ruggieri. None the less an increasing interest in anecdote, coupled with borrowings from the Flemish painters, makes it clear that a change in the artistic climate was already under way.

A new art was to make good beginning in the last decade of the century in the work of a group of younger men. Though artistic activity had never entirely ceased during the Wars of Religion, it was not until Henry IV came to the throne and peace was gradually restored that it regained its former vigor. The king decided to proceed with the Fontainebleau decorations but at the same time set his artists to work on other royal residences, the Louvre and his new Château at Saint-Germain-en-Laye. Within a few years three artists succeeded each other or collaborated on these enterprises, each of whom after his fashion cuts the figure of a pioneer: these were Toussaint Dubreuil, Ambroise Dubois and Martin Fréminet. Their respective œuvres have greatly suffered from changes in taste; even more so than those of their predecessors, the leaders of the first School of Fontainebleau. Nowadays they are often spoken of slightingly, but this is probably doing them injustice considering how little is known of this art and how few examples of it have survived.

Toussaint Dubreuil, the first of these painters, was born in Paris in 1561. Nothing is known of his early training except that he studied along with Fréminet under the same master, perhaps the latter's father, probably an imitator of the Fontainebleau Italians. Dubreuil was too young to have come in contact with Primaticcio or Niccolò dell'Abbate and it was chiefly by way of artists of the intermediate generation, such as Caron or Francken, that he made acquaintance with their art. He is mentioned as being in the service of the French court from 1588 on, and he was soon employed on large-scale works. Thus he completed the *Life of Hercules* begun by Ruggiero de Ruggieri in the Pavillon des Poêles at Fontainebleau. He made the decorations of the Petite Galerie (now Galerie d'Apollon) in the Louvre, in collaboration with Jacob Bunel, younger brother of François Bunel II (1558-1614). Of the series of seventy-eight compositions at Saint-Germain-en-Laye very few have survived. Along with some brilliant drawings in the Cabinet des Dessins at the Louvre, they are our only data for an appraisal of his œuvre. Of the two other sequences of paintings by this artist, one was destroyed in the eighteenth-century rebuilding, the other in the fire of 1661. Van Mander, concurring with Sauval, states that Dubreuil usually contented himself with giving his Flemish collaborators drawings by his hand to copy and, when they had finished work, adding some final touches—mostly the emphatic shadows for which he seems to have had a predilection. Actually, as Sylvie Béguin has rightly pointed out, the few surviving fragments of the Saint-Germain decorations are executed in very different manners and fail

Ambroise Dubois (1543-1614).

Calasiris, Theagenes and Chariclea abandoned on the Shores of Egypt, about 1608. (63¾×91¾") Château de Fontainebleau.

to give any clear idea of his personal style. However *A Sacrifice* and the *Lever d'une dame* in the Louvre and the *Two Warriors* in the Château of Fontainebleau reveal a common inspiration, accents of which are traceable in two companion pieces divided between the Louvre and the Wildenstein Collection: *Angelica and Medor* and *Leda and the Swan*.

Mannerist idioms bulk large in Dubreuil's art and he draws freely on the compositions of the first School of Fontainebleau. But whereas Primaticcio had built up a style reminiscent in most respects of that of Parma, Roman influences are more in evidence in Dubreuil's work. Nudes are treated in a more heroic style and given forceful attitudes, recalling at a far remove those of Michelangelo's figures and similar to those of the Zuccari and Spranger. In his handling of color Dubreuil gives the impression of an innovator, but perhaps this may go to the credit of his Flemish collaborators, for Sauval assures us that he personally was a very indifferent colorist. Be this as it may, he inaugurated a new system of color relations, in which cool tones not only set off the values of the warm ones but cede to them the dominant role. It is hard to form any definite conclusions regarding the personality of this somewhat neglected painter. In his work we sense a new approach and in particular a concern for balanced composition. For though his forms and figures abide by the Mannerist canon, his disposition of them shows more restraint, his mood is calmer, and in his art we find intimations, if in a small way, of the classicism of the next century.

Dubreuil died, at the age of forty, in 1602, too young perhaps to have given his full measure. It was a Flemish painter who succeeded him as leader of the Fontainebleau group. Ambroise Dubois (his real name was Bosschaert), born in Antwerp in 1543, was a considerably older man. He had undoubtedly been trained in Flanders. According to Félibien he came to France as a youth. However, it is not until the beginning of the seventeenth century that mention is made of his activities. He acquired French nationality in 1601 and in the same year married the daughter of an artist who also was of northern origin, Jean d'Hoey. His father-in-law, a little known painter, was the grandson, on his mother's side, of Lucas van Leyden. After living some fifteen years at Troyes he entered the service of Henry IV (in 1592) and in 1608 was made custodian of the royal collections of pictures at Fontaine-bleau. Presumably he helped his son-in-law with his early work and did all he could to further his interests. It was not until 1606 that Dubois was officially appointed painter to the Queen but it seems unlikely that he could have produced so large a body of work between that date and 1614, the year of his death. For his services were evidently in great demand. He decorated the Queen's apartment at Fontainebleau with a series of pictures celebrating Heliodorus' romance *Theagenes and Chariclea*, then another near-by room with scenes in which Clorinda, heroine of Tasso's *Gerusalemme Liberata*, played the leading role. For the Chapelle Haute he painted two religious pictures, a *Resurrection* and a *Pentecost*, and for the Salle d'Hercule he made a portrait of Gabrielle d'Estrées posing as Diana. His *magnum opus* was the decoration of the Galerie de Diane, which came after the Galerie d'Ulysse. When in Paris, he worked with Testelin and Delrie on the decoration of the Queen's Chamber with themes derived from Tasso.

Nothing has survived of his decorations in the Galerie de Diane, which was destroyed in the nineteenth century, except some much restored fragments, now in the Galerie des Assiettes. Here he kept to the decorative scheme of the earlier Fontainebleau School. Figures of Henry IV as Mars and Marie de' Medici as Venus occupied the central place and the vault contained a series of mythological scenes allegorically depicting incidents of the life of Henry IV (as in the Galerie François I). The decorative surrounds of the scenes resembled those in the Galerie d'Ulysse and conformed to the style of Roman grotesques. On the other hand, all the information regarding Dubois' personal style that has come down to us shows that its inspiration was of a more original order. The illustrations of Heliodorus' novel in the Queen's Chamber were imbued with the same romantic, courtly quality as the contemporary adventures of Tasso's

Clorinda. Here we have another manifestation of the preciosity in vogue at the time when Honoré d'Urfé was composing *L'Astrée*. But this spirit of aristocratic elegance was interpreted in a more agitated, more Baroque style than that of the first School of Fontainebleau. Mannerism persists, but it no longer invests the figures with a delicate refinement; on the contrary, it accentuates their presentation by the use of heavy draperies or tissues floating up in all directions. Boldly stated shafts of light heighten these effects, dappling forms with clean-cut gleaming patches. These Baroque rhythms are implemented by a Flemish feeling for color—hence the curiously romantic quality of much of his work. All Dubois' compositions are pervaded with movement and this movement acts as a connecting link between them. Were it not for a slightly melodramatic insistence on the fabulation and some heaviness in the handling of garments, one might almost see in Dubois' art the beginnings of the "grand style" of Vouet and his compeers.

Third master of this second School of Fontainebleau, Martin Fréminet was in close contact with the two artists we have been discussing. According to Van Mander he had received his early training, along with Dubreuil, six years older than himself, from his father Méderic Fréminet. He was Ambroise Dubois' brother-in-law, his first wife being Jean d'Hoey's younger daughter. On his brother-in-law's death in 1614 he married his widow, sister of his first wife and bearing the same name, Françoise d'Hoey. In 1603 he was appointed painter and *valet de chambre* to the king. He then had recently returned from Italy where he had been living for fifteen or sixteen years. Much of the time he had spent in Rome where he had made a name for himself as a highly temperamental painter with a lively imagination, and something of a libertine; hence his nickname Fulminetto. There was once a *Virgin* by his hand in the church of San Luigi dei Francesi. From Rome Fréminet went to Venice, where he fell under

Martin Fréminet (1563-1619).

The Sacrifice of Noah, between 1608 and 1619. Fresco. Ceiling of the Chapelle de la Trinité, Château de Fontainebleau.

Quentin Varin (c. 1570-1634).

The Presentation in the Temple, about 1618-1620. Grisaille. (18⅛×14⅜″) Musée Départemental de l'Oise, Beauvais.

the spell of Tintoretto; also to Turin, where the Duke of Savoy had called on him to paint decorations on mythological themes. There, too, a fair number of his works once figured in local collections, but none of them is traceable today.

This painter who now came to work at Fontainebleau had obviously studied the Italian masters. We know nothing definite of Fréminet's early activities at the court but presumably they covered more or less all branches of painting, including portraiture. In 1608, however, he was assigned a large-scale commission: the decoration of the Chapel of the Trinity at Fontainebleau. This occupied him till his early death, in 1619. The restricted space of the chapel and even its proportions must have evoked Fréminet's memories of the Sistine Chapel. But his handling was resolutely Mannerist; he framed the painted motifs with elaborately molded stucco-work and made skillful play with foreshortenings. The figures on the springings, with their salient muscles and contorted postures, are not so much reminiscent of Michelangelo as free transcriptions of Goltzius, Heintz and Spranger. Though repainted in places in the nineteenth century, the Chapel of the Trinity is still black with the dirt of ages and rarely visited by tourists or art historians. But the restoration promised for the near future will certainly bring to light all its essential features and reveal it for what it is: a major achievement of European Mannerism and one of the key works of French decorative painting.

In contemporary records we find references to many other painters whose activities synchronized with those of this trio of outstanding figures of the second School of Fontainebleau. Among them were Jean d'Hoey who, to judge by some engravings that have come down to us, practised a markedly Romanizing art; Jacob Bunel, of whose œuvre we know next to nothing as things stand; Guillaume Dumée and Gabriel Honnet, who collaborated with Dubois at Fontainebleau and Paris; and a host of artists—among them Maugras, Pasquier Testelin, Jean Delrie, Louis Poisson—who are mere names to us, unassociated with any specific works. We are equally badly informed about the activities of the studios functioning in Paris. Most popular were those of Elle, a portrait painter of Flemish origin, and Lallemant, a Lorrainer who established himself in Paris in 1601. Lallemant rapidly came to the fore and remained in vogue until his death, in 1635. Copious and highly appreciated as was his œuvre, only a fraction of it seems to have survived. The portrait group of the Echevins (mayor and aldermen) of the city of Paris painted in 1611 (Musée Carnavalet, Paris), a few rather undistinguished drawings and some engravings convey at most an inkling of his style. He appears to have made great play with exotic costumes and contorted attitudes, and to have aimed at creating an atmosphere of romantically sophisticated fantasy, though on occasion—like many writers of the period—he has no qualms about indulging in touches of realistic burlesque. While his art defies any precise classification, it reflects the complexity of the influences and cross-currents operative in the first part of the century.

Paris became once again an active international art center and so many foreigners flocked to the capital that by about 1619 the French artists practising there were moved to consolidate their privileges. There was a constant influx of Flemish painters; Rubens was but the most illustrious figure of a long sequence spanning the entire century, from Van Mol to Diepenbeck, Van Somer and Bertholet Flemalle. Occasionally we find English, German and even Polish names—for example that of Jan Ziarnko who ranked high among the painters resident in Paris. Marie de' Medici imported large Florentine pictures from her homeland and that eminent artist Orazio Gentileschi, who spent two years in Paris (1623-1625), made a deep impression, it would seem, on some of the younger artists. The prints then being produced in large numbers, and some rather unusual paintings, such as the *Last Supper* preserved before the Revolution in a Paris church and now in Lille Museum, testify to the conflicting trends prevailing in the art of the period. For by no means all the works produced were in the Mannerist style. Though Caravaggism, anyhow in its extreme manifestations, had no effect on Parisian art, the reaction fostered by the Counter-Reformation, with its simplified forms and cult of structural solidity, found a congenial terrain in France. It is in the light of its resistance to the Mannerism of such men as Fréminet that we can best understand the art of Frans Pourbus, that great painter who has not yet been appreciated at his true worth.

At the invitation of Marie de' Medici, Frans Pourbus came to Paris in September 1609. In 1618 he was appointed painter to the king; he died in February 1622. Thus he spent only some twelve years in France, but they sufficed to produce a lasting effect on the evolution of French painting. Though a newcomer to the court, he was an experienced artist who had already made a great name for himself and he was in full possession of his powers. Born at Antwerp in 1569, he was the son of Frans Pourbus the Elder, whose death in 1581 left him an orphan at the age of twelve. Success came rapidly; by 1591 he held the rank of Master at Antwerp and about 1600 he was taken into the employ of the court of Brussels, where the Duke of Mantua, Vincenzo I Gonzaga, favorably impressed by his ability, decided to attach him to his household. Accordingly he quitted Flanders in September 1600 and for the next nine years remained in the service of the Gonzaga family. His patrons employed him almost exclusively on portraiture, and it was with a view to painting portraits that Pourbus went in 1603 to Innsbruck, in 1605 to Turin and finally in 1606 to Paris, where he was asked to make state portraits of the King, the Queen and the Dauphin.

Frans Pourbus the Younger (1569-1622).
The Last Supper, about 1618. (9′ 5″×12′ 2″) Louvre, Paris.

That the French court should choose a Fleming for its official portrait painter was nothing new; a precedent had been set by the Clouets. Pourbus was as familiar with Venetian painting as with Rubens' early work, and this enlargement of his vision inclined him to break with his father's rather stiff and frigid art, to adopt freer modes of execution and less schematic layouts. None the less he was obliged to conform to tradition in his official portraits, which are conventionally posed, devoid of any real life. Thus Queen Marie de' Medici is depicted in all her finery, every detail of the embroidery meticulously rendered. So compulsive was this tradition that Pourbus kept to it even in his portraits of members of the court; it is in the attitude and setting employed by François Clouet in his portraits of Henry II and Charles IX, that he represents the Duc de Chevreuse. However, the big dog sitting at its master's feet, and looking up as if expecting to be stroked, strikes a homelier, livelier note and, though the Duke's costume is treated with Flemish precision, we sense a new approach in the expression of his face. Its look of lassitude and haunting, almost neurotic anxiety tells us far more about the man himself than about his social standing. This effect is furthered by the sobriety of the decor: simple draperies, bare floorboards, cool, clear light defining volumes with rigorous precision. Philippe de Champaigne was to learn much from these superbly executed portraits.

Not all the artist's time was taken up by individual portraits. In 1614 the City Fathers commissioned a large picture commemorating the coming of age of Louis XIII; then, about 1618, a portrait group depicting the Mayor and Aldermen in attendance on the young king. A drawing, some fragments of which have survived (two are in the Hermitage, Leningrad), makes it clear that this latter work was of a very high order. To about 1616 may be dated the *Virgin and Donors*, made for the chapel of the Vic family in the church of Saint-Nicolas-des-Champs in Paris, which has been recently assigned to Pourbus by Jacques Wilhelm and Bernard de Mongolfier. Next come three religious works: the *Last Supper* made for the Saint-Leu-Saint-Gilles church in 1618; the *Annunciation* made (1619) for the Dominican friars and now in the Nancy Museum; the *St Francis receiving the Stigmata* (1620) made for the same Order and now in the Louvre. The skillful renderings of faces testify to Pourbus' long experience of portraiture, but this is not the only exceptional element in these compositions. Following the example of the great Mannerists, he practises an art of a fine spareness, without a trace of grandiloquence, and the perfection of the line is implemented by a limpid, abstract light. Such a picture as the *Last Supper* rejects with almost brutal frankness the lyrical effusion of the art of Fontainebleau. Figures are symmetrically disposed in a purposively austere setting; the sobriety of the attitudes, the immaculate whiteness of a tablecloth marked with creases showing it has just come from the linen-chest, the marble flagstones, the architecture partly hidden by a dark curtain—all conspire to emphasize the planes and to define the structure of the composition. The artist is at pains to differentiate the apostles' faces, indeed this psychological analysis tends to override the poetic values of the scene. All French "classicism" is prefigured here; Poussin had good reasons for the remark attributed to him by Sauval: that this *Last Supper* was one of the finest pictures he had ever set eyes on.

The same conflicting trends seem to have obtained in the provinces. In Nancy, where under the Dukes of Lorraine there flourished a small but brilliantly sophisticated court, the leading artist was Jacques Bellange, one of the last but not the least of the great exponents of Mannerism. Unhappily nothing remains in the Galerie des Cerfs and the Galerie Neuve of the ducal palace of the great wall decorations which, by all accounts, vied in splendor with those of Fréminet in the Chapel of the Trinity. Apart from two small panels, minor works, in the Kunsthalle of Karlsruhe, no painting can as yet be attributed to him with reasonable certainty. However F. G. Pariset, on the strength of the admirable drawings and engravings that have survived, has arrived at a convincing estimate of his artistic personality. The Chevalier Bellange (as he was called) cuts a unique figure among the Mannerists of his generation. Distinctive of his art is an acute sensibility verging often on perverseness, an elegance carried to grotesque extremes, especially in the female figures: fantastically elongated necks,

Frans Pourbus the Younger (1569-1622).

Portrait of the Duc de Chevreuse, 1610. (78×48½″) By Courtesy of The Earl Spencer, Althorp (Northamptonshire).

hair bunched up to an impossible size, "suggestive" garments, staring eyes rimmed with heavy shadows. But this cult of theatrical, exotic-erotic effects appealing to an élite, does not preclude a taste for the sordid side of life; Bellange seems to gloat over the ugliness of his blind "Hurdy-gurdy Player" and a fight between bare-foot ragamuffins.

On the other hand a great many paintings and drawings by Jean Boucher have come down to us. Utterly unlike that of Bellange, his art was much appreciated in Bourges, which in the early seventeenth century was a staid provincial center whose tone was set by merchants and jurists. Born in 1568, Boucher had studied in Rome from 1596 to 1600 or thereabouts, and had, it seems, looked for guidance chiefly to Muziano and Pulzone. Though his pictures in Bourges and the Berry region never rise to any great height of excellence, they have a simplicity and forthrightness that had long been far to seek in French art. Thus the *Adoration of the Shepherds* (1610) in Bourges Cathedral, with its naive little angels, uncouth peasants, fat sheep (of a breed peculiar to that part of France) and quiet color scheme, has a simple bucolic charm.

We have cited only two examples among many. If space permitted, we would scan, turn by turn, the many provincial centers each of which had its artists, a way of seeing peculiar to the locality. We must confine ourselves to briefly mentioning that nobly sincere portrait painter Jean Chalette of Toulouse; Guy François of Le Puy (wrongly regarded as a practitioner of Caravaggism), to whom we owe a series of powerful, finely executed canvases; Richard Tassel of Langres, maker of the *Triumph of the Virgin* in Dijon Museum; Errard of Nantes, father of the architect and painter Charles Errard; Noël Jouvenet of Rouen, first of a "dynasty" of artists of that name. Much research work would be needed correctly to appraise the personalities and to determine the merits of all these lesser masters, often too hastily judged in the light of one or two works selected at random. To illustrate the complexity of the problem, one slightly better known "case" may be cited: that of Quentin Varin. Born at Beauvais and educated by a canon attached to the cathedral, Varin moved in 1597 to Avignon to enroll in the local painters' guild and perhaps visited northern Italy during his stay there. We next hear of him at Amiens, and he also worked in Normandy; then, having made a name for himself, he ended up by settling in Paris. His art shows traces of Mannerism, but he is far from looking only to the North for guidance. Among the fragments of a rather nondescript body of work that has come down to us, we meet some agreeable surprises. The composition of the small *Presentation in the Temple* (Beauvais Museum) keeps to the methods in favor at Parma and Fontainebleau, but the child with a glowing ember on the left recalls a motif of Bassano's, also used by El Greco. In 1624 Varin painted another *Presentation in the Temple*, for the high altar of the Carmelite church in Paris, a much larger work than the Beauvais picture. Very different from its predecessor, it skillfully combines a delicate, finely wrought arabesque with the monumentalism appropriate to a large altarpiece.

Here there were obvious possibilities for the creation of a new style. And in 1612, when he was working at Les Andelys, Varin encouraged a young painter of eighteen by the name of Nicolas Poussin to persevere in his vocation. After painting a *Death of Our Lady* commissioned by the Archbishop of Paris for Notre-Dame, Poussin went to Italy at the end of 1623. In 1624 Vignon returned from Rome to Paris, soon followed by Vouet, then by Blanchard. A new generation, enriched by their Italian experience, was making good in France. So drastic was the change that after a few decades the painting of the previous fifty years dwindled to a vague memory, an uncherished legacy, with the result that modern art historians are hard put to it to recuperate even some *membra disjecta* of the previous period.

The Great Generation
of the Seventeenth Century

Valentin de Boulogne (1591-1632).

The Concert (with an Antique Bas-Relief), detail. Undated. Louvre, Paris.

IN 1590, ravaged by the Wars of Religion, France seemed on the brink of ruin; trade was at a standstill and famine conditions prevailed. Yet it was now that there arose one of the most brilliantly enlightened generations—that of Descartes—that France has ever known, and it was in this land of plundered churches that the artists who for three centuries were to assure the Europe-wide renown of French painting saw the day. The same decade witnessed the births of Perrier, Tournier and Vouet (in 1590), of Valentin (in 1591), of Callot (in 1592), of Vignon, La Tour and Louis Le Nain (in 1593), of Poussin (in 1594), of Jacques Stella (in 1596) and of Brébiette and Mellan (in 1598).

Some of our readers may be surprised to find these names grouped together. Usually Valentin and La Tour are classified as Caravaggeschi, Vouet figures in a chapter devoted to the Baroque, while Poussin and Le Sueur come under the head of Classicism. Vignon is frequently included among the Late Mannerists. On the face of it, the works of these painters may seem to have little in common, but this, to our mind, is an erroneous view. Based on dissimilarities of manner and expression, it overlooks the fundamental affinities resulting from the same historical context.

Most of them were personally acquainted with each other. They had the same contacts in Rome or in Paris; the same admirers and patrons, broad-minded enough to relish the work of all, differences notwithstanding. Thus that famous patron of the arts, Poussin's faithful friend, the Cavaliere Cassiano del Pozzo, took Vouet under his wing while he was in Rome, and when Valentin died attended his funeral. Louis XIII recalled Vouet from Rome, appointed Poussin his First Painter, and one day had all the pictures in the royal bedchamber removed and replaced by a *St Sebastian* by La Tour, on whom he conferred the title of Painter in Ordinary to the King. There is a family likeness in these men's careers. Whether, like Vouet and Valentin, they were sons of minor artists, or like La Tour and even Poussin they came from a relatively humble milieu, all alike "heard the call" of art and saw in it, not merely a source of livelihood, but a great adventure, loftiest and most exacting of all quests. Neither home ties nor personal feelings, neither patriotism nor religion could deflect them from that goal. All these men "made the journey to Italy"; every great artist of their generation found his way to Rome, that Mecca of the aspiring painter, which their successors, men like La Hyre and Le Sueur, were to disdain. Each aimed at creating an art peculiar to himself and at leading a life congenial to his temperament. Later, when the French Academy was founded with a view to enforcing rules on the artist, they made it clear that they would obey no rules but their own. For all alike insisted on that total independence which we find not only in the work of Poussin but also in that of such lesser lights as Mellan and Brébiette.

Should we see in them the last representatives of the Renaissance or, rather, the precursors of modern painting? The question is perhaps beside the mark. For while admittedly they have points in common with their great sixteenth-century forerunners and never repudiated the heritage of Fontainebleau, they ushered in a new era of French art with a long series of richly varied works in which their native genius was enriched by a wide experience of Italian painting.

Valentin de Boulogne

VIA Margutta, Via del Babuino—it was in this small district of Rome, extending from the Piazza di Spagna to the Piazza del Popolo, that for several decades French painting was to refresh its inspiration and shape its future. Most of the painters born between the years 1590 and 1600 made a stay here, and it was here that almost all the great styles which were henceforth to dominate French art took form.

What were the reasons for this attraction? One was certainly the difficulties the younger men had to contend with in Paris, where the corporation of painters and sculptors was all for tightening up its disciplines and consolidating its privileges. It was impossible for an artist to ply a brush in the French capital until he had acquired a master's certificate or had anyhow been enrolled as an apprentice in a master's studio. The only alternative was the acquisition of letters patent from the king or residence in a college or some similar independent institution, where the writ of the painters' guild did not run. Moreover, the Parisian studios were by way of losing their prestige; even Lallemant's had dwindled to a backwater, outside the main stream of European art. Moreover, artistic activity outside the capital had almost died out; the royal "workshops" which had played so brilliant a part in the previous century had little now to offer. Hence the dilemma of the young French artist eager to consolidate and perfect his talent before launching out on the high seas of art. As it so happened, Roman painting was now at the height of its renown. Though the masterpieces of Raphael and Michelangelo had lost nothing of their appeal, Annibale Carracci's decorations in the gallery of the Farnese palace and above all the dramatic art of Caravaggio were opening new horizons. Between 1610 and 1630 Rome was the Mecca of young European painters, especially those of French and Flemish extraction, and art movements in Rome were becoming more and more internationalized. Often, indeed, foreigners stepped into the leading places and, as happened in the recent past in Montmartre and Montparnasse, these exchanges and transfusions gave rise to new, exciting, often unpredictable developments.

Thanks to the scholarly researches of such authorities as Bertolotti, Hoogewerff and Jacques Bousquet, we are getting to know more about the curious and complex milieu in which many nationalities rubbed shoulders, on more or less amicable terms. No sooner had they saved up the money needed for the journey than the young artists made haste to travel to that wonder-city where (often after a series of adventures on the way) they made their début, armed with vaguely worded letters of introduction. They were determined to see all that was to be seen and nursed vast ambitions. Often two young men shared in a humble rented studio the privations of the artist's lot and made ends meet by selling small pictures or peddling marketable drawings. Poussin himself sold a *Prophet* for eight francs and for seven crowns one of the battlepieces (now in the Hermitage, Leningrad) which even in his lifetime were to command high prices. Often the young artist's health broke down and he lost heart; sometimes, however, an early success, a commission given by a church or a cardinal's patronage enabled him to rent a larger room and even to hire a man-servant. But setbacks and struggles were compensated for by a host of new, thrilling experiences: daily contacts with masterpieces, heated discussions of all the latest developments, forgatherings in studios or taverns, bold flights of fancy and a gay libertinism only half-heartedly discouraged by the papacy.

Of this proliferation of ideologies and experiments, dominated (less exclusively perhaps than used to be supposed) by the outstanding personality of Caravaggio, and whose leading spirits were not necessarily the men who afterwards achieved celebrity, few accounts have come down to us. The records have little to say and painters rarely signed their canvases. The registers contain lists of artists' names (oftener Christian names), but they do not help us to identify their works. Sometimes we find a group of pictures unmistakably by the same hand, but who and what manner of man he was there is no knowing. What, for example, was the style of the artist Jean Lhomme whose career Jacques Bousquet has succeeded in retracing? Born at Troyes about 1593, he settled in Rome in 1623, if not sooner, and was buried on January 2, 1633. He painted for San Luigi dei Francesi a *St Andrew and St John*, all trace of which was lost in the nineteenth century but which, if retrieved some day, may throw light on his manner. Then again, who was the painter whom Roberto Longhi named the Master of the Judgment of Solomon? A series of half-length apostles (in a private collection) shows that he practised a realism at once incisive and monumental, while the *Judgment of Solomon* (Galleria Borghese, Rome), after which he is named, skillfully combines reminiscences of Raphael with purely Caravaggesque procedures and has every appearance of being by a French hand. Despite ingenious solutions by modern experts, hosts of similar problems still exist—to tantalize the art historian. Fortunately the French painter most representative of this period, Valentin de Boulogne, is also the one about whom we are best informed.

"One of fortune's favorites, he came on the scene at exactly the right moment, as if at the summons of a good fairy." Thus Dézallier d'Argenville, writing of Valentin in the eighteenth century. Nothing probably could be falser, but nothing could better describe the legendary aura with which the painter was invested from the very start. We know nothing of his appearance and for a long while even his real name was a subject of speculation, some believing it to be Moïse Valentin, others Jean de Boulogne, others, again, Valentin Colombien. As is the case with most of the Caravaggeschi, there are no preliminary drawings that might throw light on the original conception of his works; those which are given his name in the Uffizi and in various great collections are either clearly by another hand or anyhow open to question. It is only comparatively recently that such eminent authorities as Victor de Swarte, Roberto Longhi, Jacques Bousquet and Michel Hoog, after establishing the facts of the painter's life, have succeeded in identifying the fifty-odd canvases now regarded as authentically his.

Valentin was born in 1591 at Coulommiers in the Brie district of northern France. The local parish register still contains the record (a few lines in Latin) of his baptism on January 3. His mother's maiden name was Jeanne de Monthyon; his father, Valentin de Boulogne (or de Boullongne), who belonged to a family resident in the region from before 1489, was a painter and stained-glass worker. Since he was given the same Christian name as his father, the boy was presumably the first-born child. It seems safe to assume that he learnt his craft from his father, who doubtless was kept busy supplying neighboring churches pillaged in the civil wars with religious images and stained-glass windows. But he must soon have become alive to a vocation and nursed loftier ambitions. Very probably he began by visiting Fontainebleau

Valentin de Boulogne (1591-1632).
The Concert (with an Antique Bas-Relief). Undated. (67×83¼") Louvre, Paris.

and Paris, but evidence of this is lacking. Sandrart, who was personally acquainted with him, tells us that he turned up in Rome some time before 1613. He was never to see again his native land or his father, who died in 1618. However, there is nothing to show that he had broken every link and that, but for an early death, would not, like Vignon and Vouet, have returned to France. He was not forgotten at Coulommiers; a legal document dated December 20, 1628 refers to his first cousin once removed, the painter Jean de Boulogne, as being "a trustee of Valentin de Boullogne, now abroad."

Nothing is known of his early days in Italy, except for Sandrart's statement that, impressed by the rapid rise of Vouet who was about the same age as himself and who came later than he to Rome, Valentin consented to become his pupil. Whether this was literally so or not, it is highly probable that he was one of the group of French artists in Rome who between 1615 and 1627 came under the spell of the young painter who so successfully combined impetuosity and charm. It was perhaps under Vouet's influence that he adopted "the brown manner," developed an interest in Caravaggio and Manfredi and a fondness for half-length figures, and discovered that a gipsy woman, a guitar player or the soldiers in a guardroom were quite as rewarding subjects as all the gods of Olympus. Anyhow his change of front must have been abrupt; not a single canvas indicating a transition or any hesitations on the painter's part has been discovered. And the change was definitive. Whereas Vouet never ceased striking out in new directions, Valentin kept to the path he had chosen once for all.

Success seems to have come slowly. In 1620 he figures in the lists of painters merely as "Valentino Bologni francese" and Mancini, the pope's physician and an art lover, does not even mention him in his *Considerazioni* written between 1617 and 1621. In 1629, however, he has become "Signor Valentino, pittore francese" and in his death certificate (1632) he is described as *pictor famosus*. The reason is that he had now won favor with Cavaliere dal Pozzo, most famous of Roman art patrons, and with Cardinal Francesco Barberini, nephew of Pope Urban VIII. The Cardinal gave him the commission for the *Allegory of Rome*, for which he was paid 113 crowns in March 1628. In this large work, charged with a singularly poetic quality, Valentin ventured into a domain of art for which one might have thought he had no qualifications. After being lost sight of for a century, it has been rediscovered in a Roman private house. On the other hand nothing is known of the present whereabouts of the *Beheading of St John the Baptist*, also painted for Cardinal Barberini, which was much admired for the diversity of its figures and brilliant execution. (Until about a hundred years ago it was in the Palazzo Sciarra.) To the good offices of the pope's influential nephew Valentin also owed that crowning success for which all young painters longed: a commission, given in May 1629, for an altarpiece in St Peter's. This was the *Martyrdom of St Processus and St Martinianus*, originally ordered from Albani. Valentin completed it in the spring of 1630. Sandrart speaks of the controversies this picture gave rise to among the local artists and critics when it was placed alongside Poussin's *Martyrdom of St Erasmus*, a work conceived in quite another spirit and marked by a very different handling of line and color. The result was "a big dispute"—which, however, did not injure Valentin's prospects in the least. On the contrary, his canvases now commanded higher prices; for the altarpiece in St Peter's he was paid 350 crowns and when late in 1630 he was asked for a picture containing "soldiers, a gipsy woman, and other women playing instruments," he fixed the price at no less than 100 crowns and refused to lower it by more than twenty.

What direction was he giving his art, now that he could follow his own bent? Some have suggested he was moving towards a sort of Classicism. Here more than ever the term tends to confuse the issues. For in the altarpiece in St Peter's the angel who is bringing to the saints the crown of martyrdom is a common-looking young person with a shock of curly hair, quite in the Caravaggesque tradition. In the *Allegory of Rome* we find dark colors, startling light effects, a wholly realistic yet poetic handling. The archeological discoveries then in progress did not necessarily preclude a Caravaggesque approach; on the contrary, Valentin makes them serve his turn. Thus in the *Allegory of Rome* he shows a young Roman girl wearing an emperor's cuirass and in *The Concert* (Louvre) places a group of topers on the ruins of an ancient altar. Valentin, it would seem, deliberately challenged the brilliant execution and bright colors employed by Vouet in his *Time Vanquished* (1627, Prado), by Poussin in his *St Erasmus* (1628, Pinacoteca, Vatican) and by a whole group of Roman painters. He aimed, rather, at a chromatic density, making play with patches of saturated color on a dark ground and with flexible yet massive volumes, their values stressed by well-placed highlights. His art is imbued with a poetic emotion kept under firm control that rules out any excess of lyrical effusion and seeks above all to render the inner life of the figures represented. It was in so far as Valentin, between 1625 and 1630, at once maintained and renewed the procedures of the Caravaggeschi, that he caught the attention of Roman art circles.

Would he have continued to stand out against "modernists" like Poussin, Lanfranco and Pietro da Cortona? There is no knowing. He died in 1632 when his talent had come to full fruition. Sandrart tells us that on a stiflingly hot day Valentin had a basin of ice-cold water brought to him from a fountain and bathed his feet in it. Suddenly developing a high fever, he took to his bed and died a week later. Baglione, writing at least ten years after the event, is less to be relied on, given his addiction to moralizing. According to him Valentin, after a long bout of drinking and heavy smoking, was seized with the grotesque idea of plunging into the waters of the Babuino fountain; probably the local gossips, after the way of gossips, had dramatized the incident. He was buried in Santa Maria del Popolo on August 20, 1632, and we are told that "almost all the high society of Rome" attended the ceremony. A fortnight or a month later Lemaire, Poussin's pupil, wrote to the Parisian dealer Langlois: "We have lost Mons. Valentin... His pictures are not to be found or if one does find any the price is four times what they cost originally."

The vogue for Valentin's work persisted. That great connoisseur Mazarin acquired several of his best canvases, including the *Judgment of Solomon* (now in the Louvre) and despite Abraham Bosse's and Félibien's reservations regarding his "dark manner," Louis XIV

Valentin de Boulogne (1591-1632).
The Judgment of Solomon, about 1630 (?). (68¼×82¾″) Louvre, Paris.

Valentin de Boulogne (1591-1632).

Herminia among the Shepherds, about 1630 (?). (53⅛×61⅝″) Bayerische Staatsgemäldesammlungen, Munich.

installed in the royal bedchamber at Versailles no less than five of Valentin's pictures, and they can still be seen there. It was only in the nineteenth century that he came to be considered a rather tedious exponent of a purely conventional realism. Yet it would be doing him a great injustice to restrict our attention to his scenes of gamblers, topers and musicians in half-length. In our opinion his finest canvases are the large religious compositions: the *Solomon* and the *Daniel* in the Louvre, that noble work the Toulouse *Judith*, the Munich *Christ Scorned* with seven figures, the *Moneychangers driven from the Temple* in the Hermitage and the Galleria Nazionale in Rome, and that *Last Supper* in the Galleria Borghese whose simple, monumental composition produced so deep an impression a century and a half later on the youthful David that he made a copy of it to send back to Paris from Rome. Valentin's gift for the orderly arrangement of complex material is demonstrated by the large *Martyrdom of St Lawrence* in the Prado, a masterpiece that has been unjustly slighted, in which fifteen figures and a horse are grouped round the naked body, treated on quite unconventional lines, of the young saint. Nothing if not versatile, he tried his hand at allegory and romance and is known to have painted several portraits. His *Cardinal Barberini holding his Handkerchief* was well known in its day and Christina of Sweden owned a *Portrait of the Cavaliere dal Pozzo* showing that nobleman wearing the robes of the Order of St Stephen. True, Valentin had a set of stock models: girls with broad chins and a smoldering gaze, fine gentlemen wearing plumed caps, *bravi* with curly locks, the long-bearded beggar who posed for Moses (in the picture in the Kunsthistorisches Museum, Vienna) and an old lyre-player whom we see in a rather sordid tavern in *The Fortune Teller* (Louvre). But to write this down as due to a lack of imagination would be to misjudge the creative processes of an artist of the stamp of Valentin. He was one of those painters who once they have built up the vocabulary of a personal language, make the most of its resources and ring the changes on it indefatigably without trying—except on special occasions—to escape from their private world.

Was Valentin's, then, an artificial world, peopled with Caravaggesque pastiches and factitious motifs? Less than is often thought today. It was from real life, from the taverns of Rome, that he drew his source material. He lived in the Via Margutta (or nearby), indulged in "orgies" of tobacco-smoking and—Sandrart goes on to say—preferred the company of Germans and Flemings, gay sparks and glorious tipplers, to that of his more sedate compatriots. He joined the club of the "Bentvogels" under the nonce-name of "Innamorato" and presumably lived up to the fraternity's motto: *Bacco, Tabacco e Venere* (Wine, Women and Tobacco)! Need more be said? Some details of a curious lawsuit in which Valentin figured as a witness have been discovered in the Roman archives. A certain Fabrizio Valguarnera, a handsome young man of gentle birth and something of a rake, had, we are told, left his hometown Palermo, his wife and family, to try his luck abroad. While in Spain he succeeded in stealing a bag of uncut diamonds which had just been brought from the Indies, then coming to Rome attempted to get rid of them in exchange for pictures, a less dangerous form of merchandise with greater speculative possibilities. Valentin (along with Poussin and Lanfranco) was one of the artists he approached with this in mind. The records of the trial give a vivid picture of this young sprig of the nobility, with his dark hair and long moustaches, his black satin costume and turquoise-blue, silver-spangled jerkin. In the background we have glimpses of his boon companions, of a little red-haired valet, of needy artisans and a host of minor characters all "on the make." This curious document, written and attested in 1631 by the court clerk, has much to tell of the company in which Valentin spent his leisure hours and which he depicted not as an ironic observer but with the gusto of a participant.

Needless to say, this was only a "partial portrait" of the Rome of his time—as was Lautrec's Montmartre of the Paris of the late nineteenth century. But this was the Rome that fascinated Valentin; the peasant from Coulommiers found in it a world quite to his taste. Yet, like Lautrec among his street-walkers and in the cabarets of the "sacred hill," he never felt at home in it. The vulgarity of the gamblers, drabs and bullies jarred on him and he did his best to give these scenes a certain dignity, even nobility. When we turn to the "Banquets" and "Concerts" of his northern contemporaries—Honthorst, Baburen, even Terbrugghen— we find a very different atmosphere: flushed faces, overturned glasses, breasts shamelessly exposed. There is nothing of this sort in Valentin's art. In his tavern scenes there is no ribaldry, no laughter; only a pensive melancholy, as if all these persons were lost in an inner dream, nursing some incommunicable grief. Even the children's wide-open, wistful eyes show that their thoughts are far away.

To all his figures Valentin applies this keenly analytic scrutiny, ruling out anecdote and infusing new, deeper significance into every theme. The "Judgment of Solomon" ceases to be a quaint Old Testament fable; the child is a flesh-and-blood child, Solomon a youth with a preternaturally serious gaze and the competing mothers are typical young peasants from the neighborhood of Rome, who have completely lost their temper. Then, again, Herminia in the shepherd's hut forgets to be the bellicose heroine of a romantic tale and cuts the figure of a tired young woman whose unlooked-for apparition at nightfall has startled a family of peasants. We have only to observe the tallest of the youngsters in the center of the picture and to mark the look of mingled mistrust and admiration that he casts at the alluring stranger to realize the uniqueness of Valentin's renderings of such incidents.

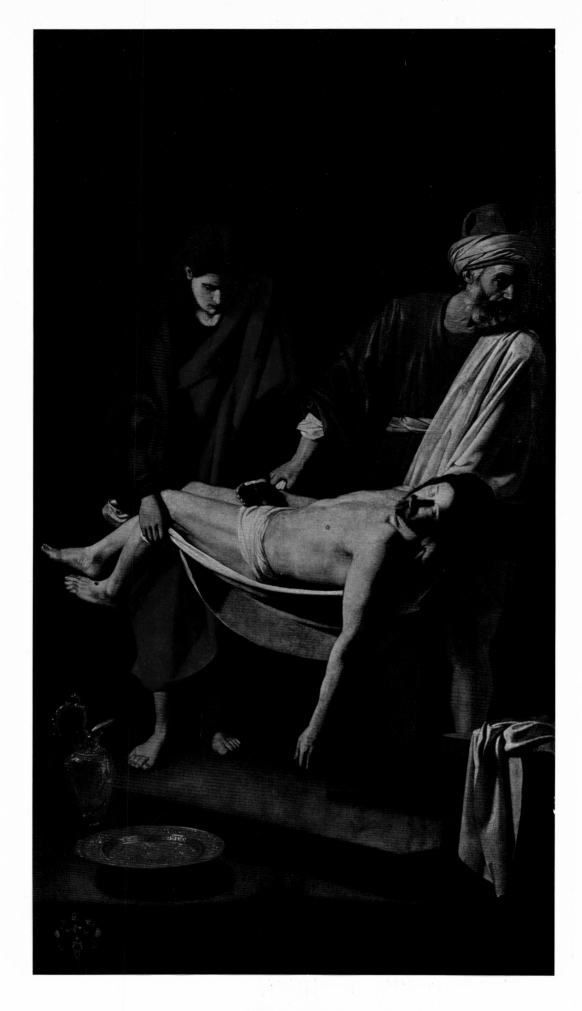

Nicolas Tournier (1590-after 1657).

The Entombment, about 1656-1657 (?). (120¼×60⅝″) Musée des Augustins, Toulouse.

Valentin's realism is no concession to the facts of visual appearance but, rather, a means of access to the secret places of the heart. Even when in the *Concerts* in the Louvre the figures he portrays are singing lustily, or jostling each other as in the *Moneychangers driven from the Temple* (Hermitage, Leningrad), they give the impression of being rapt in a sort of trance. For Valentin instinctively aligned himself to the noble example given by Caravaggio in his *Martyrdom of St Matthew*; he set out his volumes in agitated, sometimes tempestuous rhythms, in which diagonals play the leading role (*Christ Scorned*, Alte Pinakothek, Munich), but without detracting from the monumental spirit of the composition as a whole. The simplification and spaciousness of the forms may seem to imply geometric schematization but, paradoxically enough, far from entailing a static mode of presentation (as with Georges de La Tour), they implement the expressive vigor characteristic of Valentin's major works. Thus even at the moment when a brutal act is taking place we can sense within each of the actors in the scene a core of reticence and silence, hinting at, but never quite disclosing, that inner self which keeps inviolate the secret of every human personality. It is a striking fact that at the outset of this century which was to sponsor a purely abstract analysis of the impulses of the human heart, Valentin was almost the only artist who had the gift of thus combining violent action with acute psychological insight.

Something, however, of this gift can be found in the work of Nicolas Tournier. He is sometimes described as Valentin's pupil; actually he was slightly older than he. Tournier was born on July 12, 1590, at Montbéliard and in his case yet again the influences and contacts which shaped his art are to be sought for in the coterie of French artists residing in Rome. The records show that he lived there from 1619 to 1626. But, unlike Valentin, he returned to France, in 1627. He began by working at Carcassonne, then moved to Toulouse in 1632 and spent the rest of his life there. In the course of his long career he worked chiefly for churches and monasteries in or around Toulouse. His œuvre has not yet been precisely determined. It seems that, when in Rome, Tournier painted pictures in the vein of *Sinite Parvulos* (Galleria Nazionale), a solidly constructed work with half-length figures, but lacking Valentin's emotive power. However there are a number of admirable religious pictures in which a deeper insight is evident. In *Judah prostrated before Joseph*, signed and dated 1655 (Narbonne Cathedral), *Christ Crucified* (Church of Saint-Paul-Serge, Narbonne) and another picture on the same theme made for the Minims of Toulouse (now in the Louvre), the *Deposition*, the *Entombment* and the amazing *Battle of the Red Rocks* (all three in the Musée des Augustins, Toulouse), he has collated to good effect the lessons of his Italian sojourn. Rhythms are firmer, forms simplified, colors less broken and expression better disciplined. It was to the French provincial milieu that he owed what is most satisfying in his work: a serene restraint that may sometimes produce an effect of stiffness or gaucherie, but behind which lies a finely tempered feeling for spiritual values.

Claude Vignon (1593-1670).
The Adoration of the Magi (detail), 1624-1625. Church of Saint-Gervais and Saint-Protais, Paris.

Claude Vignon

VIGNON and Valentin knew each other. Both belonged to the group of artists gravitating around Vouet at the close of the second decade of the seventeenth century, and they probably became friends. But one can hardly conceive of two more different temperaments. Valentin ploughed a lonely furrow, never left Rome and died young. Vignon was one of the most traveled painters of the day and he died in Paris at the age of seventy-seven.

Vignon was baptized on May 19, 1593, in the parish church of Saint-Saturnin at Tours. In 1617 we hear of him in Rome; there are reasons to believe he had been living there for some six or eight years. In 1619 he was residing in the Vicolo della Croce. In 1623, with his *Marriage at Cana* (Potsdam), he won the first prize in an open competition organized by Prince Ludovisi. Next, he traveled in Spain. At Barcelona he was attacked by eight cut-throats, one of whom dealt him a sword thrust that entering just above his nose crossed his head and came out at the back of his neck. The wound, a severe one, healed in three days; the man responsible for this miraculously quick cure claimed to have effected it solely by using certain "mysterious words of power." Vignon returned to France, married in 1624 and rapidly made a great name for himself. Richelieu thought highly of him, Louis XIII "did him the honor of commending his work," the goldsmiths' guild commissioned him to make four *Mais* for Notre-Dame, the Jesuits sent paintings by him to their provincial seminaries, booksellers plied him with orders for frontispieces and plates by his hand. He was not only a painter, engraver and picture dealer but a recognized art expert. Marie de' Medici sent him to Spain and Italy "to buy pictures and works in marble." Among his friends was the famous dealer Langlois and a letter he sent to Langlois shows how wide was the circle of his contacts. "You will greatly oblige me," he writes, "if when in London you convey my kind regards to that famous painter Cornelius Poelenburg and to my other friends there. If Sir Anthony van Dyck happens to be in London, please remember me to him as well. When you are passing through Holland and at The Hague do not forget to give my greetings to that most excellent painter, Moïse van Wtenbrouck and to bring back some of his landscapes. Bring back, too, some works by Sieur Cornelius, you will have no trouble in finding them in London and at Utrecht. When in this last-named town, would you be kind enough to remember me to Sieur Gerard Honthorst and, when in Amsterdam, to Sieur Rembrandt. Try to procure some work by his hand and tell him that yesterday I made a valuation of his picture of the Prophet Balaam, the one that Sieur Lopez recently bought from him. For the rest, I leave it to your judgment to give my remembrances to all the other gentlemen we may have known in Italy, in Paris or elsewhere."

Claude Vignon (1593-1670).
The Adoration of the Magi, 1624-1625. (65×103¼″) Church of Saint-Gervais and Saint-Protais, Paris.

Evidently the man himself was like his work: bubbling over with life, perhaps a shade self-assertive. He is described as a loyal friend, honest in all his dealings and a hard worker. Modest he was not. The correspondence relating to his decorations in the Château de Torigni-sur-Vire has been preserved (in the archives of Monaco) and from it we gather that Vignon had no small opinion of his talent. Indeed one almost gets an impression that he was something of a boaster and determined to cut a figure.

How can we wholly trust the word of this painter who tells us he was cured almost instantaneously of what was evidently a very serious wound by a faith-healer's "words of power"? That is enough to put the historian on his guard. Vignon's biography was compiled by the official historiographer of the Academy, Guillet de Saint-Georges, who based it, so far as can be judged, on documents supplied by the family. When it was read to the Academicians in December 1690, the painter's son and many of his personal friends were present. But some of the salient facts of his early career as recorded in the biography do not carry entire conviction. According to Guillet, Vignon went to Rome when he was fifteen or sixteen and was escorted by two friars who, struck by the boy's gifts, decided to take him to Italy to study art. But their chief purpose was "to prevent his being brought up by Protestants." Yet we learn from his baptismal certificate that he was a Catholic by birth, son of Elisabeth Papillon and Guillaume Vignon, maker of silverware for the Court and *valet de chambre* first to Henry III, then to Henry IV. However, at the turn of the century, religious prejudices were still less drastic than is commonly thought and there is little question that the boy was apprenticed to Jacob Bunel, who, like his wife, was a Calvinist. It was seemingly from the household of this painter that the friars "rescued" him. There is nothing unusual about Vignon's departure to Italy at this early age. True, Mariette says that Vignon was accorded the rank of Master in the Paris guild of painters and sculptors in 1616. But he might quite well have made a hasty trip to Paris, then returned to Rome—and in any case readings of dates in records of this period are rarely conclusive. That Vignon made a long stay in Italy—he wrote and spoke Italian fluently—is a well-attested fact. His early artistic education in Paris, however, where the Late Mannerist style still prevailed, left an indelible mark on his art. In later life he never forgot his debt of gratitude to Bunel or lost his admiration of the artist whose apprentice he had been. But at quite an early stage his horizon was enlarged by a wide and lucid comprehension of the painting practised south of the Alps.

It is doubtless of less importance to learn that Vignon had no less than thirty-four children, seventeen by his first wife Charlotte Le Leu, who died in May 1643, and the same number by Geneviève Ballard, sister of Robert Ballard, "printer of music for the King," whom he married on January 11, 1644. Jal failed to find traces of more than twenty-four of them, but these were surely enough to lead the harassed paterfamilias sometimes to ply his brush with feverish haste. This is another reason for the disapproval often voiced in judgments of his work. In view of the host of inferior canvases attributed to Vignon because they reflect his style, there has developed a tendency to write him off as a slapdash painter capable on occasion of flashes of inspiration but by and large a mediocrity. Obviously he had acquired a "hurried manner"—but this does not mean that he was satisfied with daubs. One day he made a wager that he would paint in twenty-four hours for a friend of his, a goldsmith, a large

Claude Vignon (1593-1670).
King Solomon and the Queen of Sheba, 1624. (31½×46⅞″) Louvre, Paris.

picture with twelve figures on the theme of "St Catherine refusing to worship Idols." Vignon won the bet, which created quite a stir among the Parisian dilettanti and brought him in a hundred crowns. We, too, are ready to bet that the work was not in any sense scamped, despite the speed at which it was painted. Vignon's son, who was a member of the Academy, thought it one of his father's best works and it was much admired in the days of Le Brun. We should note, however, that Vignon had a team of studio assistants who made copies of his compositions, sometimes of his engravings, not to mention those of other artists. Doubtless some of his many children also worked in his studio, and several of them achieved a certain renown: Nicolas, Philippe (a portraitist) and more especially Claude-François Vignon; also their sister Charlotte, who specialized in flower pieces. Presumably we should attribute to some other "specialist" the Vignonesque canvases with a profuse display of jewelry such as the Sarasota *Anthony and Cleopatra*, and to one of his pupils, perhaps Lemaire, those with majestic architectural vistas in which we see small pages strolling, wearing the velvet caps for which the master had a predilection. Of an immense output very little has survived; less than a dozen of the hundred or so major works listed by Guillet have so far been identified, and the gallery of the Château de Torigni, containing the chief of Vignon's large-scale decorations, was burnt down recently and not even photographs of it are available. Quite possibly other works will be brought to light in the near future but meanwhile we must peremptorily exclude the many marginal and inferior canvases and base our judgment of Vignon solely on the signed works; and also on the numerous engravings which familiarized a wide public with his work. Only then do we see him in his full stature as one of the outstanding artists of the age.

We have but to look at the *Martyrdom of St Matthew*, Vignon's earliest known picture, painted when he was twenty-four, to realize how exceptional was the gusto, the lyrical emotion and the driving power of the young artist. It is true that the composition is puzzling, confused, overcrowded, but the figures of the half-naked adolescent, with the enormous, sun-tanned fist clutching the sword and driving it through the old man's chest, and of the disheveled young angel handing the saint an absurdly meager palm branch, the crimson gush of blood, the pile of tattered books and even the strained, oddly colored soles of the martyr's feet have a strength of effect of a quite unusual order. In this mingling of realism and exaggeration, marked less by sensuality than by a sort of nervous tension, we have a prefiguration of all Vignon's art. Blunders and clumsiness were the price he paid—more or less deliberately—for an almost frantic urge to get his emotive responses on to canvas, before the "first fine rapture" had subsided.

Little would be gained by searching out the influences that shaped Vignon's art. He was acquainted with all the painting of his time and of the past, and regarded as an expert on the subject. "He was frequently consulted," the historian Roger de Piles (who certainly knew him personally) informs us, "both as to the manner and the market value of pictures"—those, Guillet adds, "of the Italian masters and those of other lands." Vignon was, it seems, one of the few Frenchmen of the period to be something of an authority on Spanish art. His taste had been shaped originally by Bunel's Mannerism and he was deeply impressed by the work of the Roman followers of Caravaggio in the second decade of the century, as is evident in the *St Matthew*. Moreover he was interested enough in Vouet to make an engraving of the *Two Lovers* in 1618. But Venetian art also played a leading part in his artistic education; in particular, as Charles Sterling has pointed out, the art of Domenico Feti. It was, indeed, to Feti that some authorities attributed the *Adoration of the Magi* (now in the Art Museum, Dayton, Ohio), of which Vignon himself made an engraving, dated 1619. At a very early stage Vignon developed a technique peculiarly his own. "He had a way," Roger de Piles tells us, "of laying in his colors without binding them together, and inserting new ones, as he painted, without mixing them by the movement of the brush, with the result that the surfaces of his pictures are extremely rough." Rich impasto, translucencies, sweeping brushstrokes, dabs of vivid color —all these tokens of the Venetian "joy of painting" Vignon introduced to Paris.

Claude Vignon (1593-1670).

The Martyrdom of St Matthew, 1617. (56×37¾″) Musée Saint-Vaast, Arras.

Claude Vignon (1593-1670).

St Paul the Hermit and St Anthony Abbot. Undated. (61¾×48⅜″) Musée Départemental des Vosges, Epinal.

Yet the vast range of his knowledge did not lead him to eclecticism. Rather, it tended to safeguard a personality which, in a diversity of expressions and experiments, always remained true to itself. It is interesting to compare the Dayton *Adoration of the Magi* of 1619 with another version in the Galleria Sabauda, Turin, whose romantic vein of fantasy prefigures Rembrandt's earliest works. But the emotive lyricism pervading *St Peter and St Paul in a Common Sepulchre*, known only by an engraving made in 1620, is of a very different order. To the same year, 1623, belong the *Marriage at Cana* (Potsdam, destroyed in 1945), a large canvas striking a more sustained note, the *Martyrdom of St Andrew* whose engraved reproduction reminds us of Ribera, *Jesus among the Doctors* (Grenoble), which has something of the strange, tragic atmosphere of a Tiarini, and that wholly charming *Esther and Ahasuerus* (Private Collection) whose execution is thoroughly Venetian. No less varied are the works of 1624-1625; this multiplicity of trends may be due partly to recent contacts with Spanish art and partly to a wish to catch the attention of Parisian connoisseurs. The *Pasce oves meas* (Rijksmuseum, Amsterdam) is an austere, powerful work; the *Adoration of the Magi* recently discovered *in articulo mortis* by Bernard de Mongolfier in a church loft, with its sickly, quite unconventional Child and its huge turbaned Moor, has a poetic charm peculiar to itself. *Solomon and the Queen of Sheba* (Louvre), glittering with jewels, on the other hand, is a "show piece" in the best sense. It also comes as a surprise; in it all the refinements of the Venetian style are skillfully combined with the traditional Mannerism of such artists as Lallemant, with which Vignon had resumed contact in Paris. And this picture is at a far remove from the *Martyrdom of St Matthew* and the *Martyrdom of St Andrew*, though they were painted only a few years before.

A host of studio works exploited this brilliant, somewhat facile, eminently pleasing vein. But some major works and a series of fine engravings of pictures no longer extant prove that the effect of Vignon's contacts with the Parisian milieu was, rather, to elevate and consolidate his style. In the *Circumcision* painted in 1627 for the high altar of Saint-Martin-des-Champs (now in the church of Saint-Jean, Lyons), the artist evidently had some trouble in conforming to the architectural disciplines of a large retable; but in the *Croesus* (1629, Musée des Beaux-Arts, Tours) a new firmness in the handling implements the textural richness and the splendor of the colors. Characteristic of the *Beheading of St John the Baptist*, the *St Paul* and the *Godefroid de Bouillon* still to be seen *in situ* in Parisian churches is a conjugation of expressive power with boldly stated forms, whereas the somber intensity of *St Paul the Hermit and St Anthony* (Musée des Vosges, Epinal) derives from a masterly use of chiaroscuro. The versatility of Vignon's imagination and his gift for romantic evocation can be seen in the *Baptism of the Eunuch Candaces*, a scene of Oriental magnificence traversed by great bursts of light, painted as a *Mai* for Notre-Dame in 1638 (only an engraving of this work is extant); as also in the *Adoration of the Magi* in the parish church of Fère-en-Tardenois (Aisne).

Though a master painter in the Paris guild of painters and sculptors and on three occasions a member of the selection committee, Vignon did not take part in the founding of the Academy in 1648. None the less he was thought highly of by the Academicians and when the two institutions were amalgamated (in 1653) he was promptly nominated to the Academy, the painter Errard ceding to him his official rank of foundation member and professor. When there came a break between the two corporations, Vignon retained these titles and continued to teach. But he did not feel obliged to "tone down" his style; though few of the works of his last years are known, such canvases as the *Circumcision* (1651, Private Collection) and the *Washing of Feet* (1653, Nantes) are utterly unlike the works then being produced by Bourdon, Le Sueur and Le Brun. Rather, we find in them a continuation of the poetic art of his last years in Italy and a sort of dreamworld shot with strange silvery gleams and peopled with theatrical personae. There is, in fact, every reason to believe that Vignon's art retained to the end the qualities we find in his earliest canvases: a soaring imagination, amazing facility, little order, a lavish prodigality of his almost superabundant means.

Following Lallemant, he gave pictorial expression to the romantic fantasies that bulked so large in the literature of the period, from *L'Astrée* to *Clélie*, works couched in a style that at once delights and irritates the modern reader. Yet, though its lyrical effusion often strikes us as theatrical and exaggerated, it is sometimes infinitely delicate and tender. In Vignon's œuvre we have equivalents of the works of such authors as Hardy, Gomberville and Tristan —full of gusto, quite undisciplined, yet often brilliantly successful.

> La règle me déplaît, j'écris confusément,
> Jamais un bon esprit ne fait rien qu'aisément.

Théophile de Viau who wrote these lines had nearly the same age as Vignon and when he says that "rules displease him" and "a good mind" does everything easily, he might be voicing Vignon's theory of art. But the rhythms and imagery of the poets of that age often seem sadly old-fashioned or ineffective, whereas Vignon's colors have retained all their freshness and visual appeal. Deriving from the great Mannerists no less than from Rome, his art brought to the seventeenth century that light-hearted zest and sense of freedom of which it stood as much in need as of Poussin's high seriousness and Le Sueur's studied elegance.

Vignon was not the only artist to exploit this lyrical, romantic vein; what has saved him from oblivion is the very copiousness of his œuvre and his habit of signing his pictures. No canvas by Pierre Brébiette, who had several traits in common with him, has survived. Born at Mantes in 1598, Brébiette is recorded in Rome in 1617; he too returned to Paris (in 1626), where Vignon stood godfather to his first son in 1631. He had fertile inspiration and a penchant for mythology; his recorded pictures bear such titles as *Niobe*, the *Assembly of the Gods, Cupid Asleep*. He made his reputation in Paris as an etcher; his etchings, the only works that have survived, combine an elegant inventiveness with lively execution, and justify our ranking him among the most attractive little masters of French art. Another artist famed for his draftsmanship was Saint-Igny (born at Rouen), who kept more closely to the traditions of Lallemant and Parisian Mannerism. In his two large grisailles, the *Adoration of the Shepherds* and the *Adoration of the Magi* (1636, Musée des Beaux-Arts, Rouen), fancy costumes, plumes and oddly distorted postures are rendered with a bravura comparable to Vignon's.

If more were known about the various provincial art centers, they would doubtless be found to have included many artists of a similar caliber. A notable example is the *St Nicholas of Tolentino consoled by Angels* (Musée des Augustins, Toulouse) signed and dated 1650 by Fr. Ambroise Frédeau. At Nancy, Claude Deruet practised a stylish art whose charm was all on the surface and which struck a contrast with Bellange's violent distortions. Still we are at a loss to see the reasons for its widespread vogue. However, there are some exceptions; in the *Crucifixion* (Mainz) painted for Anne of Austria the skillful crowd effects and the careering horsemen strike a vigorously dramatic note, while the *Four Elements* suite (Musée des Beaux-Arts, Orléans), painted for Cardinal Richelieu, contains some charming passages in the ballet scene, also some court portraits enlivened with witty allusions. Best of all are the small canvases depicting scenes of the *War of the Amazons* (Private Collection and Musée Jeanne d'Aboville, La Fère), in which we see lithe horsewomen with plumed helmets deploying in picturesque, thickly wooded landscapes. Callot, who specialized in etching, falls, strictly speaking, outside the scope of the present work. Mention may be made, however, of his numerous drawings, recently collated by Daniel Ternois. They show that by reason of his Florentine training he, too, belonged to the Late Mannerist tradition. His sketches for a *Martyrdom of St Sebastian* have a rapidity of execution, an inventiveness, and a lively handling of chiaroscuro reminding us of Vignon. The vigor of the preliminary drawings was tempered by the patient labor of the engraver and his closely analytical treatment of the material. And this strict discipline, Callot's firm determination to follow his chosen path, despite a brilliantly successful start, in the provincial seclusion of Nancy, points the way towards the art of that other Lorrainese master: Georges de La Tour.

Georges de La Tour

SINCE 1915, the year of his "resuscitation" as one of the great French masters, La Tour has held a place apart. Everything about him seems out of the ordinary: a brief spell of brilliant success, followed by a sudden, total eclipse lasting two centuries and a half, a meteoric rise to fame, the surprising fewness of the canvases discovered and the fabulous prices they soon commanded on the market. So lofty is the inspiration of this œuvre, so complete its unity, that it can easily be isolated from its historical context, viewed as a unique case, and appraised on its own merits. But is it really "sacrilege" to relate it to its period, to the contemporary œuvres of Vignon, Vouet, Poussin? Thanks to the painstaking and scholarly research work of recent years, notably that of F. G. Pariset, we now know much of the life story of the man, as well as of the guiding principles behind his art. Yet in the result it well may seem that this new information, far from dispelling the mystery shrouding the genius of Georges de La Tour, suggests that it has depths behind depths as yet unplumbed.

La Tour was born on March 19, 1593, at Vic in Lorraine. His father Jean de La Tour was a baker, his mother's father and brother were also bakers, and the family, if of humble rank, was fairly well off. Vic, a large and prosperous town, had several schools and young Georges, it seems, attended one of them. Nothing is known of the circumstances which led him to make painting his vocation, nor of his early training, but we may assume that he soon showed signs of a precocious talent. In October 1616 he is recorded as being still at Vic; he now was twenty-three and on the point of getting married. His first child, Philippe, was baptized on August 5, 1619. Next year he moved to Lunéville, his wife's hometown, was granted rights of citizenship, engaged an apprentice and set up as a master painter in that city.

From the few surviving records we gather that he got off to a good start and was always much esteemed in official circles. In 1623 and 1624 the Duke of Lorraine bought two of his works; for a *St Peter* he was paid 150 francs, a large sum for the period and out of all proportion with those usually paid to "little masters" in the provinces. After the occupation of Lorraine by the French, we hear of La Tour again; he now (in 1639) bears the title of Painter in Ordinary to the King (i.e. Louis XIII), which thereafter figures constantly after his name. In 1644 a *Nativity*, presented by Lunéville to the Duke de La Ferté, French governor of Nancy, was paid 700 francs, so large a sum that it is no surprise to find him described as "the celebrated painter" in a legal document of that year. But this was not a unique case; in 1648 he was again paid 700 francs for a *St Alexis* presented to the Duke by Lunéville; in 1649 his *St Sebastian*

Georges de La Tour (1593-1652).

Job taunted by his Wife. Undated. (57×39″) Musée Départemental des Vosges, Epinal.

Georges de La Tour (1593-1652).

Woman catching a Flea. Undated. (47¼×34⅝″) Musée Historique Lorrain, Nancy.

(another gift made to the Duke) cost the municipality 868 francs, and we are told that the town council had to "beg" the painter to undertake this work. La Tour seems to have achieved everything an artist could desire: celebrity, high fees, a comfortable income. He was still at the height of his popularity when in January 1652 he, his wife and his valet were carried off by an epidemic within the space of a few days.

Given his successful career, La Tour must surely have felt thoroughly satisfied with life and with himself. But we live in a sentimental age; hence a tendency to picture him as a sort of Lorrainese Rembrandt, a man who, deeply scarred by life, had withdrawn into himself and elected to live in a provincial backwater, meditating on the problems of his art and of the human situation. The records tell a very different tale, and though no self-portrait has come down to us, there is nothing whatever to suggest that he suffered, for example, from any physical blemish or infirmity. Everything goes to show that he had a happy family life and with advancing age he could rely on the co-operation of his son Etienne, who had made painting his career and later, like his father, was accorded the title of Painter in Ordinary to the King. From 1646 on Etienne's name figures alongside his father's in legal documents. With the characteristic thriftiness of the French peasant, La Tour had built up a substantial fortune, thanks to which he ranked as one of the leading citizens of Lunéville. At the age of twenty-four he married Diane, a young woman two years his senior, and his wife's father, Jean Le Nerf, was the Duke's Treasurer, a wealthy man of noble birth. The baker's son led the life of a country squire, got himself exempted from taxation, from military duties and the billeting of troops in his house, and even kept a pack of hounds. A petition submitted to the governor in 1645 sets forth that the "Sieur de La Tour, painter, is making himself obnoxious to everyone by the great number of dogs, greyhounds and spaniels, he keeps, acting as if he were a Lord of the Manor, sending his dogs after hare into the standing crops, which they trample down and ruin." Evidently the favorite recreation of our great painter was hunting. Thus we are less surprised at the traces of callousness, almost brutality, in some of his works. When a famine was raging in 1626 he refused to contribute his quota to the poor and the local authorities had to give orders to force open the door of his granary. Then, again, in 1648 he belabored a sergeant-at-arms and in 1650 assaulted a peasant so savagely that the man had to call in a physician. A violent man—but this was an age of violence, of wars, famine and pestilence, and in this respect La Tour differed little from such men as Vouet and Poussin, neither of whom had the reputation of being particularly kind-hearted or good-tempered.

The surprising thing is that a painter so affluent and highly thought of, patronized by King Louis XIII himself, did not choose Paris or anyhow Nancy as the scene of his activities. Evidently he preferred a semi-peasant life in a small, out-of-the-way town. Lorraine, however, was a crossroads, more than ever in this period, linked up as it was by dynastic ties with Italy (by way of Florence) and in constant touch with Paris, Flanders and the German courts. By living in Lunéville he was able to perfect an art exactly to his liking, unaffected by the fashions of the day—but this does not mean that it was in any sense provincial.

There was no dearth of painters in Lorraine. Did he study under Bellange, most famous of them, whose flowing, calligraphic signature he imitated? Some aspects of his art suggest that this was so. But others quite as clearly point to Italian influences: the Caravaggism in vogue in Rome between 1615 and 1620. An example is the *Fortune Teller* (since 1960 in the Metropolitan Museum, New York), a new version of Caravaggio's picture on the same theme (Louvre): a theme that was also employed by Vouet during his sojourn in Rome (Ottawa) and by Valentin (Louvre). There is every likelihood that La Tour visited Italy—perhaps between 1614 and late 1616, a period in which we find no trace of him at Vic. True, his name is not mentioned in any Roman archives, but this is easily accounted for if we assume that he went there in the suite of some official envoy. Alternatively he may have gone not to Rome but to Florence, a city much in favor with Lorrainers; or to Bologna and Venice.

Georges de La Tour (1593-1652).
St Sebastian tended by St Irene. Undated. (63×50¾″) Staatliche Museen, Berlin.

Georges de La Tour (1593-1652).
The Penitence of St Jerome (detail). Undated. Musée de Peinture et de Sculpture, Grenoble.

Georges de La Tour (1593-1652).
St Sebastian tended by St Irene (detail). Undated. Staatliche Museen, Berlin.

Indeed he may have owed as much to Gentileschi and Saraceni as to Caravaggio. Two seventeenth-century documents describe La Tour as "Guido's pupil," and it was precisely at this time that Guido Reni was working at Bologna. Nor can we rule out possible contacts with Gerard van Honthorst, whose early "Romanizing" style has striking affinities with some of La Tour's procedures.

There are several years in the course of his career for which we have no sure evidence of his presence in Lorraine, and one is tempted to fill the gaps by suggesting that they were spent in traveling—which would account for other aspects of his work. Did he, then, go to Flanders or should the reminiscences of northern art in some of his work be ascribed to a parallel derivation from the same sources, seconded by an acquaintance with Flemish engravings? Somewhat surprisingly perhaps, the solution may lie in Paris. When, after the invasion of the Duchy of Lorraine by French troops and the partial destruction of Lunéville, La Tour was nominated Painter in Ordinary to the King, it is more than likely that he went to Paris to receive the letter of appointment from the king's hand. It was probably on this occasion, and not during the king's visit to Nancy (some years before), that he presented Louis XIII with a *St Sebastian* "in such perfect taste that His Majesty had all the other pictures removed from his bedchamber and kept there only La Tour's." In that year (1638) Richelieu and Louis XIII were extending patronage to artists on a larger scale than ever and it is not surprising that La Tour was given the title of King's Painter. As a matter of fact the least word of recommendation, however motivated, from some highly placed personage, was considered enough to justify its award. La Tour's art must have come as a surprise in Paris in the days of Vouet and Stella, and may well have found admirers. On the other hand the masterpieces of French art he must have seen in Paris do not seem to have made any impression on him. Nor, for that matter, was he any more impressed by Callot, who was active in his time at Nancy, or by Deruet, a painter much in vogue at the ducal court.

Here lies the paradox of La Tour's art. On the one hand it is essentially a product of its age. There is perhaps not a single one of his procedures that has not a parallel in the work of his contemporaries; not one item of his thematic material whose genealogy we cannot trace, whether it stems from the Caravaggesque repertory (e.g. the Penitence of St Jerome, St Peter denying Christ, the Fortune Teller) or from the stock-in-trade of the religious painting of the day (e.g. the Martyrdom of St Sebastian and the Death of St Alexis). Yet, on the other hand, La Tour is superbly and supremely faithful to his private vision and so complete is this commitment that he gives an impression of being impervious to outside influence.

It was long the custom to regard the "night pieces" as fundamental to his œuvre and to see in him a dedicated follower of Caravaggio. Yet is not the finely poetic quality of his art more evident in such works as *St Sebastian tended by St Irene* (Staatliche Museen, Berlin), and is not the technical perfection of his handling seen to better advantage in such works as the Grenoble and the Stockholm *St Jerome?* Here the nervous vitality of the line, flicked in with the tip of the brush, stresses plastic values, while masterfully incisive drawing sharply defines volumes. Color is subtly modulated through an ascending scale of browns, beige and reds, and in his treatment of the hair and beard La Tour employs a technique that is frankly calligraphic. When we turn to the night pieces it comes as a surprise to find a geometric precision that rules out accidentals and renders forms in simple, clean-cut planes, as if carved in wood, reducing every figure to its schematic equivalent—almost as drastically as in Luca Cambiaso's drawings. When we compare the head in the Grenoble *St Jerome* with the woman's face in the Berlin *St Sebastian*, we cannot fail to be struck by the differences of handling. In one the painter has let his hand rove freely over the surface of the canvas and every brushstroke remains visible; in the other the rendering of volume is, so to say, intellectualized, no trace is left of the brushwork, color is used solely to emphasize the interplay of values and everything is deliberately subordinated to an effect of timelessness, verging on abstraction.

Georges de La Tour (1593-1652).

The Penitence of St Jerome. Undated. (61¾×39⅝″) Musée de Peinture et de Sculpture, Grenoble.

It has been suggested that the "daylight" pictures should be assigned to an early phase of La Tour's career. But the consummate mastery apparent in such works as the *St Jerome* (Grenoble) and the *Hurdy-Gurdy Player* (Nantes) makes this unlikely. The dates of the *St Peter Repentant* (1645, Cleveland) and the *St Peter denying Christ* (1650, Nantes) show that he was producing his most "cubist" night pieces in the last years of his life. Are we then to assume that in the 1640s he harked back to this "youthful" style and had not been employing it on occasion from his earliest days? Actually the chronology of his œuvre is purely conjectural and it may well be that he practised both styles more or less simultaneously. In *Job taunted by his Wife* (Musée des Vosges, Epinal) we find a curiously disconcerting synthesis. Here the artist, greatly daring, has combined with a rendering of the skirt in broad, architecturally ordered planes, a minutely detailed profile treated as a pure arabesque; yet so skillful is the handling that we are never for a moment troubled by this anomaly—to which indeed is due the otherworldly atmosphere of the scene. Better perhaps than any other work, this picture brings home to us La Tour's complete mastery of his creative means.

But in a restricted field of action. That mastery involved deliberate selectivity, a limited range of subjects. Few as are the works that have survived, they include two or three, sometimes very similar, versions of *Mary Magdalen Repentant*, *St Sebastian* and the *Penitence of St Jerome*. The figures, often isolated, are always few in number. La Tour's repertory is singularly small, the same type-figures constantly recur; the models were probably members of the artist's household. This is borne out by the articles of apprenticeship drawn up in 1648 in terms of which the boy in question was to act when his master so desired as a model "for making paintings or drawings of his person." Very few animals figure in La Tour's pictures, a cock in the Cleveland *St Peter*, a lamb in the Louvre *Nativity*, a marmot in the Bergues *Hurdy-Gurdy Player*—just enough to show that this keen hunter's understanding of animal life was as acute as his insight into the human personality. Accessories, too, are few; there are no landscapes, no buildings, and all perishable things such as fruit, flowers or trees (with the exception of an almost invisible oak-tree in the *St Sebastian*) are rigorously excluded. La Tour's world is perhaps the narrowest ever created by a great painter.

This economy, evidently deliberate, throws light on La Tour's *ars poetica*. When he isolates these few figures, these few objects, it is in order to wrest from them a simple truth too often garbled by the complexity of the everyday world. Occasionally, as in *The Brawl* (Private Collection, England; studio copy at Chambéry) and *St Peter denying Christ*, he organizes his composition in terms of contrasting rhythms, but as a rule he selects the simplest possible attitudes, juxtaposes figures, does away with settings and perspective. Unlike so many Caravaggeschi he employs a chiaroscuro that helps define volumes instead of blurring them, and sometimes serves to emphasize the curve of a hand, the flawless line of a child's face. Light, in short, plays a secondary role. Usually the fixity of the attitudes is paralleled by the downward gaze of the figures, which become rather presences than vehicles of expression.

"Presences" not merely physical, for in each a soul is immanent. A hundred years ago, in his *Carnets de Voyage*, that highly perceptive, and unduly neglected writer Hippolyte Taine eulogized at length the *New-born Babe* (Musée des Beaux-Arts, Rennes). After observing that the true painter is "simply a maker of bodies," he embarks on a description of the infant's face: "pink flushing into crimson, full-blooded, chubby, almost fluid, set off by a snow-white expanse, the broad folds of the swaddling-cloth." In this "profound, all-engulfing slumber" he sensed "a complete submersion in the vegetative life" and "the essential mystery of birth." Though he attributed the picture to some unidentified Dutch master and knew nothing of La Tour, Taine instinctively grasped the purport of his art. For this realism, which on occasion does not shrink from cruelty, is bound up with so deep an insight into the human situation that it is charged with high significance. Take, for example, this half-naked, rather plain young woman who is squeezing between her thumbs a flea in the light of a candle standing

Georges de La Tour (1593-1652).
St Joseph's Dream. Undated. (36⅝×31⅞″) Musée des Beaux-Arts, Nantes.

Georges de La Tour (1593-1652).
St Peter denying Christ, 1650. (47¼×63″) Musée des Beaux-Arts. Nantes.

on a chair beside her—how is it that so vulgar a theme when treated by La Tour has all the elevation of his most austere religious compositions? This quality of nobility is not due only to a masterly arrangement of the picture elements in which horizontals and verticals intersect at right angles (even on the figure), curves play only a minor part, and two red rectangles tell strongly out against a subtly modulated monochrome ground. It is the fine spareness of his art, unparalleled in that of any contemporary artist, that enables La Tour to give an unwonted value to quite trifling details; the girl's jade bracelet, the pattern formed by the nails on the back of the chair *exist* in their own right. Uncompromisingly realistic is the rendering of the woman's gaping nightdress, her ungainly legs, her big feet and swollen belly. This ruthless depiction in so strictly geometric a language compels attention to such a point that we hardly give a thought to the anecdotal element. There is no question here of amusing the spectator or pleasing the connoisseur. We are invited to enter into communion with the human being bodied forth in this wholly passive attitude, more revealing than nudity itself and less fraught with indiscreet suggestions; with a simple creature of whose life we know nothing, glimpsed in one of those lonesome moments of the night which seem morsels of eternity. Here even compassion plays a minor part; in virtue of that faculty of sublimation which distinguishes the truly creative artist, this seeming-trivial work transcends the purely human and participates after its fashion in the divine love of all living beings.

But though we can still respond to this appeal, for a full appreciation of La Tour's message we must allow for its period and its background: the endless wars, famines and pestilences which devastated Lorraine in the first half of the century. Writing in 1636 Père Fourier, who was La Tour's compatriot and whom he certainly met, remarked that "people have almost lost their fear of death; it has become so familiar that they take it for granted." That year a nephew of the painter and an apprentice died in his house of the "red pest." Two years later Lunéville was burnt and pillaged, for the onslaughts of the plague were no less disastrous than those of the French and Swedish soldiery. Miracles, diabolic manifestations, outbursts of collective madness were everyday occurrences, and famines called into play man's lowest instincts. Documents of the period (these have been the subject of an able compilation by François-Georges Pariset) prove how all decent human feelings went by the board in Lorraine in those tragic years. In 1638 the Justice of the Peace at Vic recorded the fact that "a son had eaten his dead father and when he too died his mother partook of his body." Elsewhere he tells of women saying to each other: "Today I shall eat yours; tomorrow you shall have a piece of mine"—meaning their children.

La Tour had lived through all this when he painted the *New-born Babe*. True, he survived into better days, but a country's wounds heal slowly, certain memories can never be effaced. Callot elected for objective renderings and let the facts speak for themselves. La Tour, though he never directly alluded to the horrors of the age, perhaps struck deeper. For he commemorated only the rare, serene moments when these poor stricken souls regained something of their human dignity. In the scenes of St Joseph's dream, the penitence of St Jerome, St Irene's silent grief as she gazes down at the body of St Sebastian, everything essential is conveyed by quite simple attitudes. As for the source of illumination in the night pieces, a solitary candle, this might be written off as a mere studio device, were it not that its light is shed not only on forms and features but—and how revealingly!—on the most secret places of the heart.

Simon Vouet (1590-1649). Wealth (detail). Undated. Louvre, Paris.

Simon Vouet

UNLIKE La Tour, Vouet was never completely lost sight of, though he is only just beginning to regain the place in French art that is his due. It is still the fashion to see in him an eclectic without any real personality, but gifted with an adaptability that enabled him to supply a Parisian version of the great international style known as the Baroque. A Parisian version in the sense that it still showed traces of the classical tradition, which made it acceptable to French taste.

Nothing could be more unjust. A curious sort of "eclectic," this painter whose manner can be recognized at a glance and who made so deep an impression on all his contemporaries! Like Vignon, Vouet has suffered from the long neglect of his compatriots. Worse still, all the large-scale works which, as we now know, ranked him between Primaticcio and Le Brun, were ruthlessly destroyed, one after the other. And, as it so happened, he was one of those artists who should be judged by their composite decorative schemes, not by individual canvases, however fine their execution; still less by fragments of decorations often mainly the work of studio assistants. The destruction or disappearance of these major works is remedied to some extent by the survival of a number of admirable drawings and engravings made for the most part under Vouet's personal supervision. Pictures by him are gradually being brought to light and nearly a hundred canvases out of what was an immense body of work can now be safely attributed to his hand. Quite recently publication of the first full-length study of his œuvre, by William Crelly, has shown that he is now by way of recapturing something of his former renown. Little by little his personality is emerging: as that of one of the leading painters of the first half of the seventeenth century, a man who made his name at Rome in the days of Guido and Lanfranco, took Paris by storm in the reign of Louis XIII and dominated the Parisian art world, in the teeth of keen competition, for over twenty years. Vouet was the first to renew in Paris the glorious episode of Fontainebleau, to give new heart to French painting, to prepare the way for the eminence it was to achieve before the century was out.

His forceful personality made amends for a rather unprepossessing appearance. He was a small man, who put on weight and grew slightly bald as the years went by; had short-sighted eyes, a sensual mouth, a long, oddly shaped nose with quivering nostrils. But he was full of zest and self-assurance, aggressive to the point of rudeness on occasion. "He was never content," one of his contemporaries tells us, "with anything short of a recognition of his absolute superiority." Another describes him as "a cantankerous man, always ready to fly into a rage, determined to make his way *per fas et nefas.*" He would brook no rival in Paris and to safeguard his prestige resorted to every kind of expedient, from flattery to sarcasm. None the less he had a natural charm which captivated all who came in touch with him, from his fellow-students at Rome to his pupils in Paris; from Pope Urban VIII to King Louis XIII.

For the first time in the annals of French painting we find a "love interest" exercising a formative influence on an artist's work. (One is reminded of the case of Rubens.) In 1625 when Vouet was still in Rome, lodging in a house on the Via Ferratina, a family from Velletri came to live near by. The father was a painter, the daughter, Virginia da Vezzo, exactly corresponded to the type of buxom young brunette, with sparkling eyes and a rather protuberant forehead, that Vouet had been depicting for some ten years. This coincidence was so singular that several authorities have been misled into discovering likenesses of Virginia in pictures made by Vouet long before he came to Rome. She became Vouet's pupil, he married her and brought her with him to France, where the young Italian lady soon won favor with the court, and with Louis XIII in particular. Virginia gave her husband four children and when she died in 1638 Vouet had a medal engraved in memory of her. Two years later he married Radegonde Béranger, a Parisienne, and her young beauty is reflected, it seems, in the new elegance and frankly sensual appeal of the pictures of his last phase.

Vouet had no taste or aptitude for religious or intellectual speculation; painting *per se* sufficed him. Born in 1590, son of a sculptor in a small way, he must have taken to drawing almost from the cradle, and as a boy picked up the makings of a fairly extensive culture. This is borne out by the fact that when only fourteen he was commissioned to go to England and paint the portrait of a lady "highly esteemed both for her noble birth and for her beauty." When he was twenty he accompanied de Harlay, the French ambassador, to Constantinople, with a view to making a portrait of the Grand Turk who, as a pious Mohammedan, firmly declined to sit for the young artist. Vouet turned the difficulty by observing him closely at an audience and making a likeness of him from memory, which won plaudits on all sides. But fretting for the company of artists, which meant so much to him, the young man applied for leave. He went not to France but to Italy and after studying some months at Venice proceeded to Rome where he was given an allowance by the King. He soon won a leading place in the small group of French artists and the esteem of local connoisseurs: the poet Marino, the Cavaliere dal Pozzo and Cardinal Barberini. When Urban VIII became pope, he was in the full tide of success, received an order for a picture for St Peter's and—crowning honor—was commissioned to paint the fresco behind Michelangelo's famous *Pietà.* Completed in 1627, this composition, which provided a large-scale Baroque setting for the marble statuary, was greatly admired. It was destroyed in the eighteenth century, but there exists a canvas in the Besançon Museum in which bold foreshortenings are half submerged by sudden bursts of light, and which may reproduce a fragment of it. In the same year, when owing to dissensions in the Academy of St Luke the then President had to resign, Vouet replaced him.

His fame rapidly spread to France. This was the time when huge fortunes were being amassed and sumptuous private residences being built in the Marais district and the environs of Paris. Early in 1627 the French ambassador, de Béthune, was instructed to propose to Vouet that he should return to Paris. Vouet agreed and after a brief stay in Venice, en route, reached Paris on November 25. He soon became popular at Court and won the outspoken approval of Louis XIII and the Queen Mother—though not of Richelieu who seems to have regarded him as an upstart. He had now a huge studio, hosts of pupils, more orders than he could cope with. The king made a habit of commissioning him to paint portraits of members of the nobility in his retinue, and it became the fashion to have one's portrait done by Vouet in oils or pastel. We can gauge the mutilation Vouet's work has undergone by the fact that only one well-authenticated portrait by him, that of Canon Michel Le Masle (Musée Carnavalet, Paris), has survived, and moreover it seems probable that even this is a copy.

"There are hardly any churches, palaces or large houses in Paris," Félibien could declare half a century later, "which are not adorned with works by Vouet." It was to him that the orders were given for large altarpieces in the churches of Saint-Nicolas-des-Champs, Saint-Merry, Saint-Eustache, in the monastery and Noviciate of the Jesuits, in the Abbey of Pont-aux-Dames, and in the church of the Minims on the Place Royale. A tapestry in eight pieces illustrating Old Testament themes, woven in the Louvre factory, inaugurated a new phase in the long history of French tapestry. But it was in the field of large-scale decorative schemes that he was most active. These figured in the royal palaces and in private houses and châteaux in Paris and the suburbs; from the Louvre to Saint-Germain, from the Luxembourg to the Palais Cardinal; from Chilly to Rueil and the Hôtel Bretonvilliers. For Bullion, the Surintendant des Finances, he made the decorations of the Galerie d'Ulysse, the Grand Cabinet de Diane (what seem to be vestiges of this have survived) and the Galerie des Amours de Renaud et Armide, whose recent reconstitution in a private house in Paris gives an idea of its lost magnificence. Another decorative scheme of his, in the grotto of Bullion's Château de Wideville, has by some happy chance escaped destruction. For Séguier he decorated the chapel, library and a gallery of his residence in Paris with compositions which were undoubtedly his finest work in this domain, but all we know of them today comes from Dorigny's engravings and some sketches. For the Queen Mother he decorated the Cabinet des Bains at Fontainebleau with a brilliant sequence of mythologies which, while in the tradition of Rosso, Primaticcio and Dubois, carried it a stage further and pointed the way to the decorations of eighteenth-century Salons. Despite this intense activity Vouet found time to paint some easel pictures, notably a series of canvases on the theme of the Virgin and Child, all different but

Simon Vouet (1590-1649).

The Birth of the Virgin. Undated. (85½×129") Church of San Francesco a Ripa, Rome.

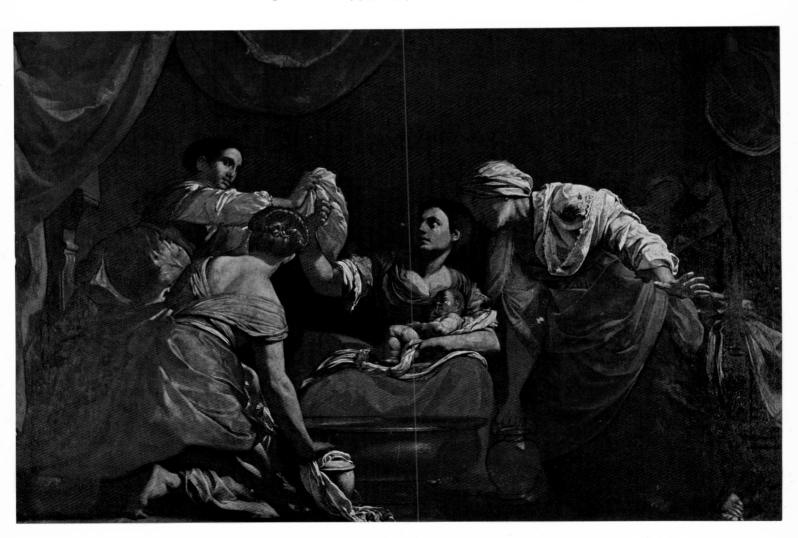

Simon Vouet (1590-1649).

The Birth of the Virgin (detail). Undated. Church of San Francesco a Ripa, Rome.

Simon Vouet (1590-1649).
Wealth. Undated. (67×48¾″) Louvre, Paris.

Simon Vouet (1590-1649).
Armida carrying the Sleeping Rinaldo. Undated. (63×47″) Private Collection.

equally delightful for their exquisite interpretation of the young Mother's flawless beauty. These pictures were much sought for by connoisseurs, taken at once by their masterly execution and the delicate sentiment without a trace of mawkishness to which they owe their charm.

Only on two occasions was his ascendancy imperiled. In 1640 Richelieu called Poussin to Paris to assume the post of First Painter which Vouet reasonably enough believed was his by right. Then, in 1647, when a group of young artists founded the Academy, they carefully refrained from inviting him to join, knowing his despotic character. On both occasions Vouet quickly regained the upper hand. Poussin went back to Italy in September 1642; Vouet, who had met him there, already knew or quickly realized that the maker of the *Schoolmaster of Faléries* was unsuited for the tasks he was expected to undertake and would soon rebel against them. The second incident must have given him more qualms. Many of the foundation members of the Academy had been his pupils and he cannot have failed to observe the high ability of such men as Le Sueur and Le Brun. He had to face the fact that a new generation was challenging his authority and hoping to replace him. Vouet made haste to counterattack. He took in hand the management of the old guild of painters, modernized its organization and methods of teaching to such effect that when he died, on June 30, 1649, he may well have thought the battle won. But this "flagrant breach of trust" must have darkened the last years of the great artist who died before his time, "worn out by the enormous body of work he had produced, more than by advancing age."

"When in Rome," Dézallier d'Argenville tells us, "he kept to the manner of Caravaggio and Valentin. But, in view of the number of commissions of all kinds which, as a much sought-after artist he was called on to execute, he developed a much more rapid technique. It was based on the use of large tracts of shadow and quickly laid-in color schemes; and in this he succeeded all the better owing to the extreme lightness of his brushwork." This résumé of Vouet's art is correct enough, if slightly over-simplified. It has too often been inferred from d'Argenville's remarks that when in Rome Vouet was a thorough-paced Caravaggesque; then abruptly, effortlessly, became a "Bolognese" on his arrival in Paris. This view does not allow

Simon Vouet (1590-1649).
The Three Marys at the Tomb. Undated. (54¼×66½″) Church of Davron (Seine-et-Oise).

for the greatly varied contacts of his Italian years. There is no question that Vouet was the recognized leader of the coterie of French artists in Rome who between the years 1613 and 1620 cultivated dramatic light effects, dark backgrounds and Caravaggio's skillful blend of poetic emotion and realism. Yet already in the *Self-Portrait* (Arles) and the *Bravo* (Brunswick) we can sense a desire for rendering movement at its apogee and a propensity for dashing brushwork. Moreover, there was a tendency in the French group, notably after 1620, to strike out in new directions; here once again Vouet took the lead, and all was grist to his mill. He worked in Naples, where he evidently familiarized himself with Neapolitan art, and he also put in a longish stay at Genoa (1620-1621) on the invitation of the Duke of Bracciano. On his way back to Paris he halted at Milan, Piacenza, Parma, Bologna and Florence, and was enabled to visit the chief private collections in these cities. The allegedly most Caravaggesque pictures were spaced out at fairly long intervals during his Italian period. His first large-scale commission was for the *Birth of the Virgin* in the church of San Francesco a Ripa. While the dramatically somber background is clearly reminiscent of Caravaggio, the gorgeous draperies and the swirling movement of the composition around the huge bronze basin strike a different note. There is nothing here of the inner silence of Caravaggesque Nativities; the poetic mood of this noble work has more in common with the rendering of the same subject by Cavaliere d'Arpino in the church of Santa Maria di Loreto. Some years later (in 1624) Vouet made an admirable night piece in San Lorenzo in Lucina: the *Temptation of St Francis*. It might seem that on this occasion he was pitting himself against Honthorst, as on others against Guido Reni; but in these works we can also see effects of Vouet's formative years in Paris. What he derived from Caravaggio was above all a need to work directly from the model and to enliven an abstract compositional schema with touches of reality. He did not so much practise a Caravaggism tempered by Bologna as a Mannerism "from the life." Also, one of the facets of his style was always oriented towards Venice. It was by way of Venice that he entered Italy and he spent some months there copying Titian, Tintoretto and especially Veronese. And when the summons to Paris came in 1627 it was again to Venice that he looked for guidance with a view to preparing himself for the task before him. In the *St Theodore* he painted there (this was probably the "St Louis" now in Dresden), few reminiscences of what he had learnt at Rome can be detected and the *Time Vanquished* (Prado, Madrid), dated the same year, reveals a marked addiction to vivid color, brilliant light, bold execution.

There is nothing here of the precisely formalized programs of such men as Baburen, Honthorst, Terbrugghen or even Valentin; rather an intelligent study of the various techniques of the age, soon mastered and assimilated. And now Vouet's years in France were to give a meaning to these seeming-desultory experiments; it was as if all the time he had been shaping, stage by stage, by way of ingenious, often fascinating exercises, a style of his own.

After a few essays Vouet found what he was searching for, a procedure based on strong effects of masses, bold contrasts of draperies and light, broad, rotatory rhythms sweeping the picture surface and carrying with them bodies of naked athletes, statuesque women, plump, chubby children. Rich textures, drifts of an amber-tinted haze temper the hard lines of the architecture; sometimes a finely decorative landscape unfolds itself upon a complex of interlocking planes. Here the effect of ordered arrangement is due not so much to conscious planning on the artist's part as to the lyrical emotion that guides his brush and pervades the entire composition. Thus a quite fantastic swirl of draperies envelops the figure of "Wealth" in the picture of that name (Louvre) and transposes what might have been a frigid allegory into the image of a majestic, sensual goddess, her wings outspread as if preparing to take flight with her treasure hoard into the empyrean. A *contrapposto* of parallel spirals associates the two groups—the Holy Women and the angels holding up the shroud—in the *Three Marys at the Tomb* (Church of Davron) and stresses the emotional link between them. Here details count for relatively little. Facial expressions are vague or indeterminate and the figures "mannered," with conventionally flexed arms, sinuous fingers, garments disposed in quite unnatural folds (ever since the seventeenth century Vouet has been reproached for mannerisms of this sort). But he deliberately turned his back on that representational imagery in which the interest of the gesture *per se* is subordinated to expression and the figure treated as a mere narrational element. To his mind every subject, whether the love life of Armida or the martyrdom of St Eustace, was primarily a sort of poem in which little importance attached to the "story," still less to the "moral"; all that interested him was the dynamic interplay of lines and shafts of light, which in themselves sufficed to lift the composition on to the heroic plane.

Thus Vouet introduced into French art that Baroque lyricism ("Baroque" in Wölfflin's sense) which had no place in the introspective art of such men as Valentin and La Tour, or in the figurations of such a man as Poussin. Back in Paris, Vouet imposed a form of art in the 1630s which was congenial to his temperament and came as a revelation; nothing had pointed the way to it. It is easy enough to find traces in the taste of the period of the elements which went to make the art of Vignon. Vouet's was unprecedented, and in a sense less inevitable, and its success was largely due to the artist's personal prestige.

The parallel that soon was drawn between Corneille and Vouet was based on flimsy grounds and by the same token it is vain to search the works of Malherbe, Théophile and Voiture for any qualities that match up to his inspiration or to the joyous world he conjured into being, full of abounding life, young men with muscular limbs, women with milk-white shoulders and merry children bursting with health. In his art sensuality and sentiment go hand in hand; even scenes of martyrdom (for example the *Martyrdom of St Eustace* in the church of Saint-Eustache, Paris) have more in them of triumph than of tragedy. Something of Rubens' boisterous joy in life is here, but purged of all Flemish grossness in the more refined atmosphere of Paris. Even in Vouet's most voluptuous figurations a daintily tip-tilted nose or a mischievously lifted chin strikes a lighter note, and there is more in Vouet's art of the languorous elegance of Pietro da Cortona than of Flemish forthrightness. Even in devotional scenes, even in such works as the *Temptation of St Anthony* (Grenoble), we find no hint of a sense of sin or any rankling unease. In the age of anxiety in which we live, it is easy to see why Vouet's art is often written off as superficial; yet it was none the less a magnificent *creation*, all the more remarkable when we remember that in his time conditions of life were grim indeed and Paris was filling up with maimed and starving victims of the Thirty Years' War.

Combining affability with a somewhat dictatorial temperament, Vouet was just the man to preside over a large studio. No sooner was he back in France than he enlisted teams of painters, some already trained, whom he employed on putting his ideas into execution or filling in details of landscapes, animals, ornamental passages. Among his studio assistants were Juste d'Egmont, Vandrisse, Scalberge, Van Boucle, Patel, Bellin, Cotelle and Thierry Bellangé, and it is remarkable how well these men, often of Flemish origin, adapted themselves to a style of painting largely Italian in spirit. The Old Testament tapestries and panels like the *Ceres* (National Gallery, London) testify to the felicity of this collaboration. Even Perrier, on his return from Italy, did not demur at using preliminary sketches supplied by Vouet for the decoration of the chapel of Chilly.

Vouet was also the most sought after and idolized teacher of the period. "All the painters," Roger de Piles observed in 1699, "who have found favor with the public in recent years were Vouet's disciples. There never was an artist whose manner made so lasting an impression on the minds and techniques of his pupils." He trained them "less by fault-finding than by dint of reasoning," and, proud though he was, "never paraded his superior knowledge, but transmitted it to his pupils without making them feel at the cost of what efforts he had acquired it." Among the painters who collaborated with him for long or short periods were Le Brun, Le Sueur, Mignard, Du Fresnoy, Chaperon, Poerson, Fr. Joseph, Fr. Luc, Michel Corneille, Dorigny, Tortebat, Jacques Belli, Louis Beaurepère, Du Guernier and André Le Nostre.

From 1630 to 1650 a vast quantity of work was produced in Paris in "the Vouet manner" and it is by no means easy to distinguish the various hands. Not a few of the artists concerned were young men who, after imitating Vouet for a while, broke free from the master's influence. Dorigny, who married one of Vouet's daughters, made over ninety engravings after his father-in-law's works. To begin with, his own pictures differed from Vouet's only by reason of a more compact composition, less broken up by vigorous contrasts (e.g. *Pan and Syrinx*, Louvre). Subsequently, in his decorations of the Château de Vincennes, he came nearer Le Sueur and Le Brun. Also similar in style to Vouet were Poerson (in his large *St Peter Preaching*, a *Mai* dated 1642 for Notre-Dame de Paris) and Michel Corneille, in his *St John the Evangelist and his Disciples* (only an engraving has survived). Even more similar was Le Sueur whose early works are wholly indistinguishable from those of Vouet's last period. A visit to Italy was needed for Chaperon, who in 1639 had painted the fine *Presentation of the Virgin in the Temple*, still *in situ* in the chapel of St Nicholas at Compiègne, to shake off Vouet's ascendancy. Even the work of Le Brun, though he studied under Vouet only a very short time, bore the master's imprint up to and including the *Martyrdom of St John the Evangelist* (c. 1641-1642, church of Saint-Nicolas-du-Chardonnet, Paris).

Belonging to a later generation, these painters naturally enough broke with their master's methods once they found their feet. There used to be too great a tendency to treat all those who in their early days came under Vouet's influence as his disciples and nothing more. Actually, however, most of them developed strongly marked personalities of their own and we are only now beginning to realize how diverse these were. This was the case with Valentin, in whom Sandrart saw merely one of "Vouet's pupils" in Rome. But it also applies to several other artists, for example Nicolas Régnier who seems to have been in close touch with both masters for many years. Of Flemish extraction (he was born at Maubeuge), Régnier finally settled in Venice where he took to practising a more fluent and externalized art, imbued with a sensual elegance, much to the taste of the local dilettanti, which was far from being a pale reflection of Vouet in his Roman period. This is evident in the *Death of Sophonisba* (Gemälde-galerie, Cassel). He would hardly belong to French painting were it not that his work shows a restraint rarely found in seventeenth-century Venice and also that, being a dealer as well as a painter, he was in constant touch with French artists and art lovers visiting Venice. It was at Turin, in the service of the Court of Savoy, that Charles Dauphin, another artist who had spent his formative years in Rome as one of Vouet's circle, established himself. Many large religious paintings by his hand are extant in the churches of Turin, and some fine State portraits in various castles in Piedmont. Two pictures, each a *Virgin and Child*, in Nantes and Florence respectively, prove that he had talents of an unusually high order, which have not yet won the recognition they deserve.

Charles Mellin, like Dauphin of Lorrainese extraction, who likewise had a successful career in Italy, has been more fortunate, Jacques Bousquet in a brilliant study having rescued him from oblivion. Vouet's influence is plain to see in such a work as *St Francis of Paola* (lost, but an engraving by Charles Audran has survived), though it is already attenuated in the lunettes (in poor condition) in the cloister of the Trinità dei Monti. Particularly striking in the sketch in the Château of Plessis-lèz-Tours, brought to light by Boris Lossky, is this artist's delicate execution combined with a skillful handling of light effects; we find this also in his delightful *Roman Charity* (Geneva). A successful rival of Poussin and Lanfranco in 1630, when commissions were being given for the decoration of San Luigi dei Francesi, Mellin made a series of paintings imbued with refined emotion (fragments are still *in situ*); we are conscious of a great change since Vouet's departure. The preliminary drawings, enhanced with a light wash, might be mistaken for those of Poussin. His decorations at Monte Cassino were destroyed in the recent war and no photographs exist. However two pictures recently discovered at Naples, painted on the eve of the artist's untimely death (in 1649), make it clear that he was now aspiring to a purer, austerer style and had long since abandoned Vouet's.

Jacques de Lestin (1597-1661).
The Death of St Louis (detail). Undated. Church of Saint-Paul and Saint-Louis, Paris.

The evolution of the artists who returned from Italy to France proceeded on much the same lines. Practically nothing is known of the two pupils Vouet brought back with him: Jean-Baptiste Mole (according to Félibien an Italian; he seems to have been overlooked by historians owing to the resemblance of his name to that of Pier Francesco Mola) and Jacques Lhomme who came from Troyes. A small *St Catherine* engraved by Jean Couvay throws little light on his artistic personality. Of that of Aubin Vouet, Simon's young brother, we have a better idea. A *David* and a *St Catherine* painted when he was in Italy, engravings of which are extant, indicate a more realistic temperament than his brother's; this is evident in his *Mai* of 1632, *Ananias and Sapphira* (Notre-Dame, Paris), a forthright composition with no pretensions to elegance. Of the many pictures he made for Paris churches few have survived. In his second *Mai, St Peter with Cornelius the Centurion* (1639, Notre-Dame) we find a marked advance, the rich color and skillful contrasts suggest that he had the makings of a great artist; but Aubin Vouet died two years later, in May 1641.

Jacques Sarrazin may claim a minor place beside him; this famous sculptor, who was friendly with Vouet and married his niece, sometimes plied the brush. In some pictures of the Virgin and Child (known through engravings) and the *Holy Family with St Francis of Paola*

Jacques de Lestin (1597-1661).
The Death of St Louis. Undated. (111×140″) Church of Saint-Paul and Saint-Louis, Paris.

Charles Mellin (1597-1649).
St Francis of Paola at the Feet of Pope Sixtus IV, about 1628-1630 (?). Sketch. (28¾×35¾″)
Château de Plessis-lèz Tours (Indre-et-Loire).

preserved in a monastery, the style somewhat resembles Vouet's, but thereafter it grew prog-
ressively colder. The same is true of Noël Quillerier. This painter, who was born at Orleans in
1594 and died in Paris at the age of seventy-five, is now practically unknown, though he had
a very successful career. *Valet de chambre* and Painter in Ordinary to the King, and member
of the advisory board of the Academy, he worked for the most part at Saint-Germain and
especially in the Tuileries. In the very few works that have survived we find no reminiscences
of his stay in Italy nor of his first decades in Paris. Two allegories, however, originally in the
Tuileries and now in the Mainz Museum, show that in his latest phase he had long forgotten
what he had learnt in Rome and was, rather, tending towards La Hyre's later manner.

In 1622, in the census of the parish of Santa Maria del Popolo in Rome, the name of Noël
Quillerier had figured alongside that of an artist named Jacques de Lestin. By some curious
mistake de Lestin's name was coupled with that of another of Vouet's pupils, Nicolas Ninet,
the result being that references are often made to a (non-existent) "Ninet de Lestin"—and this
misnomer persisted despite entries in official records and the fact that the painter made a point
of affixing a boldly written signature to his works. Thanks to this fortunate habit, Jacques de

Lestin's is the easiest to follow of the careers of the French artists who came under Vouet's influence in Rome. Also, it illustrates perhaps better than any other the later evolution of those talented artists who, of the same age as Vouet and like him owing much to their Italian sojourn, had independent minds and refused to be dazzled by the prestige of the king's painter. He was born in 1597 at Troyes, in the parish of Saint-Rémy, and came of a humble family—his father was an innkeeper—but Troyes had been the scene of a vigorous art revival and its atmosphere must have been propitious for a young man with a bent for painting. We hear of his presence in Rome between 1622 and 1625, when he was one of Vouet's circle and in contact with such French artists as Quillerier, Mellin and Sarrazin. By 1626, however, Lestin was back at Troyes, where henceforth he led a peaceful, prosperous and industrious life. By the time he died, on November 2, 1661, in the parish of Saint-Nizier, he had filled the churches of Troyes and its environs with large canvases by his hand. Many are still in place, but unfortunately they have suffered greatly from the ravages of time and—worse still—from repaintings. He also received commissions from other parts of France (for example for the *Presentation in the Temple* in the church of Saint-Pierre at Nevers) and from Paris where he was highly thought of. Of his *Mai* for Notre-Dame, *St Paul and St Barnabas*, only an excellent engraving by Bosse has survived, the original having been destroyed when the Museum of Strasbourg went up in flames in 1870. More fortunate, his *Death of St Louis* has been restored to its place in the Church of Saint-Paul and Saint-Louis. This highly original work, rhetorical without redundance, has a robustness all its own, enhanced by an adroit handling of light and the textural richness of the brushwork.

Jacques Blanchard (1600-1638).
Angelica and Medor, about 1631-1633 (?). (48×69⅝″) The Metropolitan Museum of Art, New York.
Gift of George A. Hearn, 1906.

Jacques Blanchard (1600-1638).

Charity, about 1637 (?). (42×54″) By Courtesy of the Trustees of the Goodwood Collection (Sussex).

Probably Lestin owed this commission to the good offices of Vouet, who saw in him an ally and with whom he may well have collaborated occasionally. Jacques Blanchard, on the other hand, had never studied under Vouet and must have cut the figure of a rival in the Parisian art world. Born on October 1, 1600, Blanchard turned up in Rome in 1624, some ten years after Vouet. His experience of Italy was to affect him very differently; from the start his work had something of the refinement, the studied grace, that was to reach its acme in the art of La Hyre. His quickly won success in Paris, beginning in 1629, two years after Vouet's return, and cut short by an early death, reminds us of the life stories of many of his elders. He and Vouet constituted one of those pairs of creative artists whose temperaments and achievement are at once opposed and complementary, and who figure so frequently in the long history of French art and literature.

Compared with Vouet's huge output, his seems meager; only some hundred pictures are recorded and of these, despite Charles Sterling's painstaking researches, only a quarter have been so far discovered. Blanchard rarely undertook large-scale decorations; only two are mentioned: a small gallery in the Hôtel Barbier and the lower gallery of the Hôtel Bullion, both of which were long ago destroyed. Sauval describes Blanchard as "a very worthy man, gentle, good-natured, friendly and obliging" and we can well believe that he made no attempt to deprive Vouet of his big commissions. A portrait of him, engraved by Edelinck, shows a man with a finely molded, rather sensual face touched with a shade of melancholy. He was only thirty-eight when he died, perhaps of consumption. Some large religious compositions such as the *Descent of the Holy Spirit*, a *Mai* dated 1634 and now restored to Notre-Dame, show that he was capable of tackling works of large dimensions, but it would seem that he put the best of himself into his easel pictures—which soon were in great demand.

For in the art world of Paris in the 1630s his manner was as great a novelty as Vouet's. Nephew and pupil of the painter Nicolas Bollery, Blanchard had been trained in the Mannerist tradition. After three years' study at Lyons (1620-1623) under Horace Le Blanc, he arrived in Rome at the end of October 1624, but stayed there only eighteen months. By then the enthusiasm for Caravaggio had waned, and the younger men rated the art of Domenichino, Guido and Lanfranco above the productions of the Tenebrosi. Thus, somewhat later, when Blanchard painted his *St Jerome* (two versions, Bar-le-Duc and Budapest), he was obviously under the influence of Guido Reni. He made haste to go to Venice, where he stayed two years and it was the paintings by Titian, Tintoretto and Veronese which he saw there that shaped his style, though he also owed something to Domenico Feti and Jan Lyss. On his return to Paris his "fresh and agreeable" manner of painting soon won widespread admiration. His choice of subjects contributed to his success. Before long he was being described as "the French Titian"; this was due in part to his brilliant handling of color but also to his gift for depicting beautiful women, reminiscent of Titian's *Venus* and *Flora*. The story went that love was Blanchard's ruling passion, and he indulged in it with equal zest in his life and in his art. "He much enjoyed painting naked women," as Félibien discreetly put it, "and such was his facility that he is known to have painted an entire figure, life-size, in two or three hours." The frankly sensual appeal of some of Blanchard's female figures (which often shocked the prudish-minded members of the public) can be seen to fine effect in such works as *Venus and the Graces caught unawares by a Mortal* (Louvre), a symphony of luscious flesh tints under a crimson canopy, the still more voluptuous *Danaë* (Palace of Tsarskoe Selo), the more finely conceived *Angelica and Medor* (Metropolitan Museum, New York), and the delightful *Bacchanal* dated 1636 (Nancy). That he was also capable of a more discreet approach, guided by modesty and simple human feeling, is evident in his handling of such subjects as *Charity* of which Blanchard painted several versions (Louvre, Paris; Courtauld Institute, London; Goodwood, Sussex); the *Holy Family* (two versions, Cherbourg Museum and Louvre); the *Virgin and Child* (lost, but several drawings or engravings are extant). Most of his pictures reveal a predilection for brunettes with complexions whose creamy whiteness is set off by a straying lock of hair. In Blanchard's pictures even more than in Vouet's we see a realization of the Fontainebleau ideal of beauty, modified however by the lessons of Venetian art, and, when the subject lends itself to this, the intellectual elegance of Primaticcio and his disciples is invigorated by a robust sensuality congenial to the seventeenth-century temperament.

Thanks to Blanchard French art assimilated a quality of the art of Venice that Vignon and Vouet seem to have disregarded. Vignon had taken over from it the dashing execution and sudden bursts of light that appealed to his romantic, highly strung temperament; Vouet elected for vast decorative schemes, and his color was directed to broad effects, dynamic contrasts, suitable for altarpieces and walls. For Blanchard, however, the picture *qua* picture was his chief concern. What he wanted was to create an atmosphere of tranquil beauty in which color and modeling reigned supreme, and he borrowed from the Venetians their delicate transitions, their golden harmonies in which here and there a touch of vivid red sings out. Cool greys set off the crimsons and emphasize the softly glowing flesh tints kindling into pink where the blood flows beneath the skin, and passages of shadow are shot with amber glints. Thus painting in Paris gravitated between two poles and, drawing inspiration from both in equal measure, found in Blanchard and Vouet the pioneers of its renascence.

Nicolas Poussin

THE favorable conditions to which such men as Vouet and Blanchard largely owed their brilliant success soon attracted to Paris the French painters who had remained in Italy. Official patronage of the arts was a contributing factor. Louis XIII genuinely liked painting and Richelieu saw its prestige value. In 1630 Perrier returned; in 1634, when Jacques Stella was about to enter the service of the King of Spain, Richelieu forbade him to leave France; in 1636 Mellan came back to Paris and was soon followed by Rémy Vuibert. At the end of 1642 Poussin, yielding to official pressure, returned to the capital. Though none of these artists seriously endangered Vouet's ascendancy, they familiarized Paris with a style utterly unlike his and stood for a type of painting in which his lyrical effusion had no place. Here there can be no question that Poussin played the leading role, but it is a mistake to overlook, as some have done, the influence of other artists who had come back before him and prepared the way for a drastic re-orientation of French art.

Among them was François Perrier. In point of fact he seems to have played a less conspicuous part in the development of the new style. It was only the works produced at the end of his career that won him a reputation equaling Blanchard's and caught the public eye. Son of a goldsmith, Perrier studied at Lyons, went to Rome in early youth, and entered the studio of Lanfranco. About 1630 he returned to France and executed a number of religious decorations at Lyons and near by, before moving on to Paris. To start with, he worked under the aegis of Vouet, made paintings after his designs in the Chapel of Chilly, and canvased attention with a series of excellent engravings (*Beheading of St John the Baptist*, 1633, *St Sebastian tended by the Holy Women*, 1633). His style developed much on the lines of Vouet's; though lacking the master's brilliancy and sensual appeal, it contained broader, stronger accents, which seem to have impressed Le Brun in his early period. But success was slow in coming and Perrier went back to Rome. When he published a series of etchings of the most famous ancient statues, their clarity and simple but lively execution soon found many imitators. While retaining its dramatic accents, his style was gradually affected by his study of classical antiquity and he developed a new sobriety in the handling of forms and attitudes. After his return to Paris in 1645 he became a foundation member of the Academy, collaborated in the decoration of the Hôtel Lambert and painted the gallery at the Hôtel La Vrillière (now the Banque de France). The ceiling of this gallery, long regarded as one of the finest French paintings of its kind, was piously restored by Vien in the eighteenth century, then ill-advisedly dismantled and replaced by a copy in the nineteenth. When Perrier died at the height of his success in 1650, it seems that art in Paris had not been influenced as much as might have been expected by his style. Adapted equally to large-scale decorative schemes and to easel painting, it was less austere than Poussin's and sparer than Pietro da Cortona's.

Barely a dozen pictures by Perrier's hand have come down to us and his reputation is based in the main on his engravings. Claude Mellan (1598-1688) would be even more forgotten, were it not that his engravings rank him as one of the ablest French practitioners of that branch of art. But he was a no less assiduous painter and plied the brush from the time of his Italian sojourn, which began in the same year as Poussin's, 1624, up to his death at the age of ninety, well on into the reign of Louis XIV. In the work of his early years in Italy Vouet's influence predominated, and he soon became Vouet's interpreter and close friend. After 1627, however, his style evolved rapidly and numerous engravings after paintings demonstrate the importance and originality of his innovations. Unfortunately the attribution to him of that strange work, *Joseph interpreting a Dream* (Borghese Gallery, Rome), is purely conjectural. After his return to Paris he aligned his style to that of Le Sueur and Le Brun—but none of these paintings has survived and we have only engravings to go on. Of his later career, too, surprisingly little is known. He spent the last years of his long life in strict seclusion, working industriously, neither frequenting the Academy nor courting official recognition, the result being that he is rarely mentioned in contemporary records. That his engravings anyhow exercised considerable influence seems certain but its scope is difficult to estimate.

Jacques Stella was more in the public eye. He was the son of a Flemish painter, Frans Stellaert (some fine landscape drawings by his hand are in the Louvre), who after a sojourn in Rome moved to Lyons. His mother Claudine de Masso, daughter of a notary in the Bresse region, was a capable woman who kept the family afloat after her husband's death, and her son Jacques Stella was all his life deeply devoted to her. Born in 1596, he went in early youth to Italy and began by visiting Florence where Cosimo de' Medici took the young artist under his wing; his stay in Florence left an indelible imprint on his art. In 1623 he moved to Rome, but continued working on independent lines (not to be accounted for by his lasting friendship with Poussin). In 1634 Richelieu gave him peremptory orders to return to France, accompanied by signal marks of favor: the title of Painter to the King, an allowance of a thousand livres a year, lodgings in the Louvre and the award of the Collar of the Order of St Michael. Though he never tackled large-scale decorations of galleries, Stella continued producing, up to his death (in April 1657), a series of altarpieces and easel pictures of a sobriety and power unparalleled at the time. Among these were *St Anne bringing the Virgin to the Temple* (Rouen), in which the marked austerity of the large, statue-like figure of the saint, animated only by a few touches of cool color, seems like a challenge to the art of Vouet; the monumental *Joseph and Mary finding Jesus in the Temple* (Church of Les Andelys), which might well pass for a "manifesto" even more intransigent than the *Miracle of St Francis Xavier* painted opposite it by Poussin (1641-1642); and *Clelia crossing the Tiber* (Château de Fontainebleau), whose curious blend of grace and frigidity calls inevitably to mind the works of David's followers. Once Stella's works, hitherto regrettably neglected, have been collated and it becomes possible to assess his œuvre in its entirety, he will be seen in his true stature as one of the most original, most engaging artists of the time.

It seems a pity that the artists we have mentioned are so little known and have been so little studied that we have but an imperfect idea of their respective careers. Yet they are entitled to a place alongside Valentin and Vouet in any survey of this generation and the marked differences between them help us to realize the remarkable complexity of the period. At this point we must confine ourselves to a brief mention; however, when we come to deal with the developments of art in Paris under Louis XIII and during the Regency, their art and the influence it exerted will be discussed at greater length. This applies, too, to Monnier, who like Stella stayed at Florence before going on to Rome; also to Louis Le Nain who,

Nicolas Poussin (1594-1665).

The Sacrament of Extreme Unction (detail), about 1638-1640 (?). By Courtesy of The Duke of Rutland,

Belvoir Castle (Leicestershire).

given the date of his birth, belonged to the same generation. Actually, however, his known œuvre is so strictly confined to the years 1640-1648 and his art links up so closely with that of his brothers—Antoine, his elder by some five years, and Matthieu, his junior by nearly fifteen—that it seems best to deal with him in the next volume.

Happily the greatest of these artists, Nicolas Poussin, has fared better and, despite the loss of his youthful works, enough of his pictures and drawings have come down to us (only a third are lost) to form a coherent whole and to give a clear idea of the evolution of his art. This is facilitated by his letters, some of which have been preserved, and by descriptions of him by contemporaries. The portrait that emerges is not only that of a dedicated painter but also that of one of the finest minds of the age.

Three facts may here be mentioned which, though needless to say they do not account for Poussin's genius, help to an understanding of some of the special features of his art. First, he acquired quite early in life a culture much superior to that of most of the painters of his generation. Secondly, he made a late start; he was thirty when he came to Rome and thereafter he spent almost all his active life in Italy, differing in this respect from his French brother-artists who usually stayed in Italy till they were about thirty and then returned for good to France. Lastly, his work is marked by a creative freedom soon achieved and zealously safeguarded, an independence almost unparalleled in the art of the century.

All his contemporary biographers express admiration of Poussin's "learned conversation" and his knowledge of classical antiquity. Doubts have sometimes been cast on the scope of this knowledge; but surely the question whether he had or had not the erudition of a Peiresc or a Naudé is beside the mark. His father Jean Poussin, ruined by the civil wars, had served in the royal army before marrying the widow of an attorney owning a small estate at Les Andelys, a prosperous market-town in Normandy. He came of a good family having connections with the magistracy at Soissons. Born in 1594, Nicolas was an only son and we are told that his parents hoped he would enter the legal profession or qualify for some high official post, and with this in view they encouraged him to study. Quite soon he realized that his vocation lay elsewhere, but his family refused to hear of his taking up art. In 1612, after watching a visiting artist, Quentin Varin, working on some pictures for the parish church of Les Andelys (*Martyrdom of St Clara* and *Martyrdom of St Vincent*, still *in situ*) the boy ran away from home. Hew as only eighteen and apparently had not so far had any training in art or in any other craft. Gifted with unusual intelligence, he had picked up a good working knowledge of Latin, could read the classical authors and probably some modern works in that language.

It seems clear that, well before going to Rome and sharing in the passion for Antiquity that prevailed in the Cavaliere dal Pozzo's circle, Poussin determined to perfect his understanding of the classics by intensive private study. Not being a painter's son and not having passed through the apprentice stage in the studio of an accepted master, he was not qualified to practise painting in Paris, except in some privileged institution. If his choice fell on the Collège de Laon to begin with, this was perhaps because he had friends there and looked forward to mixing with the classical students. It was, however, for another college, that of the Jesuits, that he made the pictures which brought him his first public success; these were six tempera paintings celebrating St Ignatius and St Francis Xavier on the occasion of their canonization. It was now that he came in contact with Alexandre Courtois, *valet de chambre* to Marie de' Medici and, according to Bellori, the "Court mathematician." Soon the Italian poet Giambattista Marino, famed for the delicate refinement of his work, who was then living in Paris, became the bosom friend of the comparatively unknown young painter. We may be sure that Poussin would never have been introduced to the author of *L'Adone*, still less won his regard, had he been no more than a struggling painter lacking social polish. Mancini, writing (in Rome) in or about 1626-1627, described Poussin as "a man of noble mien and

Nicolas Poussin (1594-1665).

The Martyrdom of St Erasmus (detail), 1628-1629. Pinacoteca Vaticana, Vatican City.

Nicolas Poussin (1594-1665).
The Massacre of the Innocents, about 1625-1626 (?). (58×60⅜″) Musée Condé, Chantilly.

manners and, what is more important, with a very wide knowledge of literature, and so conversant with all that counts in history, mythology and poetry, that he can give expression with his brush—and how felicitously!—to themes deriving from them."

The setbacks of his youth and the fact that he did not pass through any of the usual official channels in his formative years account in part for the tardiness of his début. When Poussin was so much impressed by Quentin Varin when he saw him working at Les Andelys, he probably knew little about the painter's craft; yet he was at the age when Vouet and Le Brun had already made a name for themselves in Paris. Perhaps after leaving home he began by halting at Rouen; the Jouvenets proudly declared that Noël Jouvenet, ancestor of a famous "dynasty" of painters, taught Poussin the rudiments of drawing. In any case he was soon in Paris, but he stayed there only a few months, dissatisfied with the teaching in the studios of Lallemant and the Flemish portrait painter Ferdinand Elle. A young nobleman from the Poitou district, who was staying in the capital, kept him in funds, then took him back with him to his château. The imbroglio that followed has often been described.

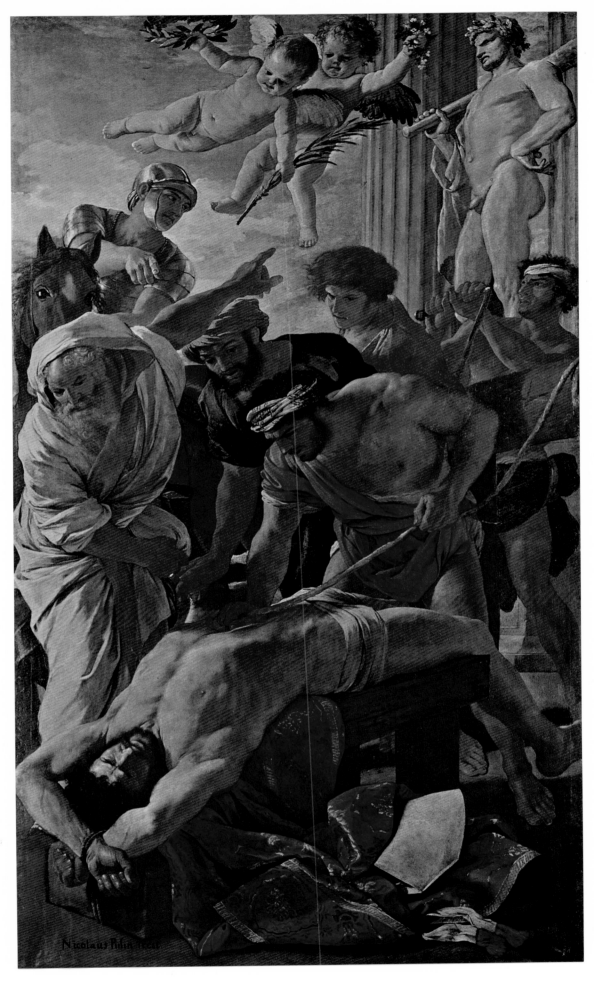

Nicolas Poussin (1594-1665).
The Martyrdom of St Erasmus, 1628-1629. (76¾×58″) Pinacoteca Vaticana, Vatican City.

Annoyed by the presence of this "parasite," the young patron's mother set him to menial tasks and Poussin promptly left the château. He made his way back to Paris on foot, earning a little money on the way as an itinerant artist, and when the prodigal son finally reached his father's house, his health was seriously impaired. But soon he was on the road again. He managed to keep body and soul together by making pictures at starvation prices, sometimes in country towns, sometimes in Paris in the "privileged establishments" we have spoken of, where the Painters' Guild could not prevent his working. Almost certainly he visited Fontainebleau and was duly impressed by the works of Primaticcio, Dubois and Dubreuil. He made several attempts to get to Rome, but the first two were abortive; he got no further than Florence and Lyons. However this was probably enough to familiarize him to some extent with the work that was being done south of the Alps. When finally he reached Rome in 1624 Poussin was in his thirtieth year, had mastered his art and had even enjoyed a brief hour of fame. For, after he had made some decorations for a festival at the Jesuit College, he was commissioned by the Archbishop of Paris, Jean-François de Gondi, to paint a picture for Notre-Dame. This work, a *Death of Our Lady*, has been lost since the beginning of the nineteenth century but a watercolor (Collection of Sir William Worsley, Hovingham Hall, Yorkshire) is thought to be a copy of it. Though there are reminiscences of Dubreuil and Pourbus, in this work Poussin already strikes a personal note. By the time he arrived in Rome the enthusiasm for Caravaggio's art had waned; artists were now less interested in strong light effects than in Venetian color and in a return to the great masters, Raphael and Giulio Romano. On his arrival Poussin assuredly gave more attention to the Vatican Stanze than to the Tenebrosi. Probably painted about 1624-1625, his *Victory of Gideon over the Midianites* (Vatican Museum), though a night piece, owes nothing to the art of Caravaggio. It was a study of Titian's famous Bacchanals, then in the Ludovisi collections, that took most effect on Poussin during his first years in Rome. He was almost entirely unaffected by that very special art climate in which most of the leading French artists of his generation, Blanchard, Stella and Mellan excepted, had put to the test their budding talents.

When Poussin arrived in Rome, provided with a letter of introduction from the Cavaliere Marino describing him as *un giovane chi a una furia di diavolo*, he applied this "demonic" energy to building up in Rome the reputation he had left behind in Paris. In 1624 and 1625 things went far from easily; as ill luck would have it, the patrons he had counted on were away from Rome and his highly personal style must have taken aback the Roman public. But the young painter soon found supporters and in 1628, like Vouet some years earlier (and before him Valentin), he was accorded the signal honor of being commissioned to make a picture for St Peter's. This, the *Martyrdom of St Erasmus*, brought him into prominence, but his path was far from smooth during the next few years. For one thing he fell ill, so seriously that but for the devoted care of a French cook, Jacques Dughet, who had settled in Rome, he would not have pulled through. Moreover he had to face keen competition, aggravated by the fact that, being the man he was, Poussin aimed at nothing short of a foremost place in the painting of the day. Pietro da Cortona, his junior by two years, who had however come to Rome much sooner, was now in the ascendant, tackling more and more ambitious compositions with outstanding success. In 1630 it was Charles Mellin, instead of Poussin, who was commissioned to decorate a chapel in the French church in Rome, San Luigi dei Francesi. Now aged over thirty-five, Poussin felt the hour had come to strike out in a new direction, and he brought to bear on the problem all the acumen of a man of the generation of Descartes.

We do not know if his decision was made suddenly; in any case a great change came over Poussin's life in 1630-1631. He married Dughet's daughter, Anne Marie (out of gratitude, it was said). This humble marriage proved that he had ceased to have social ambitions, and also had resolved to stay in Italy. Large-scale compositions such as the *Martyrdom of St Erasmus* (Vatican) and the *Apparition of the Virgin to St James* (Louvre) now gave place to works reduced in size and with small figures, suitable for private collections. Rarely was Poussin

Nicolas Poussin (1594-1665).
The Education of Bacchus, about 1630. (53⅛×66⅛″) Musée Condé, Chantilly.

to revert to life-size figures, as in the *St Margaret* (Galleria Sabauda, Turin) and the *Large Holy Family* executed for his friend Chantelou, and he left it to Pietro da Cortona to paint the huge ceiling in the Barberini Palace and indulge in vast decorative schemes. Hence there was no longer any need for him to seek commissions for churches or royal patronage, or even to cater for the tastes of individual clients. His works were beginning to fetch relatively high prices; in 1631, for his *Philistines stricken with the Plague* (Louvre), he was paid 110 scudi, and 90 for the *Realm of Flora* (Dresden). Soon there was no limit to the prices he could command for his paintings, and it was he himself who kept them down to figures often lower than their market value. Commissions poured in and his problem was to choose between them; his acceptance of one came to be regarded as a favor. When in 1652 a Sienese collector, Pandolfo Salvini, wanted a picture by his hand, he did not approach Poussin directly but asked an acquaintance of his to get in touch with Cassiano dal Pozzo, a close friend of the painter, and to beg him to put forward the proposal. Salvini only ventured to intimate that he would like a picture on a Biblical theme and left the artist free to choose the subject and dimensions of the work; nor was he discouraged when told he would have to wait at least two years before delivery. This total independence is one of the explanations of the highly personal note that Poussin developed more and more as the years went by.

Quite aware of his privileged position, Poussin hesitated for some time about accepting the proposals made in 1640 by Sublet de Noyers and transmitted by Chantelou, for his return to Paris, where Richelieu was impatiently awaiting him. That after two years in Paris he went back to Rome, ostensibly to fetch his wife, but probably with little intention of returning to France, was not only due to the intrigues of the Vouet clan or to the severity of the Parisian climate to which he now was unaccustomed. Like the hard-headed Norman he was, he might well have put up with these drawbacks in view of the honors showered on him and his many friends at court. The trouble was that he never had any leisure for those long hours of meditation on the problems of his art which meant so much to him. He was pestered by calls on his time, compelled to leave the execution of his projects to studio assistants, to move on without a moment's pause from the decoration of a ceiling to a tapestry cartoon or a frontispiece. This atmosphere suited well enough such men as Vouet and, later, Le Brun, but Poussin could never get used to it. It was, then, a great relief to resume his tranquil life in Rome and more than ever, during the twenty years that remained to him, he refused to let himself be rushed. He created slowly, guided solely by the rhythm of his inspiration, working without assistants and almost exclusively for friends. He made a point of setting apart a portion of

Nicolas Poussin (1594-1665).

The Sacrament of Extreme Unction, about 1638-1640 (?). (37¾×48″)

By Courtesy of The Duke of Rutland, Belvoir Castle (Leicestershire).

the day for reading books of many kinds and kept some hours clear for a morning stroll in the Campagna or on the Pincio, or an evening walk in the city, accompanied by friends, young artists and foreign visitors to Rome who came to pay their respects to the famous "Monsieur le Poussin."

Such is the nobly dignified figure presented to the reader by Poussin's first biographers, Bellori and Félibien, who knew him in his middle age. And perhaps it was thus the artist wished himself to be remembered; the two self-portraits in Berlin and in the Louvre, more particularly the latter, show us a man who is haughtily aloof, lost one would say in philosophic meditation. And this conception of him became crystallized with the passing of the years. Segla's bust (1782) in the Pantheon gives the master's face a truly Olympian serenity. But we must not forget that there had been another Poussin: the courageous youngster who ran away from home; the itinerant, almost unschooled artist who trudged the roads of France living from hand to mouth; the youth whose sparkling verve delighted the Cavaliere Marino; the ambitious artist who did not disdain the aid of eminent patrons in his struggle to make good in Rome. Until about 1630 Poussin's personality is colorful, full of contradictions (perhaps of secrets), beyond all doubt as picturesque as that of Valentin or Vignon. His path of life was far from easy, much of it marked by illness and adversity. The earliest of his extant letters (dating, it seems, to the beginning of his sojourn in Rome) contains a pathetically humble request addressed to Cavaliere dal Pozzo, the man who was one day to become his loyal friend and sometimes his obligee. "I beg you most fervently to help me out, as I am in the direst need. Most of the time I am ill and I have nothing to live on except what little I can earn with my hands." One of his last letters (August 1660) voices the sadness of an aging man. "I get through hardly a day without pain, and every year my limbs get shakier and shakier." But Poussin did not make of his infirmities a pretext for retiring from the fray. His lucidity and self-control were not limited to the practice of his art; beneath the Sage in the antique manner there lay the Norman peasant with his down-to-earth commonsense. Poussin was habitually plain-spoken, enjoyed good company and good fare, and had no dislike for compliments even a shade fulsome. He accepted the honors heaped on him provided they did not overmuch disturb his way of life. He handled words without prudishness, money without disdain, people without illusions. As for politics, he found all he needed in Montaigne and declared that a painter had no business to meddle in affairs of State—though there were times when he expressed his opinion with surprising frankness.

But this level-headedness, echoes of which are found in his correspondence (sometimes we almost seem to catch the very tone, somewhat peremptory and curt, in which he aired his views), was only one aspect of his personality, its outer husk. His inner life was of a far subtler nature; he was capable of fine shades of feeling and a delicate sensitivity, especially in all that touched his art.

Hardly any of the paintings Poussin made before he was thirty have survived. That even the drawings in the Massimi Album (Windsor Castle), which according to Bellori he made for Cavaliere Marino, date to the time of Marino's stay in Paris is far from certain. It seems more likely that they were made when Poussin met the poet again, in 1624, in Rome, just before Marino's departure for Naples. None the less, in this small series of drawings we find intimations of the two conflicting themes which were to haunt the artist's mind throughout his career; on the one hand we are shown the wretchedness of the human situation, man's struggle with his fellows and with his destiny; on the other hand, the joy of life celebrated in a sort of hymn to music, to wine, to the beauty of young naked bodies—an aftermath, it seems, of the joyous paganism of the Renaissance. His subjects, culled from Ovid's *Metamorphoses*, in which delicate sentiment and cruelty are so strangely intermingled, reflect this ambivalence: *Acis and Galatea taken by surprise by Polyphemus*; the *Metamorphosis of Acis*, the *Birth of Adonis, Chione slain by Diana*. His earliest pictures, too, illustrated the age-old

Nicolas Poussin (1594-1665).
St Matthew and the Angel, about 1643 (?). (39×53⅛″) Staatliche Museen, Berlin.

universal themes of Love and Death. The two *Battles of Joshua* (1624-1625, Hermitage, Lenin-grad, and Pushkin Museum, Moscow), of relatively small dimensions, are crowded with repre-sentations of physical horror, daggers transfixing naked flesh, dead bodies, severed heads, streams of blood. Yet, painted apparently at almost the same time, *Rinaldo and Armida* (Moscow) evokes a golden moment of romantic love. Then, a little later, comes the *Massacre of the Innocents* (Musée Condé, Chantilly), made for Prince Giustiniani, probably about 1625-1626, which gives the impression of being a "show piece" meant to attract the attention of connoisseurs. Here the brutal gesture of the soldier is contrasted with the harrowing gaze and posture of the mother (placed exactly in the center of the composition) and the tiny —but how poignant!—jet of blood, painted in pure vermilion, spurting from the child's body. Very different is the *Triumph of Flora* (Louvre), believed to have been executed at the end of 1626 or in 1627; here all is in the gentle mood of Titian's Bacchanals. With its canopy of blue sky against which a branch of an apple tree in flower tells out, and, below, lovers embracing in a meadow, it celebrates an exquisitely happy moment. In this delightful work Poussin has resolutely closed his eyes to the dark side of life and nature.

For a while he seems to be seeking to combine these dual inspirations in the lyrical effusion of the Baroque. It was a study of Venetian art and also the example set by Vouet that led him to develop, about 1628-1629, the highly unusual style of the *Martyrdom of*

St Erasmus. There is a tendency to disregard this masterly composition, but Poussin never repudiated it. Reproduced here in color for the first time, it displays not only the artist's vigorous handling of light effects, vivid colors, diagonals and foreshortenings, but also his capacity, when so minded, for creating scenes of appalling brutality, a raw, well-nigh barbaric realism. What indeed could be more horrifying than this depiction in full light of the victim's belly slit open by the executioner? Sandrart tells us that this work gave rise to much controversy and was sometimes unfavorably compared with Valentin's picture exhibited alongside it. In any case Poussin soon abandoned this style. The *Apparition of the Virgin to St James* (1629-1630, Louvre), while equally forceful, differs in its darker, denser color, and in the superb *Education of Bacchus* (Musée Condé, Chantilly) Poussin returns to a wholly static composition. A year later—perhaps, as Denis Mahon thinks, following the lead of Sacchi—we find him tending towards pale, softly glowing color schemes like that of the *Realm of Flora* (1631, Gemäldegalerie, Dresden), all in light carmines, tender greens and flaxen blues; indeed in his mythologies, whether smiling or tragic, there seems to linger a faint aroma of the bygone art of Fontainebleau.

It is now that a new conception of the picture makes its appearance in Poussin's art; or, rather, a conception more precisely affirmed and more systematically applied by him than by any other painter. It was after a close study of Leonardo's treatise on painting (brought to his notice by Dal Pozzo), combined with the discussions of aesthetics then in vogue in Rome, that he arrived at a "theory of art," fragments of which are disseminated in his letters and in documents published by Bellori. To Poussin's thinking, the work of art should not be

Nicolas Poussin (1594-1665).
The Blind Orion searching for the Rising Sun, 1658. (46⅞×72″)
The Metropolitan Museum of Art, New York. Fletcher Fund, 1924.

an expression of the artist's personality, in which he aims at creating a private world or at regaling the beholder with surprise effects of form and color. On the contrary, the painter must be dominated by his *subject*. Therefore he must choose a *noble* one (i.e. one providing a field for worthwhile meditation) and also *new*, or anyhow capable of embodying original ideas. Next, the artist must think out the theme at length and this mental operation is the mainspring of the creative act. It is here that the painter's genius reveals itself and here that we find in action that element of art which cannot be reduced to any formula, but, as Poussin put it, "may be compared to Virgil's Golden Bough which no man may find or pluck unless he be guided by Destiny." Moreover the artist has to bring all his painterly resources to bear on the chosen subject, and since every theme calls for a special kind of treatment, the handling of colors and arabesques must never be conditioned by a personal, invariable "manner." Poussin's well-known theory of Modes (equivalent to the ancient modes of music) was a corollary of this objective conception of the picture and it led him to examine all available compositional formulas. Thus a series of short lines, or clashing colors set out in harsh, syncopated rhythms (the Phrygian Mode) was suitable for depicting the chaotic movement of a battlefield, whereas long arabesques, broad tracts of color, discreetly harmonized (the Dorian Mode), were suitable for "solemn, severe, philosophic subjects."

Far from being a merely literary conception, Poussin's theory of art was given practical application. Nor was this all. Always keenly interested in history, he had a habit of including in his pictures archaeological details wrought out with loving care. But the ruling interest of the seventeenth century was a searching analysis of the human heart and Poussin's greatness lies in his creation of a pictorial language equivalent to that of Tragedy, in which abstract type figures are shown at grips with emergencies involving a clash of passions. ("Passions," not in the modern sense, but in the meaning given it by Descartes, i.e. as covering all human responses to the impact of events.) Here we have the vital core of Poussin's later art. There is no denying that this method was apt to lead to a frigid, almost mechanical handling of the pictorial data—and this in fact is what it did in the case of some of his mediocre followers at the end of the seventeenth century and in the eighteenth. In Poussin's case it was his prime concern, from the preliminary, intellectual planning of the picture to his final, almost physical participation in the birth of the work. There is a revealing passage in a letter he wrote in 1646, in which after completing a "Crucifixion" he refused to undertake a "Bearing of the Cross." "I have not enough joy or health left me to cope with harrowing subjects of this kind. The Crucifixion made me ill. I took great pains over it, but the Bearing of the Cross would literally kill me. I couldn't stand up against the solemn, agonizing thoughts with which one needs to fill one's heart and mind when dealing with subjects so sad and gloomy in themselves."

We see this theory of art put into practice in a long series of famous works: from the *Philistines stricken with the Plague* (Louvre) to the *Judgment of Solomon* (Louvre), the *Rape of the Sabines* (Metropolitan Museum, New York, and Louvre) to *Coriolanus* (Les Andelys Museum). For "pleasant" subjects, such as *Pan and Syrinx* (Dresden) and *Moses saved from the Waters* (two versions, Louvre) he usually employs an "amiable" style, charged with sensuous appeal. Sometimes, however, his handling is austere to the point of harshness, as in the *Schoolmaster of Faléries* (Louvre). In such works his manner hardens, figures tend to be heavier and the composition tenser, colors are more subdued. But always he shows Man facing up to his destiny and resolved, cost what it may, to master it. This applies not only to the figurations of Moses, whose life of constant struggle was one of Poussin's favorite themes, but even to the scenes in which Pan takes part. Thus the "Bacchanals" are not treated in the Flemish manner, as manifestations of unbridled sensuality; on the contrary, a lucid intelligence presides over these seemingly chaotic revels, Mind dominates Matter. But, as the years went by, this impulse towards movement subsided, Poussin's figures now seem to be standing up against the onrush of events rather than trying to direct their course.

Nicolas Poussin (1594-1665).
The Blind Orion searching for the Rising Sun (detail), 1658. The Metropolitan Museum of Art, New York.
Fletcher Fund, 1924.

Groups are spaced out and confront each other in a static dialogue (e.g. the *Continence of Scipio*, Hermitage). Intimations of a brief lull, preceding the new tension which made its appearance in Poussin's art when he was in his fifties, can, we believe, be seen in the first set of the *Seven Sacraments* painted for Dal Pozzo between about 1638 and 1642. Here the successive stages of a Christian life from birth to the grave are treated with profound feeling and understanding; indeed, despite the liturgic content, what lies behind these noble works is less a meditation on the mystery of the sacraments than on the most solemn moments of man's earthly existence. What we see here is not so much a supernatural intervention in the affairs of men, but a revelation of humanity sublimated by the sacramental rite.

Now, however, Poussin was gradually moving in a direction that was to lead him far from the art of his contemporaries and to the creation of works quite out of keeping with the spirit of the age. That they found favor with the élite was due solely to the fact that to admire Poussin had become a sort of dogma. Landscape now bulked ever larger in his paintings. To begin with, his approach was purely intellectual; the landscape in which the apostle and angel are located in the Berlin *St Matthew* is sparely indicated, indeterminate. But round about 1647-1648 Poussin discovered in nature a deeper life, more secret and more solemn than that of the settings of the Bacchanals of his earlier days. The conflict between violence and sensual pleasure, between joy and death, which had inspired his "heroic" scenes acquired a

Nicolas Poussin (1594-1665).
Apollo and Daphne, 1664.
(61×79¼″)
Louvre, Paris.

Nicolas Poussin (1594-1665).
Apollo and Daphne (detail), 1664. Louvre, Paris.

new significance. No longer merely incidental to the human situation, it now becomes assimilated to the contrast between the endless, carefree life of Nature and the pathetic brevity of man's lot on earth. Thus Poussin moved on from the tragic sense of life to an art of purely poetic inspiration. The *Funeral of Phocion* (Collection of the Earl of Plymouth) is located in a vast, indifferent countryside where men are going placidly about their daily tasks, and in *The Ashes of Phocion* (Collection of the Earl of Derby) the hero's wife collecting his ashes is but a tiny figure dwarfed by the far-flung landscape of woodland, rocks and temples. Only the fertility of woman or the creative artist can overcome the transience of all things human; in contrast with Narcissus' sterile love, the *Birth of Bacchus* celebrates the triumph of the infant god surrounded by a joyous train of nymphs.

Poussin had a glorious old age, but not a happy one. He was more and more handicapped by the trembling of his hand, which compelled him to adopt a new manner in which the picture was built up with small dabs of the brush, lightly sprinkled on the canvas and lacking precise outlines. This was, however, compensated for by his amazing gift for harmonizing values. Poussin had several long illnesses, most of his old friends had passed away, and when Anne Marie died in October 1664, after nine months of fever, he summed up his plight in a despondent letter. "Laden with years, half paralysed, stricken with all sorts of infirmities, a lonely foreigner (for friends in this city I have none) — that is my present lot." Yet this was the year in which he completed the *Four Seasons* (Louvre).

The last works form a group apart. With advancing age Poussin applied himself more and more to studying Nature and "listening in," as we now would say, to her most secret voices. He took a new delight in rustling foliage, in sudden gleams reflected in a pool, in pebbles on the wayside, and loved them for their own sake. Thus his interest in human passions gave place to a sort of Pantheism and by the same token—in this resembling Montaigne in his declining years—his stoical attitude to life was gradually superseded by an acquiescence in the universal flux of being. Cruelty and conflict are not excluded from his art, but merged into the beneficent, unfailing fecundity of Nature. In the landscape with Orion (1658, Metropolitan Museum, New York) the blinded giant, awaiting the first rays of sunrise that will restore his sight, seems less the victim of a cruel fate than a portentous symbol of the elemental forces governing the universe. In *Hercules and Cacus* (Hermitage, Leningrad) the detail of the hero kicking aside the dead monster leaves unruffled the spacious calm of a landscape of still waters and caves half hidden in lush overgrowth. The atmosphere of the *Four Seasons* (1660-1664, Louvre) seems reminiscent of the painter's youth in Normandy and his contacts with the peasantry of that green and fertile countryside; and these scenes of vernal orchards, copious harvests, autumn fields, have all the simple gravity and delicate appeal of the bucolic poetry of Virgil and Theocritus. In that somewhat intriguing work, *Apollo and Daphne*, left unfinished at his death (a gift to Cardinal Massimi), we have the artist's testament and surely it is one of the most deeply moving pictures in the Louvre. Tricked by Mercury who has stolen his arrows, frustrated in his friendship for the youth Hyacinthus whom he himself has slain and whose body lies under the trees, baffled in his pursuit of Daphne who has fled for refuge to her father's arms, Apollo, god of poetry and painting, lords it triumphantly in his bounteous realm, amid his flocks and herds, his train of joyous nymphs. Thus, participating in the fertility of Nature, the creative spirit, unsubdued by the buffetings of fate, regained in the last works of this great master its proud serenity.

Since Poussin's departure from Paris a great change had come over French painting. Under the auspices of the younger men, Champaigne and La Hyre, Le Sueur and Le Brun, a new taste had developed. Doubtless the many pictures by Poussin that Parisian art-lovers imported from Italy played a considerable part in this change of taste, but in fact they had less influence on it than is commonly supposed. Perhaps, indeed, his prestige bulked larger, to begin with, than his art. It was in 1664, at the very time presumably when Poussin was starting work on *Apollo and Daphne*, that Colbert became Surintendant des Bâtiments and appointed Le Brun to the post he had vacated some twenty years before, that of Director of Fine Art. One of the first acts of the new "dictator of the arts in France" was to have Charles Perrault draft a letter offering Poussin the post of President of a French Academy in Rome. The letter was never sent; presumably Colbert realized at the last moment that the aged artist's health was rapidly failing and he was quite incapable of filling so exacting a post. But the fact that the offer was all but made is significant, as showing that, when in the seventeenth century Louis XIV and Colbert were establishing a hierarchy of the arts in France, it was proposed to place French painting under the aegis of Poussin.

That "great generation" of painters born in the last decade of the previous century had done more than produce a series of exemplary works; they had endowed French painting with an independence and self-confidence that were brilliantly to justify themselves for centuries to come. Indeed there were ample grounds for Félibien's statement in the preface to his *Entretiens* that they had "taken over from Greece and Italy all the skills of painting and transported them to France."

Select Bibliography

General Index - List of Color Plates

Table of Contents

Select Bibliography

SOURCE WORKS

Giorgio VASARI, *Le Vite de' piu eccellenti Architetti, Pittori e Scultori...*, Florence 1550; revised ed., 1568. — Benvenuto CELLINI, *La vita scritta da lui medesimo* (c. 1558-1566), Naples 1728. — Carel van MANDER, *Het Schilderboek*, Alkmaar 1604. — Giulio MANCINI, *Considerazioni sulla pittura* (c. 1617-1621), edited by Adriana Marucchi and Luigi Salerno, Rome 1957. — Le Père DAN, *Le Trésor des merveilles de la maison royale de Fontainebleau*, Paris 1642. — Giovanni BAGLIONE, *Le vite de' pittori, scultori ed architetti*, Rome 1642. — André FÉLIBIEN, *Entretiens sur les vies et les ouvrages des plus excellents peintres...*, Paris 1666-1688. — G. P. BELLORI, *Le vite de' Pittori, Scultori ed Architetti moderni*, Rome 1672. — Joachim von SANDRART, *L'Academia Todesca... oder Teutsche Academie*, Nuremberg 1675-1679. — Michel de MAROLLES, *Le livre des peintres et graveurs* (c. 1677), new ed., Paris 1855. — Roger de PILES, *Abrégé de la vie des peintres...*, Paris 1699. — Florent LE COMTE, *Cabinet des Singularitez...*, Paris 1699-1700. — Pierre-Jean MARIETTE, *Abécédario*, edited by P. de Chennevières and A. de Montaiglon, Archives de l'Art Français, Paris 1851-1860. — *Mémoires inédits sur la vie et les ouvrages des membres de l'Académie royale de peinture et de sculpture*, edited by L. Dussieux, E. Soulié, P. de Chennevières, P. Mantz, A. de Montaiglon, Paris 1854. — A. JAL, *Dictionnaire critique de biographie et d'histoire* (recueil d'actes d'état civil, etc.), Paris 1867; 2nd revised edition 1872.

GENERAL

André MICHEL, *Histoire de l'Art*, Paris 1907-1929. — Louis DIMIER, *Histoire de la peinture française des origines au retour de Vouet (1300-1627)*, Paris 1925. — René SCHNEIDER, *L'Art français* (Les Patries de l'Art), 6 vols., Paris 1926-1930. — A. WEESE, *Skulptur und Malerei in Frankreich in 15. und 16. Jahrhundert* (Handbuch für Kunstwissenschaft), Wildpark-Potsdam 1927. — Paul JAMOT, *La Peinture en France*, Paris 1934. — Bernard DORIVAL, *La peinture française*, Paris 1942. — Sir Anthony BLUNT, *Art and Architecture in France (1500-1700)*, The Pelican History of Art, London 1953. — Pierre FRANCASTEL, *La Peinture Française*, 2 vols., Paris-Brussels 1955. — René HUYGHE, *L'Art et l'Homme*, Vols. II and III, Paris 1958-1960.

15th CENTURY

Henri BOUCHOT, *Catalogue de l'exposition des Primitifs français*, Paris 1904. — Henri BOUCHOT, *Les Primitifs français, 1292-1500*, Paris 1904. — Comte Paul DURRIEU, *La Peinture à l'exposition des Primitifs français*, Paris 1904. — Louis DIMIER, *Les Primitifs Français*, Paris 1911. — Jean GUIFFREY, Pierre MARCEL and Charles TERRASSE, *La Peinture française: les Primitifs*, Paris 1910-1926. — A. C. BARNES and V. de MAZIA, *French Primitives and their Forms*, Merion, Pa. 1931. — Paul André LEMOISNE, *La Peinture française à l'époque gothique*, Leipzig 1931. — Louis DIMIER, *Etudes sur les Primitifs Français*, Gazette des Beaux-Arts, Paris, II, 1936; II, 1937; I and II, 1938. — Jacques DUPONT, *Les Primitifs français*, Paris 1937. — Germain BAZIN, *Les Primitifs français*, Paris 1938. — Charles STERLING, *La Peinture française, les Primitifs*, Paris 1938. — Louis RÉAU, *La Peinture française du XIVe au XVIe siècle*, Paris 1939. — Louis GILLET, *Les Primitifs français*, Marseilles 1941. — Charles JACQUES (STERLING), *La peinture française, Les Peintres du moyen âge*, Paris 1942. — Grete RING, *A Century of French Painting, 1400-1500*, London 1949. — Charles STERLING, *Les peintres primitifs*, Paris 1949. — Erwin PANOFSKY, *Early Netherlandish Painting*, 2 vols., Cambridge, Mass. 1953. — (Jean PORCHER), *Les manuscrits à peintures en France du XIIIe au XVIe siècle*, Bibliothèque Nationale, Paris 1955.

PROVENÇAL SCHOOL OF THE 15th CENTURY

Abbé REQUIN, *Documents inédits sur les Peintres d'Avignon au Quinzième siècle*, Réunion des Sociétés des Beaux-Arts des Départements, Paris 1889, pp. 118-217. — Lucie CHAMSON, *Nicolas Froment et l'école avignonnaise au XVe siècle*, Paris 1931. — L. H. LABANDE, *Les Primitifs français. Peintres et verriers de la Provence occidentale*, Marseilles 1932. — Dr. PANSIER, *Les Peintres d'Avignon au XIVe et XVe siècle*, Avignon 1934. — G. BAZIN, *L'Ecole Provençale*, Geneva 1944. — Michel LACLOTTE, *L'Ecole d'Avignon. La Peinture en Provence au XIVe et XVe siècle*, Paris 1960.

16th CENTURY

Henri de LABORDE, *La Renaissance des Arts à la cour de France*, Paris 1886. — F. HERBET, *Extraits d'actes concernant les Artistes de Fontainebleau*, Paris 1901-1902. — Louis DIMIER, *French Painting in the XVIth Century*, London 1904. — W. H. von der MUELBE, *Die erste Schule von Fontainebleau*, Breslau 1904. — M. ROY, *Artistes et Monuments de la Renaissance française*, 2 vols., Paris 1929-1934. — *Ecole de Fontainebleau*, exhibition catalogue, Galerie des Beaux-Arts, Paris 1939. — Louis RÉAU, *Les peintres français de la Renaissance*, Paris 1940. — Pierre du COLOMBIER, *Le style Henri IV - Louis XIII*, Paris 1941. — François GEBELIN, *Le style Renaissance*, Paris 1942. — Louis DIMIER, *La peinture française au XVIe siècle*, Marseilles 1942. — Pierre du COLOMBIER, *L'Art Renaissance en France*, Paris 1945. — Henri BADEROU, *Ecole de Fontainebleau*, Geneva 1947. — Catalogue of the exhibition, *Fontainebleau e la maniera italiana*, Naples 1952. — Jean ADHÉMAR, *Le dessin français au XVIe siècle*, Lausanne 1954. — Catalogue of the exhibition *Triumph of European Mannerism*, Amsterdam 1955. — Lionello VENTURI, *The Sixteenth Century. From Leonardo to El Greco*, Geneva 1956. — Sylvie BÉGUIN, *L'école de Fontainebleau. Le maniérisme à la cour de France*, Paris 1960.

THE PORTRAIT IN THE 16th CENTURY

Louis DIMIER, *Le Portrait du XVIe siècle aux Primitifs français*, Paris 1904. — Etienne MOREAU-NÉLATON, *Les Clouet et leurs émules*, Paris 1924. — Louis DIMIER, *Histoire de la peinture de portrait en France au XVIe siècle*, 3 vols., Paris 1924-1927. — Sheila M. PERCIVAL, *Les portraits au crayon en France au XVIe siècle*, Gazette des Beaux-Arts, Paris 1962, II, pp. 529-542.

17th CENTURY

Philippe de CHENNEVIÈRES-POINTEL, *Recherches sur la vie et les ouvrages de quelques peintres provinciaux de l'ancienne France*, 4 vols., Paris 1847-1862. — Werner WEISBACH, *Französische Malerei des 17. Jahrhunderts*, Berlin 1932. — Charles STERLING, Catalogue of the exhibition *Les peintres de la réalité en France au XVIIe siècle*, Musée de l'Orangerie, Paris 1934. — Alfred LEROY, *Histoire de la peinture française au XVIIe siècle (1600-1700). Son évolution et ses maîtres*, Paris 1935. — Thérèse BERTIN-MOUROT (editor), *Bulletin de la Société Poussin*, Nos. I-III, Paris 1947-1950. — Charles STERLING, Notices on French painters in the catalogue of the exhibition *Il Seicento Europeo*, Palazzo delle Esposizioni, Rome 1956. — Michel LACLOTTE, Catalogue of the exhibition *Le XVIIe siècle français*, Petit-Palais, Paris 1958 (see also *The Age of Louis XIV*, Royal Academy of Arts, London 1958 and *The Splendid Century. French Art 1600-1715*, Washington-Toledo-New York 1960). — Boris LOSSKY, Catalogue of the exhibition *Das 17. Jahrhundert in der Französischen Malerei*, Kunstmuseum, Bern 1960. — Georges ISARLO, *La peinture en France au XVIIe siècle*, Paris 1960. — Pierre ROSENBERG, Catalogue of the exhibition *Nicolas Poussin et son temps*, Musée des Beaux-Arts, Rouen 1961. — René HUYGHE, *La peinture française des XVIIe et XVIIIe siècles*, Paris 1962.

FRENCH ARTISTS IN ROME IN THE 17th CENTURY

Hermann VOSS, *Die Malerei des Barock in Rom*, Berlin 1924. — Roberto LONGHI, *I pittori della realtà in Francia, ovvero i Caravaggeschi Francesi del Seicento*, Italia Letteraria, January 19, 1935. — Roberto LONGHI, *Ultimi studi sul Caravaggio e la sua cerchia*, Proporzioni, I (1943), pp. 5-63. — Jane COSTELLO, *The Twelve Pictures "ordered by Velazquez" and the Trial of Valguarnera*, Journal of the Warburg and Courtauld Institutes, XIII (1950), pp. 237 ff. — Roberto LONGHI, Costantino BARONI, Gian Alberto DELL'ACQUA, Mina GREGORI, Catalogue of the exhibition *Caravaggio e Caravaggeschi*, Milan 1951. — G. J. HOOGEWERFF, *Via Margutta, centro di vita artistica*, Istituto di Studi Romani, Rome 1953. — Raffaello CAUSA, Catalogue of the exhibition *La Madonna nella pittura del 600 a Napoli*, Naples 1954. — Nolfo di CARPEGNA, Catalogue of the exhibition *Caravaggio e i Caravaggeschi*, Palazzo Barberini, Rome 1955. — Jacques THUILLIER, *Poussin et ses premiers compagnons français à Rome*, Actes du Colloque International Nicolas Poussin, Paris 1960, I, pp. 71-116.

MONOGRAPHS

Beaumetz: Charles STERLING, *Œuvres retrouvées de Jean de Beaumetz, peintre de Philippe le Hardi*, Bulletin des Musées Royaux des Beaux-Arts, Brussels 1955, pp. 57-82.

Bellange: François-Georges PARISET, *Jacques de Bellange, Origines artistiques et évolution*, Bulletin de la Société d'Histoire de l'Art Français, 1955, pp. 96-109. — François-Georges PARISET, *Jacques de Bellange*, L'Œil, No. 93 (Sept. 1962), pp. 42-49.

Blanchard: Charles STERLING, *Les peintres Jean et Jacques Blanchard*, Art de France I (1961), pp. 76-118.

Boucher (de Bourges): Philippe de CHENNEVIÈRES-POINTEL, *Recherches...*, op. cit., II, pp. 85-120. — Jacques SOYER, *Documents inédits sur Jean Boucher, peintre berruyer, maître de Pierre Mignard*, Mémoires de la Société des Antiquaires du Centre, XXV (1901), Bourges 1902.

Boulogne (Valentin de): Victor de SWARTE, *Le peintre Valentin, 1591-1634*, Revue des Sociétés des Beaux-Arts des Départements, 1899, pp. 77-82. — Roberto LONGHI, *A propos de Valentin*, La Revue des Arts, 1958, No. 2, pp. 58-66. — Jacques THUILLIER, *Un peintre passionné : Valentin de Boulogne*, L'Œil, No. 47 (November 1958), pp. 26-33. — Michel HOOG, *Attributions anciennes à Valentin*, La Revue des Arts, 1960, No. 6, pp. 267-278.

Bourdichon: D. MacGIBBON, *Jean Bourdichon, a Court Painter of the Fifteenth Century*, Glasgow 1933.

Brébiette: Léon ROSENTHAL, *Pierre Brébiette, graveur français*, Gazette des Beaux-Arts, 4e période, tome 5 (1911). — Jacques THUILLIER, *Brébiette*, L'Œil, No. 77, May 1961, pp. 48-56.

Callot: Daniel TERNOIS, *L'art de Jacques Callot*, Paris 1962. — Daniel TERNOIS, *Jacques Callot. Catalogue complet de son œuvre dessiné*, Paris 1962.

Caron: Jean EHRMANN, *Antoine Caron, peintre à la Cour des Valois*, Geneva-Lille 1955. — Jean EHRMANN, *Drawings by Antoine Caron of the Valois Tapestries in the Uffizi*, Art Quarterly, Detroit 1958.

Charonton: see Quarton.

Chrétien (Pseudo Félix): Jacques THUILLIER, *Etudes sur le cercle des Dinteville. I: L'énigme de Félix Chrétien*, Art de France I (1961), pp. 57-75.

Cousin: Maurice ROY, *Les deux Jehan Cousin*, Paris 1909.

Clouet: Irene ADLER, *Die Clouet, Versuch einer Stilkritik*, Jahrbuch des Kunsthistorisches Museum in Wien, NF III, 1929, pp. 201-246.

Deruet: A. JACQUOT, *Notes sur Claude Deruet*, Revue des Sociétés des Beaux-Arts des Départements, XVIII (1894), pp. 763-943. — François-Georges PARISET, *Les débuts de Claude Deruet*, Bulletin de la Société d'Histoire de l'Art Français, 1947-1948. — François-Georges PARISET, *Claude Deruet*, Gazette des Beaux-Arts, 1952, I, pp. 153-172. — D. H. FERSENDEN, *The Life and Works of Claude Deruet*, Brooklyn N.Y. 1952. — François-Georges PARISET, *Les Amazones de Deruet*, Pays Lorrain, 1956, pp. 97-114.

Fouquet: Henri FOCILLON, *Le style monumental dans l'art de Fouquet*, Gazette des Beaux-Arts, 1936, I, pp. 17 ff. — Klaus G. PERLS, *Jean Fouquet*, Paris 1940. — Otto PAECHT, *Jean Fouquet: a Study of his Style*, Journal of the Warburg and Courtauld Institutes, London 1940-1941, pp. 85-102. — Paul WESCHER, *Jean Fouquet und seine Zeit*, Basel 1945.

Hay: Erwin PANOFSKY, *Jean Hey's "Ecce Homo", speculations about its author, its donor and its iconography*, Bulletin des Musées Royaux des Beaux-Arts, Brussels 1956, pp. 94-138.

Lallemant: François-Georges PARISET, *Documents sur Georges Lallemant*, Bulletin de la Société d'Histoire de l'Art Français, 1952, pp. 169-176. — François-Georges PARISET, *Georges Lallemant, émule de Jacques Bellange*, Gazette des Beaux-Arts, May-June 1954, pp. 299-308. — Robert LE BLANT and François-Georges PARISET, *Documents sur Georges Lallemant*, Bulletin de la Société d'Histoire de l'Art Français, 1960, pp. 183-192.

La Tour: Paul JAMOT, *Georges de La Tour*, Paris 1942; new enlarged edition, 1948. — François-Georges PARISET, *Georges de La Tour*, Paris 1948. — Vitale BLOCH, *Georges de La Tour*, Amsterdam 1950. — Marcel ARLAND, *Georges de La Tour*, Paris 1953. — François-Georges PARISET, *La servante à la puce*, Pays Lorrain, 1958, No. 3, pp. 100-108.

Le Clerc: François-Georges PARISET, *Note sur Jean Leclerc*, La Revue des Arts, 1958, No. 2, pp. 67-72.

Lhomme: Jacques BOUSQUET, *Un compagnon des caravesques français à Rome, Jean Lhomme*, Gazette des Beaux-Arts, February 1959, pp. 79-96.

Limbourg Brothers: Comte Paul DURRIEU, *Les Très Riches Heures du duc de Berry*, Paris 1904.

Master of 1456: Jean PORCHER, *L'homme au verre de vin et le Maître de Jouvenel des Ursins*, Revue française, Paris, July 1955, p. 17. — Jacques

DUPONT, *Le portrait de Zaccaria Contarini, ambassadeur de Venise à la cour de Charles VIII*, Bulletin des Musées Royaux des Beaux-Arts, Brussels 1955, pp. 121-127.

Master of the Aix Annunciation: Louis DEMONTS, *Le Maître de l'Annonciation d'Aix et Colantonio*, Mélanges Hulin de Loo, Brussels 1931 and Revue de l'Art ancien et moderne, Paris 1934, pp. 131-138. — Anne LIEBREICH, *L'Annonciation d'Aix en Provence*, Gazette des Beaux-Arts, Paris 1938, I, p. 63. — Jean BOYER, *Le maître d'Aix enfin identifié*, Connaissance des Arts, Paris, February 1958, pp. 38-43. — Jean BOYER, *Documents inédits sur le triptyque de l'Annonciation d'Aix*, Gazette des Beaux-Arts, Paris 1959, II, pp. 301-314. — Jean BOYER, *Personnages représentés sur les volets du triptyque de l'Annonciation d'Aix*, Gazette des Beaux-Arts, Paris 1960, II, pp. 137-146.

Master of Moulins: Friedrich WINKLER, *Der Meister von Moulins und Hugo van der Goes*, Pantheon, Munich 1932, pp. 241-248. — Paul DUPIEUX, *Les Maîtres de Moulins*, Moulins 1946. — Madeleine HUILLET d'ISTRIA, *La peinture française à la fin du moyen âge. Le Maître de Moulins*, Paris 1961. — Jacques DUPONT, *Jean Prevost, peintre de la cour de Moulins*, Art de France 1963, pp. 75-89. — Albert CHÂTELET, *A Plea for the Master of Moulins*, The Burlington Magazine, London 1962, pp. 517-524.

Master of the Rohan Hours: Jean PORCHER, *Les Grandes Heures de Rohan*, Geneva 1948. — Jean PORCHER, *The Rohan Book of Hours*, London 1959. — Jean PORCHER, *Le Portrait de Louis II d'Anjou*, Art de France 1961, pp. 290-292.

Master of St Giles: Max J. FRIEDLAENDER, *Le Maître de Saint Gilles*, Gazette des Beaux-Arts, Paris 1937, I, pp. 222-228.

Master of St Sebastian: Charles STERLING, *The "Master of St Sebastian" (Josse Lieferinxe?)*, Gazette des Beaux-Arts, New York 1942, pp. 135-148. — E. HAVERKAMP BEGEMANN, *Een onbekend werk van de meester van de Hl Sebastian*, Bulletin des Musées royaux des Beaux-Arts, Brussels 1958, pp. 18-28.

Master of the Lovesick Heart: O. SMITAL and Emil WINKLER, *Herzog René von Anjou, Livre du cuer d'amours espris*, Vienna 1926. — Otto PAECHT, *René d'Anjou et les Van Eyck*, Cahiers de l'Association internationale des études françaises, Paris 1956, No. 8, pp. 41-47.

Malouel: Friedrich GORISSEN, *Jan Maelwael und die Brüder Limburg*, Gelre, 1954, pp. 153-221. — Friedrich WINKLER, *Ein frühfranzösisches Marienbild*, Jahrbuch der Berliner Museen, Berlin 1959, pp. 179-189. — Millard MEISS and Colin EISLER, *A New French Primitive*, The Burlington Magazine, London 1960, pp. 133-140.

Mazerolles: Antoine de SCRYVER, *Philippe de Mazerolles*, Art de France, 1964. — Albert CHÂTELET, *Le retable du Parlement de Paris*, Art de France, 1964.

Mellan: see Jacques THUILLIER, *Poussin et ses premiers compagnons français à Rome*, Actes du Colloque International Nicolas Poussin, Paris 1960, I, pp. 86-96.

Mellin: Jacques BOUSQUET, *Un rival inconnu de Poussin: Charles Mellin dit "Le Lorrain"*, Annales de l'Est, 1955, No. 1. — Boris LOSSKY, *Le peintre Charles Mellin dit "le Lorrain" et les musées de Tours*, Bulletin de la Société d'Histoire de l'Art Français, 1956 (1957), pp. 50-58.

Niccolò dell'Abbate: F. REISET, *Niccolò dell'Abbate et les peintres de l'école de Fontainebleau*, Gazette des Beaux-Arts, Paris 1859, III, pp. 193-209 and 266-277. — Sylvie BÉGUIN, *Niccolo dell'Abbate en France*, Art de France, 1962, pp. 112-145.

Penni: Lucile GOLSON, *Luca Penni, a Pupil of Raphael at the Court of Fontainebleau*, Gazette des Beaux-Arts, Paris 1957, II, p. 171.

Perréal: F. ROLLE, *Jean de Paris*, Archives de l'Art français, Paris 1861, pp. 15-142. — Jacques DUPONT, *A Portrait of Louis XII attributed to Jean Perréal*, The Burlington Magazine, London 1947, pp. 235-247. — Grete RING, *An Attempt to reconstruct Perréal*, The Burlington Magazine, London 1950, pp. 255-260. — Charles STERLING, *Une peinture certaine de Perréal enfin retrouvée*, L'Œil, No. 103, August 1963.

Pietà d'Avignon: James G. FORD and G. Stephen VICKERS, *The Relation of Nuño Gonçalves to the Pietà d'Avignon, with a consideration of the iconography of the Pietà in France*, The Art Bulletin, 1939, pp. 5-43. — Germain BAZIN, *La Pietà d'Avignon*, Geneva 1941. — Hélène and Jean ADHÉMAR, *Quelques hypothèses au sujet de la Pietà d'Avignon*, Revue des Arts, 1953, pp. 16-19. — Charles STERLING, *La Pietà de Tarascon*, Revue des Arts, Paris 1955, pp. 25-46.

Pourbus: Jacques WILHELM and Bernard de MONTGOLFIER, *La Vierge de la famille de Vic et les peintures de François II Pourbus dans les églises de Paris*, La Revue des Arts, 1958, No. 5, pp. 221-228. — Jacques WILHELM, *Pourbus, peintre de la municipalité parisienne*, Art de France, III (1963), pp. 114-123.

Poussin: *Correspondance de Nicolas Poussin publiée d'après les originaux par Charles Jouanny*, Paris 1911. — Otto GRAUTOFF, *Nicolas Poussin*, 2 vols., Munich 1914. — Emile MAGNE, *Nicolas Poussin, Premier peintre du Roi*, Brussels-Paris 1914. — Walter FRIEDLAENDER, *Nicolas Poussin, Die Entwicklung seiner Kunst*, Munich 1914. — Walter FRIEDLAENDER, Anthony BLUNT, etc., *The Drawings of Nicolas Poussin. A Catalogue Raisonné* (3 volumes published since 1939). — *Bulletin de la Société Poussin*, edited by Thérèse BERTIN-MOUROT, Nos. I-III, Paris 1947-1950. — Paul JAMOT, *Connaissance de Poussin*, Paris 1948. — Georges WILDENSTEIN, *Poussin et ses graveurs au XVIIe siècle*, Paris 1957. — *Nicolas Poussin. Actes du Colloque International Nicolas Poussin*, edited by André CHASTEL, Paris 1960. — Anthony BLUNT and Charles STERLING, Catalogue of the exhibition *Nicolas Poussin*, Musée du Louvre, Paris 1960, 2nd revised ed. — Denis MAHON, *Réflexions sur les paysages de Poussin*, Art de France, I (1961), pp. 119-132. — *Poussin*, special issue of the Gazette des Beaux-Arts, July-August 1962 (Denis MAHON, Doris WILD, etc.). — Denis MAHON, Notices on Poussin in the catalogue of the exhibition *L'ideale classico del Seicento in Italia e la pittura di paesaggio*, Bologna 1962.

Primaticcio: Louis DIMIER, *Le Primatice*, Paris 1900. — Louis DIMIER, *Le Primatice*, Argenteuil 1928.

Quarton: Charles STERLING, *Le Couronnement de la Vierge par Enguerrand Quarton*, Paris 1939.

Rosso: Kurt KUSENBERG, *Rosso fiorentino*, Paris 1931. — Paola BAROCCHI, *Il Rosso Fiorentino*, Rome 1950. — Dora and Erwin PANOFSKY, *The Iconography of the Galerie François Ier at Fontainebleau*, Gazette des Beaux-Arts, Paris 1958, II, pp. 113-190. — Guy de TERVARENT, *Les énigmes de l'art. IV, L'art savant*, Bruges n.d.

Saint-Igny: Philippe de CHENNEVIÈRES-POINTEL, *Recherches...*, op. cit., I, pp. 161-182.

Stella: see Jacques THUILLIER, *Poussin et ses premiers compagnons français à Rome*, Actes du Colloque International Nicolas Poussin, Paris 1960, I, pp. 96-112.

Tournier: Henri BADEROU, *Un échange d'œuvres d'art entre les musées de Paris et de la province sous la Révolution*, Bulletin de la Société d'Histoire de l'Art Français, 1935, pp. 168-202. — Robert MESURET, *L'œuvre du peintre Nicolas Tournier*, Gazette des Beaux-Arts, December 1957, pp. 327-345.

Valentin de Boulogne: see Boulogne.

Varin: Philippe de CHENNEVIÈRES-POINTEL, *Recherches...*, op. cit., I, pp. 215-236. — Abbé REQUIN, *Notes biographiques sur Quentin Varin*, Revue des Sociétés des Beaux-Arts des Départements, 1888, pp. 340 ff. — Emile DELIGNIÈRES, *Notes complémentaires sur Quentin Varin, peintre picard*, ibidem, 1903, pp. 259-281. — Gaston VARENNE, *Essai sur la vie et l'œuvre du peintre Quentin Varin*, Beauvais 1905.

Vignon: Charles STERLING, *Un précurseur français de Rembrandt, Claude Vignon*, Gazette des Beaux-Arts, 1934, II, pp. 122-136. — Georges WILDENSTEIN, *Deux inventaires de l'atelier de Claude Vignon*, Gazette des Beaux-Arts, March 1957, pp. 183-192. — Claude GRÉGOIRE-BESNARD, *Les Vignon et la Galerie de Torigni-sur-Vire*, Gazette des Beaux-Arts, July-August 1960, pp. 57-70. — Bernard de MONTGOLFIER, *Deux tableaux de Claude Vignon*, Gazette des Beaux-Arts, June 1961, pp. 315-330. — Wolfgang FISCHER, *Claude Vignon (1593-1670)*, Nederlands Kunsthistorisch Jaarboek 13 (1962), pp. 105-148.

Villeneuve Pietà: see Pietà d'Avignon.

Vouet: Louis DEMONTS, *Essai sur la formation de Simon Vouet en Italie*, Bulletin de la Société d'Histoire de l'Art Français, 1913, pp. 309-348. — Hermann VOSS, *Die caravaggeske Frühzeit von Simon Vouet und Nicolas Regnier*, Zeitschrift für bildende Kunst, 1924, I-II, pp. 56-67; III, pp. 121-128. — Jacques BOUSQUET, *Documents sur le séjour de Simon Vouet à Rome*, Mélanges d'Archéologie et d'Histoire, LXIV (1952), pp. 287-300. — Jacques THUILLIER, *Un peintre du grand siècle, Simon Vouet*, L'Œil, No. 29 (1957), pp. 52-57. — William CRELLY, *The Painting of Simon Vouet*, New Haven and London 1962.

General Index

List of Color Plates

Contents

THIS VOLUME OF THE COLLECTION "PAINTING ○ COLOR ○ HISTORY" WAS PRODUCED BY THE TECHNICAL STAFF OF EDITIONS D'ART ALBERT SKIRA. FINISHED THE TWENTY-FIFTH DAY OF SEPTEMBER NINETEEN HUNDRED AND SIXTY-THREE.

TEXT AND ILLUSTRATIONS PRINTED BY

COLOR STUDIOS
IMPRIMERIES RÉUNIES S.A., LAUSANNE

PLATES ENGRAVED BY GUEZELLE & RENOUARD, PARIS

PHOTOGRAPHS BY

L. R. Adrion, Paris (pages 53, 54, 132, 168, 170, 196, 197, 201, 202, 222-223, 224), Maurice Babey, Basel (pages 10, 16-17, 27, 32, 41, 47, 51, 82, 83, 96, 98, 100, 104, 109, 113, 118, 122, 125, 127, 130, 131, 138, 142, 145, 147, 148, 150, 156, 161, 163, 171, 173, 174, 178, 179, 185, 188, 190, 195, 203, 212, 215), Henry B. Beville, Washington (pages 103, 120, 204, 219, 221), Joaquim Blauel, Munich (page 164), Conzett & Huber, Zurich (pages 48, 49), A. C. Cooper, London (page 91), John R. Freeman & Co., Ltd., London (pages 84, 105, 135, 144, 152, 205, 209, 216), Marc Garanger, Lyons (pages 36, 39, 62, 64, 70, 73, 166, 182, 187), Giraudon, Paris (pages 23, 143), Kurt Haase, Bergen bei Frankfurt (page 114), Louis Loose, Brussels (pages 45, 74, 78), P. Marzari, Schio, Italy (pages 92, 193, 194, 211, 213), Ruppert Roddam, Glasgow (page 24), Walter Steinkopf, Berlin (pages 19, 183, 218), and by the photographic services of the Staatliche Museen, Berlin (page 44) and the National-bibliothek, Vienna (page 57).

PRINTED IN SWITZERLAND